wo

Social Administration: Social Work

BEHAVIOUR MODIFICATION
IN
SOCIAL WORK

Behaviour Modification
in
Social Work

DEREK JEHU

Director, School of Social Work, University of Leicester

PAULINE HARDIKER, MARGARET YELLOLY and MARTIN SHAW
Lecturers, School of Social Work, University of Leicester

WILEY—INTERSCIENCE

A division of John Wiley & Sons Ltd.

LONDON · NEW YORK · SYDNEY · TORONTO

Library of Congress Catalog Card No. 70-37111

ISBN 0 471 44140 6

Reprinted 1975

Printed in Great Britain
By Unwin Brothers Limited
The Gresham Press, Old Woking, Surrey.
A member of the Staples Printing Group.

Contents

Acknowledgements

The authors wish to acknowledge the co-operation of the following for granting permission to reproduce diagrams and tables from their publications:

Academic Press, Inc.
Figure 3 (Hawkins et al, *Journal of Experimental Child Psychology,* 1966, **4,** pp. 99-107 and reproduced by permission).
Figure 16 (Tharp and Wetzel, *Behavior modification in the natural environment,* Academic Press, New York, 1969).

Aldine. Atherton, Inc.
Figures 8 and 9 (Reprinted from George W. Fairweather, David H. Sanders, David L. Cressler and Hugo Maynard, *Community Life for the Mentally Ill* (Chicago: Aldine Publishing Company 1969: copyright © 1969 by the Aldine Publishing Company, reprinted by permission of Aldine. Atherton, Inc.).

American Psychological Association
Figure 2 (C. D. Williams, The elimination of tantrum behavior by extinction procedures: Case report. *Journal of Abnormal and Social Psychology,* 1959, **59,** p. 269. Copyright 1959 by the American Psychological Association and reproduced by permission).

Family Service Association of America
Table 3 (Muller, *Social Casework,* 1968, **49,** pp. 546-551).

McGraw-Hill Publishing Co. Inc.
Figure 17 (Adapted from Kanfer and Saslow, *Behavior therapy: Appraisal and status,* McGraw-Hill, New York, 1969, reprinted by permission).

Pergamon Press Ltd.
Figure 4 (Ayllon et al, *Journal of Behaviour Therapy and Experimental Psychiatry,* 1970, **1,** pp. 125-138 and reproduced by permission).

The Psychological Record
Figures 10 and 11 (Burchard, *The Psychological Record,* 1969, **19,** pp. 259-261).

Society for the Experimental Analysis of Behavior, Inc.
Figures 5, 6 and 7 (Ayllon and Azrin, *Journal of the Experimental Analysis of Behavior,* 1965, **8,** pp. 357-383. Copyright 1965 by the Society for the Experimental Analysis of Behavior, Inc.).
Figures 12 and 13 (Phillips, Achievement place, *JABA,* **1,** 1968, pp. 213-223. Copyright 1968 by the Society for the Experimental Analysis of Behavior, Inc.).
Figures 14 and 15 (Ayllon and Azrin, *Journal of the Experimental Analysis of Behavior,* 1964, **7,** pp. 327-331. Copyright 1964 by the Society for the Experimental Analysis of Behavior, Inc.).

Society for Research in Child Development, Inc.
Figure 1 (Allen et al, *Child Development,* 1964, **35,** pp. 511-518. Copyright 1964 by the Society for Research in Child Development, Inc.).

Dr. E. J. Thomas
Table 1 (*Building Social Work Knowledge,* National Association of Social Workers, New York, pp. 38-48).

Part 1

A Behavioural Approach
in
Social Casework

Introduction

The essential characteristic of a behavioural approach in casework is an attempt to apply systematically certain principles established in experimental psychology to the explanation and modification of problem behaviour. This does not entail commitment to any specific psychological theory and the principles used may be derived from many fields of pyschology including motivation, perception, cognition, learning, attitude change and problem solving. These principles are deployed to amend and extend traditional casework methods so that they accord better with the available body of psychological knowledge, rather than simply to describe these methods in a different language. Thus the application is a priori rather than post facto.

For casework, the approach offers a corrective to the situation described by Shoben (1953) in which: 'the "applied" science of psychotherapy has been essentially divorced from the "pure" science that presumably should most nourishingly feed it, general psychology... this seems most unfortunate. Certainly medicine would not have made the striking advances it has were it not for underlying developments in physiology and biochemistry, nor would engineering be capable of its dramatic accomplishments were it not for the growth of physics' (p. 121). The potential advantages of exploiting a large body of empirical, systematic and cumulative knowledge from a broad field of experimental psychology seem obvious, but there are also certain restrictions which need to be recognized. These include the limitations in the data, principles and theories which constitute contemporary psychology, the inadequate and incorrect derivation of knowledge from psychology for treatment purposes and the practical difficulties of converting such knowledge into usable casework techniques. These restrictions, and some of the advantages of exploiting experimental psychology for casework purposes, are discussed and exemplified in the ensuing chapters.

It is emphasized that a behavioural approach in casework concerns only certain aspects of social work theory and practice rather than the whole field. Thomas (1964) identifies four areas of relevant knowledge which need to be considered at five levels of human aggregation to yield the twenty cells in Table 1.

Behaviourally oriented casework is restricted to the individual level and it

Table 1—*Behavioural Science Knowledge Potentially Relevant for Social Work* (*Thomas 1964*)

Level to which subject matter applied	SUBJECT MATTER			
	Normal behaviour	Abnormality and deviation	Growth, maturation, and change	The helping process
Individual	1	2	3	4
Group	5	6	7	8
Organization	9	10	11	12
Community	13	14	15	16
Society	17	18	19	20

contributes especially to cell 4. This may be particularly valuable because it is the first three cells that have received the greatest attention to date. Nevertheless, it is important to recognize that a behavioural approach in casework has no direct relevance to large areas of social work theory and practice.

D. JEHU

1

Explaining Problem Behaviour

Problem behaviour may be analysed in terms of the way a client is responding to certain conditions. These might be aspects of his own physiological or psychological processes, or features in his environment including the behaviour of other people towards him. The problematic responses may be physiological, motor, perceptual, cognitive or emotional and examples of each are given below. To anticipate discussion in Chapter 4, they are defined as 'problematic' on the basis of their unacceptability to the client or the society in which he lives.

DETERMINANTS OF PROBLEM BEHAVIOUR

Such problematic responses may be regarded as a function of somatic factors, previous learning experience and contemporary events.

Somatic Factors

This group of determinants includes heredity, injury and infection. In some types of problem behaviour, the influence of such factors is ascertainable either by observing the presence of an associated somatic disorder or from genetic investigation. Cases of physical handicap, organic psychiatric disorder and certain types of subnormality would fall into this category. Somatic factors may also contribute to some other types of problem behaviour, but there is no detectable somatic pathology associated with them and the genetic influence appears to be less strong. In this category, one might include functional psychoses such as schizophrenia and manic-depression, together with the neuroses and personality disorders.

Even when somatic factors do contribute to certain types of problem behaviour, these are still influenced by the client's previous learning and current conditions. For example, the contents of a psychotic's delusions are learned, and a current stress might precipitate a neurotic disorder.

Previous Learning Experiences

In a behavioural approach special attention is paid to any learning procedures which might contribute to problem behaviour, although this does not mean that the influence of somatic factors or contemporary events is neglected or denied. The learning procedures likely to be involved have been outlined elsewhere by the present writer (1967), and they are discussed here only very selectively, with special reference to their possible contribution to the development and maintenance of problem behaviour. It should be noted that the same learning procedures are involved in the acquisition of both acceptable and problem behaviour, although there are differences in the *conditions* of learning in each, case. Problem behaviour may develop in conditions such as aversive stimulation, conflict, exposure to deviant models or reinforcement patterns, or when there is insufficient opportunity to learn more acceptable ways of behaving. These conditions are illustrated below, and the learning procedures concerned are considered in the categories of classical conditioning, instrumental conditioning, observational learning and cognitive learning.

Classical Conditioning

This is the learning procedure made famous by Pavlov (1927). Before conditioning, his dogs salivated when food was placed in their mouths but not when a bell was rung. The conditioning process consisted of ringing a bell immediately before the presentation of food on a number of occasions, after which the bell alone evoked salivation. As the elicitation of salivation by food was not conditional upon learning, Pavlov called them the unconditioned response (UCR) and the unconditioned stimulus (UCS). The new link between the bell and salivation being conditional upon learning, they were termed the conditioned stimulus (CS) and the conditioned response (CR). Once a conditioned stimulus reliably elicits a conditioned response then higher order conditioning can occur. This means that a neutral stimulus which accompanies a conditioned stimulus can itself become a conditioned stimulus. Furthermore, a response which is elicited by an unconditioned or conditioned stimulus tends to be evoked by similar stimuli also, a process known as stimulus generalization.

This kind of learning is especially important in the acquisition of problematic emotional responses, such as anxiety or fear. A well-known paradigm of this is the experiment by Watson and Rayner (1920) with an eleven-month-old infant named Albert. Prior to conditioning, a white rat (CS) evoked no fear in the child, but he was afraid (UCR) of loud noises (UCS). The experimenters gave Albert a white rat to touch, while at the same time making a loud noise behind his head. After several such pairings, fear (CR) was evoked by presentation of the rat alone. This fear persisted for at least a month and generalized to similar stimuli such as rabbits, dogs, a fur coat, cotton wool and human hair. The results of several other experiments with human subjects accord with those of Watson and Rayner (Campbell et al. 1964, Jones 1931, Krasnogorski 1925, 1933, Moss 1924) and there is clinical evidence of traumatic experiences being followed by relevant phobias (Clark 1963a, Freeman and Kendrick 1960, Friedman 1966, Grinker and Spiegel 1945, Kraft and Al-Issa 1965, Kraft and Burnfield 1967, Kushner 1965,

Lazarus and Rachman 1957). However, many other contributory factors in addition to classical conditioning processes are likely to be involved in the acquisition of neurotic fear, especially the less specific kinds such as chronic anxiety states or agoraphobia (Marks 1969).

A second example of the contribution of classical conditioning to problem behaviour is the experimental establishment of a sexual fetish in several young, male, unmarried psychologists (Rachman 1966, Rachman and Hodgson 1968). Their degree of sexual arousal was measured by continuous plethysmographic recording of the blood volume in the penis (erections). Initially the subjects were aroused by coloured slides of nude women, but not by similar slides of a pair of women's black knee-length boots. The conditioning process consisted of presenting a slide depicting the boots followed immediately by another of a nude woman. After a number of such pairings, all the subjects exhibited sexual arousal in response to the slides of the boots, and this generalized to slides of black shoes but not of other forms of footwear. (The fetishistic responses were subsequently extinguished in all subjects.) At present there is a lack of direct evidence on the role of classical conditioning in the acquisition of fetishes outside the laboratory, although McGuire et al. (1965) have included it in their theoretical explanation of sexual deviations and Clark (1963b) has reported a suggestive clinical case.

In summary, the processes of first and higher order classical conditioning together with stimulus generalization result in existing responses being evoked by previously neutral stimuli. They are especially important in the acquisition of problematic emotional responses, although usually in conjunction with other contributory factors.

Instrumental Conditioning

In this procedure, what a person does in a situation determines the consequences for him. There is a response-consequence contingency. For instance, in order to obtain reward or avoid punishment he must make some specific response which already exists in his repertoire. The conditioning process consists of altering the probability of the occurrence of this response in future by attaching to it certain consequences which have the effect of increasing or decreasing its frequency.

Two major distinctions are commonly drawn between the classical and instrumental conditioning procedures. In the case of the former, the reward is not dependent on the organism's behaviour, for example, Pavlov's dogs received the food whether or not they salivated to the bell, and the psychologists were shown the nude slides quite irrespective of their degree of sexual arousal in response to the boots. In instrumental procedures, however, it is the subject's own behaviour which is 'instrumental' in determining the consequences for him. He exercises some degree of active control over the situation rather than merely responding to certain stimuli in a fairly automatic way. The second distinction concerns the kinds of responses which are conditionable by each of the two procedures.

Relatively involuntary reflexes and responses mediated by the autonomic nervous system, such as those involved in emotional behaviour, seem to be subject to classical conditioning mainly, while instrumental conditioning applies primarily to voluntary responses mediated by the central nervous system, such as speech and skeletal movement. In recent years, however, evidence has been advanced for the instrumental conditioning of autonomic responses also, but there is considerable controversy over the significance of these findings (Katkin and Murray 1968).

A form of instrumental conditioning called 'reward training' involves increasing the future probability of a response by following it with a reward or positive reinforcer. In this context, these two terms are used empirically to refer to any event which increases the probability of a particular response recurring in a similar situation and the controversial theoretical issue of why they have this effect is by-passed (Kimble 1961).

There is a good deal of evidence that reward training does play a part in the development and maintenance of problematic responses. Patterson (1971) has presented data showing that the parents of deviant children provided attention, interest, approval and positive physical contact as a consequence of behaviour like shouting, hitting and disobedience. Any aversive consequences attaching to such behaviour were usually mild and consisted of nagging, scolding or threats rather than more severe punishment. Table 2 shows that during ten hours' observation of each of seven families, the children's behaviour attracted substantial proportions of positive reinforcement, sufficient apparently to offset any aversive consequences. Incidentally, the child who received reinforcements for only 1% of his deviant responses was a problem in school rather than at home.

Table 2—*Average Proportions of Positive and Aversive Consequences for Deviant Behaviour* (*Patterson 1971*)

Family	Positive (%)	Aversive (%)
1	43	20
2	44	13
3	1	10
4	36	52
5	14	43
6	22	13
7	22	33

An individual illustration of the positive reinforcement of problem behaviour is the case of a four-year-old boy, Peter S., whose treatment by Hawkins et al. (1966) is discussed later. 'He is the third of four children in a middle-class family. Peter had been brought to a university clinic because he was extremely difficult to manage and control. His mother stated she was helpless in dealing with his frequent tantrums and disobedience. Peter often kicked objects or people, removed or tore his clothing, called people rude names, annoyed his younger sister, made a variety of threats, hit himself and became very angry at the slightest frustration. He demanded attention almost constantly, and seldom co-operated with Mrs S.... He was described as having borderline intelligence, as being hyperactive, and possibly brain-damaged.... The experimenters, observing the mother and child in the home, noted that many of Peter's undesirable behaviours appeared to be maintained by attention from his mother. When Peter behaved objectionably, she would often try to explain why he should not act thus; or she would try to interest him in some new activity by offering toys or food.... Peter was occasionally punished by the withdrawal of a misused toy or other object, but he was often able to persuade his mother to return the item almost immediately. He was also punished by being placed on a high chair and forced to remain there for short periods. Considerable tantrum behaviour usually followed such disciplinary measures and was quite effective in maintaining mother's attention, largely in the form of verbal persuasion or arguments.' (p. 99).

Another example, also considered later from a treatment point of view, is the case reported by Holder (1969) of a three-year-old girl named Maria who was indulging in tantrum crying on going to bed. Her mother 'described her attempts to get Maria to sleep at night as "a battle of wills", and said ruefully that her parents said she "had made a rod for her own back!".' She stated that she had had toxaemia badly when Maria was born, and when she took Maria to her cot as a baby, she had been in the habit of lying on the bed in the same room as Maria, partly in the hope of soothing the child to sleep by her presence, and partly to rest because of her own ill-health. She had continued to do this when she was recovered from the toxaemia, and Maria had grown used to her mother's presence and now refused to go to sleep unless mother was in the room.' (p. 8).

Similar evidence on the positive reinforcement of problem behaviour has been gathered in school settings. Allen et al. (1964) found that the degree of solitary behaviour exhibited by a withdrawn nursery school child was systematically related to the reinforcement practices of her teachers (Figure 1). It was observed that when the child isolated herself, the teachers gave her a great deal of attention and encouraged her to play with other children. When she did so, the teachers withdrew their attention. It was decided to alter the reinforcement contingencies so that teacher attention was given only when the child interacted with other children, and this change was followed by an increase in social play and a decrease in solitariness. In order to check the relationship between this modification in behaviour and the change of reinforcement contingencies, the teachers then reverted to their previous practice of attending to the child when she was alone, with the result that social play decreased and solitariness increased. The treatment condition of attending only when the child interacted with other children was then reinstituted, and again the proportion of social play increased.

Studies such as those by Allen et al. are especially valuable because they do provide correlational evidence that the positive reinforcement is systematically

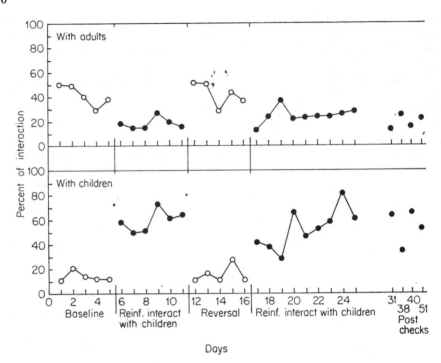

Figure 1. Percentages of time spent in social interaction during approximately two hours of each morning session (Allen et al. 1964).

related to *increases* in problem behaviour, whereas the evidence cited earlier merely establishes that such behaviour is often accompanied by events which are arbitrarily deemed to be positively reinforcing although their strengthening effect is not actually demonstrated.

There is similar indirect support for the operation of reward training in the development and maintenance of a wide variety of other conditions. Ayllon and his co-workers (Ayllon and Michael 1959, Ayllon and Houghton 1962, 1964) show that psychotic symptoms, such as delusional talk, are influenced by the attention, interest and support they attract from nurses. If these social reinforcers are made contingent upon rational rather than psychotic behaviour, then the latter is reduced. Various deviant sub-cultures reward their members for indulging in behaviour such as prostitution (Greenwald 1958), homosexuality (Caprio 1954, Henry 1941, Hooker 1961), aggression and delinquency (Buehler et al. 1966, Sutherland 1937, Wolfgang and Ferracuti 1967, Yablonsky 1962). For instance, in two of the studies of institutionalized delinquents conducted by Buehler et al., some 70% and 88% of deviant acts were socially reinforced by at least one peer, while conforming behaviour was usually followed by aversive consequences. Finally, although certain forms of problem behaviour may arise from somatic factors or as means of avoiding stress they may also entail considerable secondary gains or positive reinforcement. A school-phobic child may no longer be frightened of going to school and yet still refuse to do so because of the rewards available to him at home (Ayllon et al. 1970). Lovaas et al. (1965) have demonstrated that self-injurious behaviour in autistic children is increased by responding to it with sympathy, reassurance and physical affection. In a case reported by Walton (1960) a young woman perpetuated neurodermatitis by compulsively scratching the area concerned. Her skin condition attracted a great deal of attention from parents and fiancé, including the application of ointment by the latter. Removal of this attention was followed by cessation of scratching and successful treatment.

One form of reward training is called discrimination learning. It involves reinforcing a specific response only when a certain stimulus is present, and not otherwise. After a number of such learning experiences, the subject emits the response only in the presence of the discriminative stimulus which signals the likelihood of reinforcement. In the simplest experimental paradigm of this procedure, a pigeon given a food pellet for pressing a bar when a light is on but not when it is off will soon learn to commence and to cease pressing according to the presence or absence of the light. The behaviour of some clients may constitute a problem because their responses are not guided by suitable discriminative stimuli. For instance, a schizophrenic may appear bizarre because his responses do not conform to the social conventions, or a child's behaviour may be outside the control of his parents' instructions. Such problems may sometimes arise from insufficient exposure to appropriate discrimination learning so that stimulus control is not properly established, as well as from the breakdown of previously learned discriminations due to some somatic factor or contemporary stress.

A second major instrumental conditioning procedure which may contribute to problem behaviour is termed avoidance training. In a well-known experimental example of this procedure (Soloman and Wynne 1953), a dog was placed in a compartment that was divided down the middle by a fence. On each trial a buzzer was sounded followed ten seconds later by a shock through the electrified floor on the side of the compartment where the dog was standing. If the dog jumped the fence to the other side of the compartment within ten seconds of the buzzer sounding then the shock was avoided. Within ten trials the animal had learned this avoidance response. Thus avoidance training consists of pairing a warning signal with an aversive event until the subject responds to the signal alone so that the event is avoided.

Many kinds of problem behaviour have an avoidance component. Perhaps the simplest examples are the more restricted phobias. Little Albert acquired not only a classically conditioned fear of rats and similar objects, but also certain instrumentally conditioned avoidance responses to keep the feared stimuli at a safe distance from him. These avoidance responses reduced his fear and thus were reinforced. Similarly, the claustrophobic person avoids closed spaces, the agoraphobic avoids places of public assembly, the acrophobic avoids heights and the school-phobic child avoids going to school. In each case the avoidance response is strengthened by its reduction of fear.

Obsessive–compulsive behaviour also seems to have an avoidance component in that it often reduces anxiety, while this is increased by attempts to resist or interfere with the thoughts or rituals. For example, a person may have to wash his hands a set number of times in order to dispel temporarily the obsession that he will contaminate anything he touches, together with its accompanying anxiety. Of course, this does not constitute a complete explanation of obsessive–compulsive disorders; one has still to account for the genesis of the obsessional idea as well as for the selection of a particular avoidance response (Meyer and Chesser 1970). For instance, the origin of a contamination obsession requires explanation and compulsive handwashing might arise as a rational way of removing imagined sources of contamination, as a symbolic cleansing of guilt, as an extension of a socially approved habit which has been associated with feelings of relief since childhood or as a means of preventing the performance of some unacceptable manual activity such as masturbation.

Avoidance training may contribute to several other kinds of problem behaviour. The losses of sensory or motor function without organic basis, which occur in hysterical conversion reactions, are often precipitated by traumatic conditions such as experiences in battle and they enable the person to avoid re-entry into the stressful situation (Grinker and Spiegel 1945). Similarly, an hysterical amnesia for disturbing events may represent a cognitive avoidance response consisting of 'not thinking' about the anxiety-provoking stimuli. The hypochondriac's unrealistic concern with his own health may enable him to avoid some stress, illness being an acceptable reason for evading responsibility in many spheres of life, including school, work and sexual relationships. Both alcohol and drugs have the property of reducing anxiety, thus addiction to them may in some degree constitute a means of avoiding stress. Finally, any sexual activity may arouse pleasurable feelings which counteract anxiety, and it may also shift attention away from stressful events. Thus deviant sexual behaviour may constitute an avoidance response and be reinforced by anxiety reduction. For example, Cooper (1963) cites the case of a transvestite who discovered accidentally that his cross dressing reduced the anxiety he was experiencing in relation to an examination. Thereafter, he indulged in transvestite behaviour when under many different kinds of stress.

These types of problem behaviour which involve anxiety and avoidance responses tend to be remarkably persistent and resistant to extinction. Providing that they are not reinforced by aversive events subsequently, one might expect classically conditioned fears to extinguish. In fact, the dog in the experiment by Solomon and Wynne (1954) went on jumping the fence on hundreds of occasions although the shock was switched off after twenty trials. Similarly, to have to avoid entering certain phobic situations, to spend large proportions of one's waking time in compulsive handwashing, to lose one's vision, movement or memory, to be over-concerned about one's health or to suffer the personal and social consequences of alcoholism, drug addiction, or sexual deviation, all entail considerable unhappiness and impairment of function, but some clients still persist in behaving in such ways. This self-perpetuating and yet at the same time self-defeating behaviour has been called the 'neurotic paradox' (Mowrer 1948).

Several points have been advanced to explain this phenomenon (Mowrer 1948, 1960, Solomon and Wynne 1954, Wynne and Solomon 1955). In the first place, the problem behaviour may be maintained by various secondary gains or positive reinforcers, as discussed above in the section on reward training. For instance, hysterical or hypochondriacal reactions may be rewarded by the sympathy, attention and support normally accorded to the sick. Secondly, the avoidance responses may be reinforced also by the anxiety reduction they entail. As the dog jumped the fence his fear lessened and similarly, a client's anxiety may be reduced by his performance of compulsive rituals. Thirdly, such responses prevent the extinction of fear and the discovery that the threat no longer exists. As the dog did not stay in the compartment his fear could not be extinguished by the absence of shock; similarly the claustrophobic's refusal to enter lifts means that he cannot experience their harmless nature. Finally, a rather more technical point, while classically conditioned fear may be important initially in the acquisition and reinforcement of avoidance responses, it does seem that subsequently these can be evoked directly by the warning signals mediated by the central nervous system, and thus no longer be dependent on the persistence of fear responses as autonomic mediators of avoidance.

To conclude, instrumental conditioning procedures involve the attachment of consequences to responses which alter their future probability of occurrence in similar situations. In the case of reward training, this probability is increased by following the response with a positive reinforcer, while avoidance training consists of establishing a response to a warning signal so that a subsequent aversive event is avoided. Both types of instrumental conditioning procedures may contribute to the development and maintenance of a wide range of problem behaviour.

Observational Learning

The client's observation of certain behaviour by other people and of its consequences for them is another type of learning experience which may contribute to problem behaviour. One effect of this procedure is that the observer acquires new responses by imitating the behaviour of the model. A laboratory example is a series of studies by Bandura and his co-workers (Bandura and Walters 1963) in which nursery school children were exposed to real or filmed adult models who exhibited unusual forms of aggression towards a large rubber doll. After mild frustration these children frequently imitated the model's unusual behaviour very precisely and they were more aggressive than similarly frustrated children who had not previously observed an aggressive model.

A second effect of observation learning is the disinhibition of responses already possessed by the observer. For example, Walters and Thomas (1963) asked adult subjects to assist in studying the effects of punishment on learning. These 'assistants' were required to administer shocks to 'subjects' whenever they responded incorrectly to a task set them. (In fact, the subjects were confederates of the experimenters and did not receive the shocks, although the assistants were unaware of this.) Next, the assistants were shown an extract from the film *Rebel Without a Cause* in which two adolescents engage in a knife fight, while a control group saw an educational film of adolescents performing constructive activities. After exposure to the aggressive film the strength of the shocks given by the assistants increased and were stronger than those administered by the controls.

Of course, not all the behaviour of other people is reproduced by those who observe it, and one important factor in determining whether or not imitation does occur is the consequences of the behaviour for the model. These may consist of immediate reward or punishment or be inferred from the model's possessions, prestige, status or power. An experimental example of the influence of shorter term consequences is a study by Bandura et al. (1963). They showed some nursery school children a film of an adult using aggression successfully to obtain possessions, while other children saw a film of the same behaviour leading to punishment. In a subsequent test, those exposed to the rewarded model were more aggressive than the children shown the punished model and than controls.

It is more difficult to distinguish the influence of observational learning experiences on the acquisition and performance of aggressive responses outside the laboratory, but there is some possible support in anthropological field studies (Bateson 1936, Whiting 1941, Whiting and Child 1953, Eaton and Weil 1955), in the literature on delinquent subcultures (Cohen 1955, Whyte 1937, Yablonsky 1962) and in reports of a positive relationship between aggressiveness in parents and their children (Bandura and Walters 1959, McCord and McCord 1958). There is additional support also for the relevance of the consequences of the model's behaviour as a factor influencing imitation by an observer. Several studies have demonstrated that exposure to models behaving aggressively without adverse consequences tends to be followed by increases in the frequency and degree of aggression exhibited by observers (Epstein 1966, Hartmann 1969, Wheeler 1966).

The attachment of emotional responses to certain stimuli is usually considered to result from the direct experience of pain or pleasure in association with these stimuli. However, there is evidence that emotional responses may also be acquired vicariously, by watching someone else experiencing painful or pleasurable stimulation. Thus Lazarus and his colleagues (1962) were able to elicit emotional responses in college students by showing them a film of an Australian aborigine boy undergoing a crude genital operation as an initiation rite. The degree of emotional arousal was heightened by playing the sound track of the boy's expression of pain (Speisman et al. 1964).

In this series of experiments, the observers reproduced the model's unconditioned emotional response to the unconditioned painful stimulation. If such an unconditioned stimulus is preceded by a neutral conditioned stimulus, then a conditioned emotional response can be vicariously classically conditioned in an observer. For example, Berger (1962) told a group of observers that a model would receive a shock (UCS) whenever a light was dimmed, and each time this occurred the model exhibited an arm jerk to indicate pain (UCR). A buzzer was sounded shortly before the dimming of the light signified the administration of a shock to the model, and after a number of such pairings, the buzzer alone elicited emotional responses in the *observers*.

It is possible that observational learning procedures may contribute to emotional problems in some clients. Jones (1924a) suggests that social imitation is a common source of irrational fears in children and cites the case of a child who developed a phobia of rabbits after seeing another child exhibit fear towards them. Furthermore, the similarity reported between children's fears and those of their parents and siblings (Hagman 1932, May 1950) might reflect observational learning experiences.

To conclude, in addition to direct classical and instrumental conditioning, it does seem that vicarious observational learning processes may contribute to problem behaviour. This is illustrated by work on aggression and anxiety, but the influence of such processes may well extend to many other types of problem. Much remains to be done in distinguishing this influence in naturalistic situations outside the laboratory.

Cognitive Learning

This is a more controversial category in that some psychologists would regard it as superfluous and it is relatively neglected in behavioural formulations of deviance. Little dispute exists over the importance of a person's thinking or problem-solving processes in influencing his behaviour. These processes include attending to and perceiving the relevant elements in a problem situation, storing these in short-term memory and recalling other essential information, conceptualizing the data into appropriate categories and manipulating these by inductive and deductive reasoning to yield hypotheses, rules or principles which solve the presenting problem and others of similar nature. A breakdown at any point in the whole process may prevent a client from solving his problems satisfactorily. Such breakdowns might arise from somatic factors like brain damage and/or from learning experiences.

It is at this point that controversy enters (Hilgard and Bower 1966). Some psychologists argue that instrumental conditioning and observational learning procedures provide the necessary learned component in problem solving, so that the subject simply applies solutions learned in these ways to the new problem. Others believe that this is not an adequate explanation and while not denying the importance of past learning they stress the need for a cognitive restructuring of the contemporary situation so that it is perceived and understood differently. They therefore postulate a separate category of cognitive learning in addition to those already described. This issue may be by-passed here, providing one recognizes the possible contribution of learning deficiencies to the inability of clients to solve their own problems.

This concludes discussion of the learning procedures which might contribute to the development and maintenance of problem behaviour. Their classification into the four categories of classical and instrumental conditioning, together with observational and cognitive learning, is a matter of convenience for the purposes of this book rather than being the only division (Melton 1964).

Contemporary Events

The stress in a behavioural approach upon the contribution of learning experiences to problem behaviour is noted above. Another major characteristic of the approach is the importance attached to contemporary events. Although somatic factors and past learning may contribute to the origin of behaviour, it constitutes a problem only when it represents an unacceptable way of responding to a current situation. To take a simple example, suppose someone has acquired a monosymptomatic fear of snakes, even when they are quite harmless. This represents a problem only if it involves distress and impairment of functioning in the current situation, and may never occur in countries where there are no snakes. Another example is that the effects of a physical illness or injury in the past may be maintained in the present by secondary gains or rewards, such as the prospect of monetary compensation or the avoidance of some stressful situation. Thus, the contemporary controlling conditions are another set of factors which contribute to problem behaviour. Bandura (1969) has categorized these contemporary events into three interrelated control systems: antecedent control, outcome control and symbolic control. The possible contribution of each of these to problem behaviour is discussed below.

Antecedent Control

The contributions of antecedent events include the *elicitation* or *reinforcement* of certain kinds of problem behaviour. These include emotional responses comprising subjective feelings like anxiety, guilt or anger, together with physical signs of overactivity in the autonomic nervous system such as changes in respiration, heart rate, muscular tension, gastrointestinal secretion and blood pressure. Responses of this kind may be elicited by a wide range of stimuli, as discussed in the sections on classical conditioning and observational learning.

Some psychiatric disorders represent unacceptable emotional reactions to antecedent events. The symptoms of anxiety states reflect the subjective and autonomic components of emotional arousal. Thus a client might complain of feelings of apprehension accompanied by muscle tension, palpitations and nausea. Some psychosomatic conditions may arise from prolonged emotional arousal leading to permanent tissue changes. For instance, an unduly prolonged increase in blood pressure might contribute to hypertension, or persistent gastrointestinal changes to the formation of ulcers. Finally, the inappropriateness of certain antecedent events as eliciting stimuli is perhaps most clearly illustrated by the phobic states, in which relatively harmless objects or situations evoke irrational or excessive fear.

A third function of antecedent events is to serve as *discriminative* stimuli to guide the performance of instrumental responses. As a result of the discrimination learning procedures described above, certain stimuli come to signify the likelihood of different reinforcement consequences and this influences the probability of a given response being performed. Such discriminative stimuli are to be distinguished from eliciting stimuli. The latter evoke responses in an automatic way without regard to their consequences, while the former merely modify the probability of a response being performed according to its likely outcome, rather than eliciting its occurrence. We see above that emotional responses are mainly under the control of eliciting stimuli, and that it is the performance of instrumental responses such as speech or movement which is influenced by discriminative stimuli.

Many forms of problem behaviour may involve some failure of antecedent control by discriminative stimuli. Events which usually influence the performance of responses may not do so in particular clients. For example, a parental prohibition may fail to inhibit a child's misbehaviour. In other cases, certain responses may be controlled by inappropriate discriminative stimuli. Thus the probability of a parent attending to a child may be increased by the latter's tantrum behaviour, whereas a more appropriate discriminative stimulus for parental attention would be reasonable requests by the child. Thirdly, discriminative stimuli which have guided behaviour in the past may be absent from a client's contemporary situation. This may occur if there is a marked change in his social environment, and Gewirtz (1961) has suggested that it may contribute to the inappropriate, disorganized and regressive behaviour which occurs in some children on admission to strange foster homes or institutions.

Turning now from the functions to the sources of the antecedent events that contribute to problem behaviour. They may exist in the client's external environment, as occurs when his behaviour is elicited or guided by other people. Alternatively, the antecedent events may arise in the client's own physical processes. There is now a considerable body of evidence supporting the efficacy of internal changes as eliciting and discriminative stimuli for a wide range of responses (Bykov 1957, Razran 1961, Slucki et al. 1965). A third possible source of antecedent control is the client's symbolic processes and this is discussed below.

Outcome Control

In the earlier discussion on instrumental conditioning procedures, it is noted that the future performance of many responses may be influenced by their consequences for the subject. If these are rewarding, then the responses are likely to be retained and strengthened. In contrast, responses which are followed by non-reward or punishment tend to be eliminated or weakened.

The outcome may occur in the external environment and be experienced directly by the subject. This is the case when other people reinforce problem behaviour in clients, as described above in the section on reward training. Secondly, a subject's performance of a response in future may be influenced vicariously by his observation of its consequences for a model. Examples of such vicarious reinforcement are cited in the discussion on observational learning. Thirdly, the consequences of, behaviour may occur in the client's own psychological processes and this is discussed below in the section on symbolic control.

There are several ways in which outcome control may contribute to problem behaviour. In the first place, certain harmful or culturally disapproved consequences may be rewarding to some clients. Examples of problems involving such inappropriate positive reinforcement are drug addiction, alcoholism and disorders of sexual object like fetishism, pedophilia or homosexuality. Conversely, certain consequences which customarily influence behaviour may fail to do so in some clients, including those who are autistic, anti-social or psychopathic. Thus customary social rewards such as attention, approval and affection may fail to positively reinforce behaviour, or it may not be reduced by normally punishing consequences like disapproval, criticism or censure. In other cases certain customary reinforcers may be lacking in a client's environment. This is likely to produce apathy and unresponsiveness and might be an important contributory factor to conditions of fatigue, depression and institutionalization. More specifically, lack of customary material reinforcers such as food, clothing and suitable accommodation may lead to responses of hunger, anxiety or anger. Finally, some problem behaviour may be maintained and strengthened by the rewards attaching to it in the client's social environment. Many examples of this are given in the earlier discussion on reward training.

Symbolic Control

In the discussions on antecedent and outcome control it is noted that their sources may be a person's own symbolic processes rather than his physiological changes or external environment. First, aversive thoughts, images and talk may serve as eliciting or reinforcing stimuli for problematic emotional responses. For instance, anxiety might be aroused by disturbing sexual or aggressive thoughts or by imagining a feared situation. Secondly, antecedent symbolic events may function as discriminative stimuli for instrumental responses. Thus the symbolic attribution of 'authority' to father, teacher and employer may increase the probability of hostility towards them, or the labelling of any sexual relationship as 'wrong' might contribute to the inhibition of response in conditions of impotence or frigidity.

Thirdly, the probability of certain responses occurring in future may be influenced by their symbolic consequences. A person may praise or otherwise reward himself when he behaves in ways which accord with his own standards, while disapproved behaviour is followed by symbolic punishment. Some clients have excessively high standards for self-reward and this may produce feelings of depression, worthlessness and purposelessness, together with apathy and inaction or the avoidance of situations which may entail any risk of failing to meet the self-imposed standards. Other clients may have deficient or distorted symbolic reinforcement systems so that symbolic rewards and punishments are administered inappropriately. For instance, the psychopath may not punish himself for behaviour which would make most people feel extremely guilty, or the professional criminal might reward himself for a successful theft.

Finally, the symbolic control of behaviour occurs in the processes of attention, perception, memory and reasoning. In the section on cognitive learning above, these processes are recognized as necessary components of problem-solving and this is likely to be impaired by any breakdown of symbolic control. Many psychotic symptoms, such as distractibility, hallucinations, recent memory loss and dementia, represent especially striking examples of such breakdown.

CONCLUSION

In this chapter, problem behaviour is conceptualized as unacceptable ways of responding to certain conditions and it is explained as a product of somatic factors, learning experiences and contemporary events.

As some exponents tend to play down the contribution of the first group of determinants, it is emphasized that a behavioural approach does not necessarily entail any denial or neglect of the importance of somatic influences on problem behaviour, although there is a special interest in the contributions of learning experiences and contemporary events.

However, it must be recognized that there is very little direct evidence on the nature and role of learning experiences in the origin and development of problem behaviour. As discussed in the relevant section, their contribution is largely inferred from experimental analogues and only very rarely can the origin and course of problems be traced to specific learning experiences with any degree of confidence.

Finally, the stress on the contribution of contemporary events to problem behaviour does not imply that the client merely responds to a relatively fixed environment. In fact, his behaviour to some extent influences and creates his environment, as well as vice versa, so that there is a reciprocal relationship between behaviour and its controlling conditions (Bandura 1969). For instance, it has been shown that aggressive children tended to create a hostile environment for themselves, while friendly children produced a more amicable environment (Rausch 1965). We shall see that the behavioural stress on contemporary controlling events and their reciprocal interaction with problem behaviour has important implications for treatment.

2
Behaviour Modification

The behavioural attempt to apply certain principles from experimental psychology may provide more specific guidance to social work treatment, although some limitations in the nature and use of the knowledge available are indicated in the introduction.

An additional point of note is that the principles used in the treatment of a particular problem are not necessarily those involved in its origin and development. For example, some forms of problem behaviour are modifiable by rewarding alternative behaviour, but this does not imply that the problem arose because these alternatives were not reinforced at some earlier stage. Rimland (1964) uses the analogy that because aspirin eliminates a headache one must not conclude that it was caused by lack of aspirin.

A related feature of behaviourally oriented casework is an emphasis on the contemporary events which control problem behaviour rather than those which led to its acquisition in the first place. There is a concentration on the 'here and now' instead of an historical working through of past experiences, and this may be a more practicable and appropriate approach for many problems, clients and social workers.

There are two general treatment strategies which may be implemented either singly or in combination. One is to alter a client's responses to the controlling factors in his environment without deliberately changing the latter. Assuming a family environment to be essentially satisfactory one might attempt to adjust a client to it. A second strategy is to change the controlling factors in an environment as a means of modifying problem behaviour. Thus, a client's material or social deprivations might be remedied with consequent reduction in the anxiety or aggression previously elicited by them, or a mother might be helped to respond to her child's reasonable requests rather than reinforcing his tantrum behaviour with her attention. These strategies may be implemented in interviews or natural situations, including the usual environments of clients as well as special therapeutic milieux such as residential institutions. The use of certain selected procedures within these settings is now reviewed. They are not the only procedures which might be derived from experimental psychology and the examples of their use are illustrative rather than exhaustive. The procedures are categorized according to whether they appear to operate primarily through the antecedent, outcome or self-control of problem behaviour. However, more than one form of control may contribute to a particular procedure, and often it is difficult to distinguish the operation and effect of a specific source of control.

ANTECEDENT CONTROL PROCEDURES

There are several ways in which contemporary antecedent events may be manipulated for therapeutic purposes:

1. Stimuli that *elicit* problematic responses may be removed, while those eliciting desirable behaviour may be presented and enhanced.

2. Similarly, stimuli that *reinforce* problematic responses may be removed, while the reinforcement of desirable behaviour is strengthened.

3. Finally, *discriminative* stimuli may be utilized to decrease the probability of problematic instrumental responses being performed, and to increase the probability of desirable instrumental behaviour.

These eliciting, reinforcing or discriminative antecedent events may be manipulated to modify clients' behaviour either directly, or vicariously through observational learning experiences. Some possible social work treatment procedures which appear to be based primarily upon antecedent control are now illustrated, but it is stressed that the uncontrolled case studies do not permit the necessary attribution of any beneficial changes in the client's behaviour to the procedure concerned or to the treatment programme as a whole. Aspects of the treatment other than the specific procedure or extra-therapeutic factors might have contributed to these changes but their effects cannot be distinguished. This point is discussed in Chapter 3, but it should be noted here that these case studies are described only for the purpose of illustrating the procedures rather than as evidence for their efficacy.

Reduction of Stressful Antecedent Conditions

One way of weakening responses such as anxiety, guilt or anger is to reduce the stresses that elicit or reinforce them. This may occur in interviews if clients talk about matters which evoke such responses, without incurring disapproval, criticism or punishment from the social workers. In a study of this process, anxiety over sexual matters decreased throughout a series of permissive therapeutic sessions (Dittes 1957a). Moreover, the anxiety level varied systematically with the permissiveness of the therapist: it decreased when he was gentle and attentive and increased when he reacted negatively (Dittes 1957b).

In natural situations, stress might be reduced by changing the behaviour of other people towards the client. A father might be helped to be less harshly punitive in order to weaken his child's fear and avoidance of him. A husband might be encouraged to be very controlled in his sexual behaviour towards his frigid wife, so that her anxiety over sexual activities is not reinforced while treatment is in progress. In so changing the behaviour of other people towards the client, the social worker may use any of the procedures described in this chapter.

Stress might consist also of some material or social deprivation, such as inadequate income or accommodation, or some lack of care or opportunity. When this is so, often it is more appropriate to attempt to reduce the excessive environmental stress rather than to modify the client's reactions to it.

Positive Counterconditioning

The principle of all counterconditioning procedures is the establishment of a response to a stimulus which is incompatible with and stronger than the problematic response to the same stimulus, so that the latter response is eliminated (Wolpe 1958, 1969). In the case of positive counterconditioning, certain positive responses including relaxation, eating, pleasant emotions, assertion and sexual arousal are used to eliminate negative responses, such as anxiety. The stimuli which arouse the negative response are presented in a gradually ascending sequence from the least to the most disturbing, so that the positive response is always the stronger of the two.

This procedure may be illustrated by the treatment of a three-year-old child named Peter who was afraid of rabbits (Jones 1924b). The treatment was carried out in an American residential nursery, using eating as a response incompatible with fear. But if Peter was given sweets with a rabbit near him, his fear was so strong that he ignored them in favour of escaping from the animal. To overcome this difficulty, while Peter was eating, a caged rabbit was first introduced into the far corner of the room, and then gradually over a number of sessions it was released from the cage and brought nearer to him, until finally he quite happily held the animal on his lap and allowed it to nibble his fingers. A similar example is the treatment of John D., aged eight years, for an intense fear of moving vehicles following his involvement in a car accident (Lazarus 1959). He was given his favourite chocolate as treatment progressed from talking about vehicles, to deliberate accidents with toy cars, to sitting in a stationary car, to travelling short distances, until after six weeks, at the therapist's invitation the child went one and a half miles in a car with a complete stranger to buy chocolate. There was a stage when he would not go in the car with his parents unless he was given chocolate, but this passed, and he soon enjoyed motoring.

The use of pleasant emotional reactions to eliminate fear may be illustrated first by the treatment of a year-old baby girl named Margaret, who had become very afraid of water after slipping in the bath (Bentler 1962). The pleasant responses used included attraction to toys, interest in a mirror, and affection towards her mother. Initially, toys were placed in an empty bath, and then in a sink filled with water, through which after some reluctance Margaret waded to get them. She was then washed in the sink, while playing with a favourite toy and showing great interest in a mirror. Finally the baby was washed in the bath, to which initially she objected strongly, but with parental hugging and reassurance she no longer cried and began to play normally. A second example is the treatment of Jimmy, aged ten years, for school phobia (Garvey and Hegrenes 1966). Accompanied by a social worker with whom he had a good relationship, Jimmy was gradually exposed to school situations, starting with sitting in front of the school in a car, going to the bottom and then the top of the school steps, entering the school and then the classroom, remaining in the classroom first with the teacher alone, then with one or two classmates and finally with the whole class present. Whenever any of these situations aroused fear, the session was terminated and Jimmy returned to the car. The responses incompatible with fear consisted of positive emotions aroused by the social worker's presence and his praise at the satisfactory completion of each step in treatment. After twenty days of treatment, lasting twenty to forty minutes on each day, the social worker withdrew and Jimmy attended school normally on his own. Positive emotions may be induced also in interview situations. If social workers are warm and sympathetic, if they are concerned about clients' problems and hopeful for their solution, if they are known to respect confidences and to possess professional competence and prestige, then the clients may react with feelings of confidence, trust, optimism and positive self-regard, which will be counterposed against any anxiety, guilt or self-devaluation, and may serve to countercondition these undesirable responses. This is most likely to occur if the stimuli which evoke the negative responses are discussed in a gradually ascending sequence of aversiveness, so that the incompatible positive responses evoked by the social worker remain the stronger.

Another type of positive response which is especially valuable in counterconditioning social anxieties evoked in interpersonal situations is self-assertiveness, including not only the overt expression of anger and resentment but also of friendliness and affection. Stuart (1967) has reported an example of the use of this procedure in natural situations. The client was a twenty-one-year-old girl, who presented with an anxiety state following her second abortion. She was markedly unstable both in her work history and in her relationships with men. Prior to dates, her anxiety over her physical attractiveness and her intellectual and social skills mounted to panic level, and in order to distract the man from her imagined shortcomings, she would have sexual intercourse with him as early as possible in the evening. The client was helped to alter her behaviour on dates, so that men would respond differently to her. She was instructed to behave as if she expected to be treated with respect, for example by waiting to be helped on with her coat and for doors to be opened and her cigarette lit. To avoid inappropriate sexual experiences, she was encouraged to meet her dates in public places, to remain with other people and not to invite the men into her flat at the end of the evening. These new ways of behaving were followed by more satisfying and continuous relationships with men, as well as by increased assertiveness and success in other sectors of her life. In another case Mr A. B., a twenty-five-year-old engineer, complained of excessive shyness, great difficulty in relationships with women, and certain physical symptoms. He was unmarried and living in his parents' home, which was dominated by his overprotective and restrictive mother, who even insisted on approving all his social contacts and arrangements. Mr A. B. was set a graded series of assertive tasks commencing with praising his secretary, deciding where to lunch and asking for quicker service, and moving on to his home life. Eventually he went to live in a flat on his own, and when his mother reacted with pseudo-heart trouble he treated her sympathetically but did not return home. A month after taking the flat, his physical symptoms had ended and he had established close relationships with two girls whom he had long admired. On follow-up eighteen months later, improvement was maintained and no symptoms had returned (Eysenck and Rachman 1965).

Finally, sexual arousal may be used to countercondition anxiety responses which are impairing sexual performance. The client is instructed only to attempt intercourse when he is strongly motivated, otherwise probable failure will reinforce his anxiety. The co-operation of the sexual partner is sought to indulge in sex play without expecting intercourse to follow necessarily, only if the client experiences a strong desire for it. Increasingly strong erections and successful intercourse may be achieved by this method, the sexual satisfaction being rewarding as well as inhibiting the previous anxiety responses. Wolpe (1954) cites the example of Mr S., a forty-year-old accountant who had a long history of erectile failure and premature ejaculation, both during his marriage which ended in divorce after nine years, and in many extramarital affairs. At the time of treatment he had fallen in love with a twenty-four-year-old girl who was cooling towards him because of his sexual difficulties. The institution of the procedure described was followed quickly by successful intercourse on two occasions—and by the partners' marriage by special licence; this success was consolidated, treatment ended after three months and a follow-up over a five-year period revealed no relapse.

By far the largest volume of data on the efficacy of positive counterconditioning relates to the procedure of systematic desensitization in which muscular relaxation is used as the positive response. As social workers generally are not trained or oriented to intervene directly at an organic level, this technique is not selected for discussion here. However, Paul (1969a,b) summarizes a comprehensive review of 'the application of systematic disensitization therapy to nearly 1,000 clients in the hands of over ninety different therapists. While fifty-five of these papers were uncontrolled case reports or group studies without sufficient methodological controls to establish independent cause–effect relationships, twenty of these reports were controlled experiments, and ten of the controlled experiments included designs which could potentially rule out intraclass confounding of therapist characteristics and treatment techniques. These findings were overwhelmingly positive, and for the first time in the history of psychological treatments, a specific therapeutic package reliably produced measurable benefits for clients across a broad range of distressing problems in which anxiety was of fundamental importance. "Relapse" and "symptom substitution" were notably lacking, although the majority of authors were attuned to these problems. Investigations of equal quality and scope have not been carried out with other treatment techniques deemed appropriate for similar problems, . . .' (pp. 158-9).

This last comment applies to the use of eating, pleasant emotions, assertion and sexual arousal for positive counterconditioning. To date, the evidence on the efficacy of each of these procedures consists only of case studies like the illustrations above, and there are no controlled experimental investigations. Wolpe and Lazarus (1966) have reported a collection of case studies in which sexual arousal was used to countercondition impotent men. Out of thirty-one cases, twenty-one (67·7%) achieved entirely satisfactory sexual performance, while another six (19·4%) attained a level acceptable to their partners. This appears to be the only collection of cases treated by any of the counterconditioning procedures described above which has been reported; the remainder of the evidence consists of individual case reports.

Observational Learning

Problem behaviour may be reduced and its alternatives promoted by exposing clients to real life or symbolic models whom they may imitate. In interviews, social workers often provide models of desired behaviour, either in their personal conduct or symbolically by verbal prescription and proscription. Their own behaviour may constitute a model of effective personal problem solving for clients to imitate in dealing with current and future difficulties. Symbolically, social workers provide models each time they suggest, advise or advocate a course of action to a client, what Hollis (1964) calls 'procedures of direct influence'. For example, many social workers have a parental role which requires them to present appropriate models to children and adolescents in matters such as dress, the management of money and sexual morality.

Several studies indicate that clients may be helped to acquire whatever behaviour is expected of them in interview situations by prior exposure to appropriate models. Marlatt et al. (1966) found that interviewees were more inclined to reveal their personal problems after exposure to a model admitting his problems when this was either accepted or encouraged by the interviewer, compared to the conditions of discouragement of problem admission or of non-exposure to a model. Moreover, the modelling procedure produced and maintained greater revelation of problems by the observer than reinforcing him directly for this behaviour (Marlatt 1968). In another series of studies reported by Truax and Carkhuff (1965) it was considered desirable for clients to engage in self-exploration during therapeutic interviews. A group of clients who had previously listened to tapes of models exhibiting this type of behaviour subsequently indulged in it more than another group of controls who had not been exposed to the modelling condition but otherwise were treated identically. Finally, problem-solving activities have been modelled on tape, including vocational and educational planning (Krumboltz and Schroeder 1965, Krumboltz and Thoresen 1964, Krumboltz et al. 1967) and more efficient study habits (Smith 1965).

Social workers may also constitute or promote suitable models in a client's natural environment. They might encourage good child-rearing practices in parents by actually demonstrating appropriate behaviour towards their children, perhaps by remaining calm in the face of hostility, by expressing affection or by praising achievement. One example of the promotion of suitable observational learning opportunities is the encouragement of parents to reason with their children instead of punishing them excessively, so that the children are exposed to rational rather than aggressive models. Another instance is the provision of substitute male or female models from whom children may learn the appropriate sex role if they are separated from their own parents.

The systematic application of a modelling procedure to improve a mother's handling of her child is described in a paper by Johnson and Brown (1969). Having been adopted at fourteen months, and after a long history of poor development and adjustment, David was referred for treatment at the age of six years. He had been excluded·from ordinary school and was described as over-active, distractible, tense, excitable, as having attacked other children and being defiant to authority. At home, he was excessively demanding and manipulative to the point of largely determining the conduct of the household. David was admitted to a special day school for behaviour-disordered children and his parents participated in a weekly group aimed at the fairly didactic transmission of effective child management principles. After eight months his behaviour had improved at school but not in the home, and it was decided to embark upon an individual treatment programme. As part of the assessment process, the therapists observed the mother performing certain set interactions with David. She was instructed to play with him for two minutes and then to require him to do arithmetical problems within his capacity for five minutes, this sequence being repeated. When asked to do the arithmetic he would often respond with requests for a drink or to go to the lavatory, refuse to use lined paper or indulge in unusual activities like thumb-sucking, head-banging, or crawling. Such 'off task' behaviour was almost always successful in gaining his mother's attention, whereas she rarely rewarded him when he was working at the arithmetical problems. From this and other information gathered during assessment, it seemed that David's problem behaviour was being maintained by his mother's inappropriate reinforcement practices, and it was decided to attempt to modify these by modelling. While the mother observed and recorded, the therapist attended alternately to David's on and off task behaviour, with concomitant variation in the proportion of the arithmetical period spent on each of these activities. The mother then made her attention contingent upon David remaining on task during this period, so that the proportion of off task behaviour to which she attended dropped from 98% to 20%. Further sessions of modelling and other procedures were devoted to ensuring the persistence and generalization of the changes in the behaviour of both David and his mother. She is reported as becoming more successful and positive in her relationship with her son, and five months after the modelling procedure was instituted he was able to return to an ordinary school without further difficulty. The inclusion of other procedures in the latter phase of treatment precludes identification of the specific contribution of the modelling, but it may be significant that this was followed by a degree of improvement that eight months of more didactic instruction had failed to achieve.

Controlled trials of the therapeutic efficacy of modelling procedures have been conducted in respect of several forms of problem behaviour. Especially notable is a series on the treatment of phobic conditions, by Bandura and his co-workers. In their first investigation (Bandura et al. 1967) the subjects were children aged three to five years who exhibited some degree of fear of dogs. During eight brief sessions spread over a few days some of the children were shown a four-year-old boy interacting fearlessly with a cocker spaniel. This child model carried out a carefully arranged sequence of increasingly fear-provoking actions, starting with calling the dog by name and petting it, and moving on to feeding and nursing the animal in a playpen, at first with the model outside the pen and finally climbing in with dog. One group of subjects observed this model in the context of a party atmosphere which was designed to positively countercondition anxiety. A second group observed the model in a neutral context. Two further groups experienced the control conditions either of observing the dog in a party context but without the model or of not being exposed to the dog or the model. After experiencing one of these four conditions the children were asked to carry out the sequence of interactions with the dog which was described above for the model. Those subjects who had observed the model in either the positive or neutral context were considerably less fearful than before treatment and than the children in the two control groups. For instance, 67% of the children in the modelling groups remained alone in a playpen with the dog, compared to only 32% of the controls. On follow-up one month later, the improvement in the modelling groups was maintained and had generalized to unfamiliar dogs.

In a second study (Bandura and Menlove 1968) with similar subjects, the fearless behaviour of the model(s) was shown on film rather than in real life, while a control group were shown films which did not contain a dog. Again the children exposed to the model(s) were less fearful of dogs at the end of treatment and on follow-up. Moreover, the control children who had not improved were then given the modelling treatment after which they achieved a similar decrease in fear to the original treatment group.

The subjects in the third study (Bandura et al. 1968) were adolescents and adults whose social functioning was considerably restricted by snake phobia. Two different forms of treatment which included a modelling procedure were followed by marked reduction in fear of snakes, and this occurred also in another group who were given systematic desensitization, but not in untreated control subjects. These unchanged subjects were then given one or, if necessary, both forms of modelling treatment, with subsequent complete elimination of snake phobia in all cases. The results of these controlled trials and of others reviewed by Bandura (1969) provide support for the efficacy of modelling procedures in ameliorating animal phobias and indicate their possible value in the treatment of other anxiety conditions.

Social isolation in pre-school children is another condition with an anxiety component, which has been modified by the symbolic modelling of alternative behaviour. O'Connor (1969) showed some isolated children a film depicting progressively more active social play with a child model at first watching from a distance and then joining in with positive consequences for himself. Another group of isolated children were shown a control film containing no social interaction. Immediately after seeing the film the treated group displayed a substantial increase in social participation and this reached a similar level to that exhibited by non-isolated children. In contrast, the control children remained withdrawn. This study lacks adequate follow-up data, but the improvement in the treated group seems likely to have endured provided that their new social behaviour was suitably reinforced.

Over-aggressive and domineering reactions to frustration have been modified in children by modelling alternative forms of behaviour together with the different consequences for each type of response. Chittenden (1942) presented a series of short plays in which dolls responded aggressively or co-operatively to common frustrating situations. The aggressive reactions were followed by unpleasant consequences for the dolls, while cooperative behaviour was rewarded. For example, in one play, two boys fight over a toy with the unpleasant result that it is broken, in contrast to the cooperative and rewarding alternative of taking turns to play with it. Compared to untreated controls, the children exposed to the modelling procedure became less aggressive and domineering in a test situation and in the nursery school generally, both at the end of treatment and on follow-up one month later.

Reference has been made to the application of observational learning procedures in the treatment of phobias, social isolation and aggression, and Bandura (1969) reviews their employment with many other conditions, including the reduction of autistic and transgressive behaviour and the promotion of desirable responses such as altruistic acts and helping people in distress. Thus, modelling appears to constitute a potent source of antecedent control in the elicitation, reinforcement and guidance of a wide range of responses. It acts as a catalyst in accelerating new ways of responding, which are then strengthened or weakened according to their future pattern of reinforcement. This last point is important for social work practice, and it is considered further in the following sections on outcome and self-control procedures. In this section, the reduction of stress, positive counter-conditioning and observational learning are reviewed as examples of therapeutic procedures in which the element of antecedent control appears to be especially important.

OUTCOME CONTROL PROCEDURES

In Chapter I we see that the probability of an instrumentally conditioned response occurring in future can be influenced by altering its consequences. This principle yields five basic outcome control procedures:

1. Reinforcement procedures which increase the future probability of any response they follow, and may consist of:

(*a*) the presentation of a reward or positive reinforcer, such as food, money or attention,

(*b*) the removal of aversive stimuli or negative reinforcers, such as pain, threats or reprimands.

2. Punishment procedures which decrease the future probability of any response they follow, and may consist of

(*a*) the presentation of aversive stimuli,

(*b*) the removal of rewards.

3. Extinction procedures which decrease the future probability of any response to which they are applied, and consist of discontinuing the reinforcement contingency which has been maintaining the response concerned.

Of these five possible procedures, the three more likely to be used in social work are selected for discussion here. These are the presentation of rewards or positive reinforcement, the removal of rewards or response cost procedures, and extinction. Most commonly they are offered in some combination as a differential reinforcement programme, and this emphasis is reflected in the following discussion, although each type of procedure is first considered separately.

Positive Reinforcement

Positive reinforcement or reward training procedures are a means of strengthening or maintaining desired behaviour, and an example of their employment in social work occurs in the treatment of a case of elective mutism (Sluckin and Jehu 1969). This is a rare disorder of childhood in which patients choose not to speak, or to speak only to certain people and on certain occasions, despite having normal intelligence with unimpaired comprehension of language and motor ability to speak.

Tessa, the patient, was referred to a Child Guidance Clinic by a paediatrician when she was aged four years eleven months. At about the age of four years, she had suddenly become rather shy and had restricted the people to whom she was willing to speak. When Tessa was four and a half years old, her mother fell ill, and as the child was very frightened of doctors she was assured that the doctor was not coming to see her. A few days later, however, Tessa herself had to have medical attention and it was at this point that she became totally mute, although continuing to communicate by gestures.

Tessa's early history and development had been normal, and there were no serious illnesses or any separations from home. However, both parents noticed a certain stubbornness earlier in her life, for example, her refusal to swallow food when she did not want it and becoming constipated at the commencement of toilet training.

Her parents were a young couple of average intelligence, the father being a skilled worker. They were puzzled and worried over Tessa's unwillingness to speak. Both parents appeared to be stable and mature people, the family relationships seemed good and the atmosphere was friendly, warm and indulgent. There was one other child in the family, a girl named Gina who was three years older than Tessa, and described as lively, assertive and so talkative that Tessa had complained of 'not being able to get a word in edgeways'.

Because of Tessa's fear of strangers it was decided not to see her at the clinic on referral. When the social worker visited a few days later, Tessa had spontaneously resumed talking to her family, but she remained mute with others both inside and outside her home. It became clear that the mother had been responding rather indulgently to Tessa's refusal to speak, and that both had been deriving enjoyment from this. The need to ignore the speech problem but to reward more appropriate behaviour was advocated, the parents were reassured about the outcome and management of the problem and some clarification was offered of its possible origin. The social worker continued to work along these lines for several months until Tessa commenced school.

She settled well and there were no difficulties over attendance, but throughout the whole of the first term Tessa talked to neither children nor teachers. During the second term the headmistress became concerned over the child's lack of progress in reading, and communicated her anxiety to the mother. This, in turn, led to new developments in the relationship between the mother and the social worker. With considerable emotion, the mother disclosed that as a child she had experienced a series of traumatic incidents involving people who were strangers to her, which had been all the more frightening because she had not dared to tell her mother. Remembering her own fear, she had repeatedly and persistently warned the children not to speak to strangers.

By this time the social worker had got to know Tessa quite well, and the child seemed to enjoy communicating with her in a rather flirtatious way, although she did not speak to the social worker or to her mother in the social worker's presence. Having noted Tessa's fondness for sweets, the social worker proposed that she would reward Tessa with a sweet if she would read to her mother in the social worker's presence. Initially, the child was reluctant to participate, but she seemed interested. The social worker placed herself at a distance from, and with her back to, Tessa and her mother. When the child whispered a line to her mother, the promised reward was dispensed. A similar procedure was followed for twenty to thirty minutes at a time, three or four times a week for a period of four weeks. Each session was continued only so long as Tessa enjoyed it, and she became increasingly willing to participate. During the next few weeks the task was made progressively more difficult, at first the whispering of a word being rewarded, then a line, then a page, and finally increasing audibility was required. At the same time, the social worker moved nearer and turned towards Tessa, finally sitting next to her and her mother on the settee. By the end of eight weeks, Tessa was reading and talking to her mother in loud whispers in the close presence of the social worker, who then began gradually to decrease her visits and reading sessions down to one a week.

At this point the social worker suggested that the family might tape record Tessa's voice, and a whole series of conversations, songs and poems were recorded. These were played back by Tessa, first to her family, then to the social worker and finally to the headmistress at school, in the last two cases with the mother present. Tessa appeared to enjoy hearing her own voice and the attention and approval the tapes elicited from others. From then on the mother visited the school once a week and in her presence Tessa would usually, though not always, read to the headmistress.

The social worker next attempted to get Tessa to read to her at home in the absence of the mother. Noting Tessa's liking for colours, the social worker proposed rewarding her with coloured stars for reading, and provided a special book to stick these in. The child took to the 'new game' enthusiastically, interrupting her reading only to choose a star, comment on the number she had earned and to stick them in her book. During this procedure the mother discreetly left the room and Tessa evidenced no sign of missing her. After about four such sessions over a two-week period, she was talking to the social worker directly and in her mother's absence. Within the next few days Tessa began to whisper to her headmistress at school, but not her teacher or to other children.

The summer holidays followed, during which the social worker saw Tessa only once. Her parents reported that suddenly she started to lose her shyness and began to speak spontaneously to most people. On her return to school she answered the register willingly and began to speak appropriately to teachers and children. Follow-up over a period of one year revealed no evidence of symptom return or substitution, and Tessa was behaving normally at home and at school.

Among the learning procedures utilized in the treatment were the non-reinforcement of inappropriate behaviour, the positive reinforcement of appropriate modes of behaviour, *in vivo* desensitization and the facilitation of stimulus and response generalization. The social worker helped the mother to reduce her overindulgence of Tessa's refusal to speak, while increasing the rewards consequent upon talking. Thus the reinforcement contingencies were shifted from not speaking to speaking, positive reinforcers being withdrawn from the former and attached to the latter more appropriate behaviour. Similarly in the treatment sessions, positive reinforcers in the form of sweets, coloured stars and approval by the social worker, parents and headmistress were made contingent upon Tessa talking either directly or on tape. The principle of shaping was applied in the gradual raising of the level of performance required for reinforcement. In vivo desensitization conditions were arranged by opposing Tessa's fear of strangers and of speaking with the incompatible positive emotions elicited by her mother's proximity and approval, by the eating of sweets and by the acquisition of coloured stars. To ensure that these positive emotional reactions were always stronger than the fear reactions, the social worker initially sat far from Tessa and did not look at her. Only gradually as the fear was reduced did the social worker move nearer and turn towards the child, eventually remaining alone with her in her mother's absence. Stimulus generalization was facilitated by having Tessa progress through talking to her mother in the presence of the social worker, on to a tape which the child played to the family, the social worker and the headmistress, to the headmistress in the mother's presence, and finally to the social worker alone. Among the treatment conditions likely to have contributed to response generalization were the gradually increasing audibility of speech required for reward, and the movement through reading words, lines and pages, and recording and playing back conversation, poems and songs, leading finally to spontaneous talking. This uncontrolled case report does not, of course, permit the necessary attribution of the successful outcome to the treatment programme, or the identification of any specific contribution by the positive reinforcement component. It merely illustrates the nature of such a component, with an emphasis on its application in interview situations.

In the next three examples, the emphasis is on the use of positive reinforcement procedures by family members in natural situations. Patterson et al. (1967) have reported an application of this approach. The client, a five-year-old boy, was extremely isolated, socially unresponsive, negativistic and subject to outbursts of bizarre behaviour. His stepmother was using punitive means of control and the child's behaviour was being maintained as an avoidance and escape reaction to this. His behaviour meant also that the parents received no rewarding responses from the boy for their attempts to establish social contact with him. The treatment was aimed first at increasing the positive reinforcement value of the child and his parents for each other. Attention and smiling responses to the parents were shaped up in the child, using sweets and praise as reinforcers. In turn, the parents were rewarded by a reduction in the clinic fee, for reinforcing the child appropriately. As treatment proceeded, in order to reduce his isolation the boy was rewarded for approaching and spending time with his stepmother, and to increase his cooperativeness he was reinforced for carrying out tasks as requested. The authors offer evidence in support of their conclusion that these systematic alterations in the reinforcing practices of the parents were followed by attainment of the treatment goals.

A similar approach to casework with adolescents in an American probation setting is reported by Thorne et al. (1967). One of their clients was a sixteen-year-old girl named Claire, who was referred mainly for serious truancy. In an attempt to correct this, her mother had stopped Claire's pocket money, use of the telephone and going out on dates, but had not made it clear how these privileges could be regained. The treatment plan included the school attendance officer dispensing notes to Claire if she was present at all her classes during a day, and these notes were exchangeable with the mother for certain specified privileges. It was stressed also that the mother should praise Claire when she brought a note home. Over a period of seven weeks the notes were reduced and then stopped entirely. Before treatment, Claire was absent on thirty out of forty-six days, whereas for three months after it commenced she truanted on only two occasions, and not at all during a follow-up over several months. Some improvement in her performance, attitude and interest in school was also reported.

Finally, Stuart (1969a,b,) has used positive reinforcement procedures in the treatment of marital problems. The following brief account considerably over-simplifies his approach and fails to communicate its deep roots in a substantial body of data and theory from social psychology. In the light of this material the treatment was aimed at increasing the positive reinforcement value of the marital partners for each other. There is evidence to suggest that this is likely to be accompanied by more favourable attitudes and communication between the spouses. The treatment was characterized to the couples as a 'game'. Each spouse was asked to choose three forms of behaviour which he or she would like the partner to engage in more frequently, and these were specified in detail. In some marriages it was possible to arrange for a straightforward exchange of these desired responses between partners. In other cases, a token economy system proved useful and Stuart describes the treatment of five such couples. They were aged between twenty-four and fifty-two years, and had been married for three to twenty-three years. Each sought treatment as a last attempt before obtaining a divorce. 'In each instance, the wife complained that her husband neglected her conversational needs while her husband complained that his wife refused any and all sexual advances. . . . The wife was then instructed to purchase a kitchen timer which she could carry about the house. She was instructed to set the timer as soon as her husband entered and to give him one token when the bell sounded if he met her conversational needs at her criterion level during that period. If he failed to behave at the criterion level by the end of the first thirty minutes, she was required to notify him of this and to offer constructive suggestions, cueing him as to how his performance could be improved upon. If she failed to do this, she was required to give her husband a token despite his failure to meet her conversational needs.... The tokens were exchangeable by husbands for sexual favours from their wives. A different menu was constructed for each couple, taking into account their baseline level of sexual activity, and the number of hours available for nonsexual (in this instance conversational) activity.... Accordingly, husbands were charged three tokens for kissing and "lightly petting" with their wives, five tokens for "heavy petting" and fifteen tokens for intercourse' (1969a pp. 224-6). Stuart presents data showing that the rates of conversation and sex increased during treatment and continued during follow-up periods of twenty-four and forty-eight weeks. According to inventories completed by each spouse throughout treatment and follow-up, the rate of reported satisfaction in the marriage increased in association with the changes in behaviour.

Extinction

Problem behaviour which is being maintained by the rewards it produces may be extinguished by discontinuing this inappropriate reinforcement contingency. After a period during which they are not performed, extinguished responses become available to the person again, but if the cycle of extinction, rest and spontaneous recovery is repeated a point is reached at which recovery no longer occurs. Both extinction and spontaneous recovery have an adaptive function. The former involves the abandonment of responses which are no longer producing rewards and the opportunity of trying other responses which may be more successful. If they are, the extinguished response may not be used again, but if the new responses are not reinforced then spontaneous recovery permits the possible retrial of the extinguished response.

An example of an extinction procedure is the treatment of a child's tantrum behaviour on being put to bed (Williams 1959a, 1962). For the first eighteen months of his life he had been seriously ill and received a great deal of special care and attention. On referral at twenty-one months, he was fully recovered but parental attempts to reduce his excessive dependency produced severe tantrums and other manipulative behaviour. For instance, when the parents attempted to leave his room after putting him to bed, he would scream and fuss until they stayed, so that they spent one and a half to two hours waiting for him to go to sleep. If they picked up a book to read during this period, the child would cry until they put it down again. He appeared to enjoy exercising this sort of control and it was ascertained that there was no physical reason for his behaviour.

The mother and an aunt who took it in turns to put him to bed were therefore instructed to do so in a relaxed, leisurely way, then to leave the room and not to return however much the child screamed. The outcome is shown in Figure 2. On the first application of the new regime, the child cried for forty-five minutes.

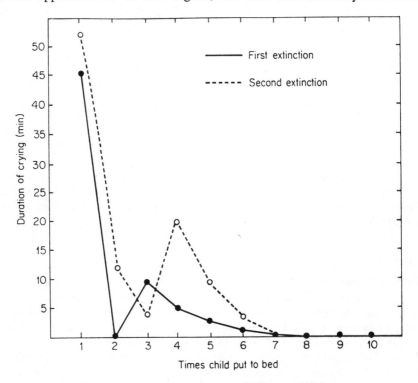

Figure 2. Length of crying in two extinction series (Williams 1959a).

Perhaps because of fatigue after this occasion, he did not cry at all when put to bed for the second time. The duration of crying then increased again to ten minutes, and thereafter progressively declined until it ceased completely, and the child was reported as smiling and making happy sounds on being left alone.

About a week later, screaming recurred after the aunt put him to bed and she reinforced it by returning and remaining in his bedroom until he went to sleep. The extinction procedure was reinstituted with the same result as in the first series, and no further bedtime tantrums were reported during a two-year follow-up period. The parents had also successfully applied extinction procedures to other manipulative behaviour, and the child was described as friendly, expressive and outgoing.

A similar example from an English Children's Department is the case of Maria, which is introduced in Chapter 1 (Holder 1969). The social worker reported that the mother 'had with varying degrees of persistence tried ignoring the child's tantrums when she left the room, keeping the child up late to tire her out, bringing her down after a period of crying, leaving the child to cry with a dummy for comfort, etc. Her husband to some degree had opted out on the problem—he was spending more time at work, and denied he could do anything to help, though he thought the child's behaviour was problematical, and agreed it was causing friction between himself and his wife. Because of the demands Maria was making on his wife's attention. Mr Duffy was determined to limit the size of the family to one child. . . .

'It was agreed that the parents would set up a consistent bedtime routine for Maria in the course of which mother would put her daughter to bed in a relaxed, non-punitive way, and would attend to all the child's needs in a predictable, routine manner before she left the room, i.e. the bedroom would be warm, safe and comfortable, all distracting stimuli would be removed. Maria would have visited the bathroom, had a drink, etc. Mother would then tell Maria a bedtime story, and then having tucked the child up, kiss her goodnight and leave the room, not returning even though the child from past history, could be expected to scream and storm. . . .' The social worker at first visited the home each evening at Maria's bedtime, in order to support the mother in maintaining the extinction regime in the face of the child's very strong reaction to it. 'After seven nights of tantrums, Maria's behaviour suddenly showed a dramatic change, with abrupt, total cessation of the tantrum. Nightly visiting was continued for two nights more, and it was interesting to note how mother and child were beginning to enjoy their consistent bedtime routine. It was then agreed that Mrs Duffy should carry out the bedtime routine alone but that she should telephone each night to report Maria's behaviour. This routine was carried out for the next ten days, during which time the Duffys reported no difficulties with Maria and no tantrums. The child was accepting mother leaving her once she was settled with no signs of distress, and the parents were now enjoying rediscovering each other's company in the evening. . . . Six months later, there has been no sign of a relapse, nor of symptom substitution . . .' (pp. 8-10).

Another example of an extinction procedure is the treatment of the case of neurodermatitis described in Chapter 1 (Walton 1960). It will be recalled that discontinuance of the social attention given to the condition was followed by the cessation of compulsive scratching and subsequent successful treatment.

Certain practical problems may arise in using extinction procedures. There may be difficulty in identifying the reinforcers which are maintaining the problem behaviour or in obtaining sufficient control to ensure their discontinuance. For instance, persistent delinquency which seems only to result in punishment might be maintained by peer approval, and this is often outside the control of a parent or social worker. Another possible source of difficulty arises from the two common side-effects of extinction. One of these is a temporary increase in the behaviour being extinguished during the early stages of this process, and the second is the occurrence of various frustration reactions such as crying or aggression. Both effects are illustrated in the cases described above, and they entail the practical problem of ensuring that they are not successful in regaining reinforcement, otherwise extinction will be prolonged and its side-effects exacerbated. Faced with this intensification of the problem and the frustration reactions, it is difficult for parents and others to maintain the non-reinforcement regime, and prior warnings and support from a social worker may be crucial—as in the case of Maria. The client's passage through this difficult period is likely to be easier if acceptable alternative ways of obtaining reinforcement are available to him, and this is one reason why the extinction of problem behaviour is usually combined with the promotion of acceptable alternatives. Another reason is that an extinction procedure on its own does not specify the form of behaviour which will replace the extinguished responses, and this may also be problematic unless the strengthening of more desirable behaviour is built into the treatment programme. Often this is accomplished by arranging for the positive reinforcement of suitable alternative ways of behaving, but if these are absent or weak in the client's repertoire then treatment may be facilitated by modelling and vicariously rewarding them.

Response Cost

A common form of punishment is the temporary deprivation of customary rewards or privileges, such as pocket money, television viewing or personal liberty, so that these unpleasant consequences constitute the cost of performing problem responses (Weiner 1962). A distinction needs to be drawn between response cost and extinction procedures. The latter involve the non-presentation of the rewards which maintain the problem behaviour, while response cost procedures consist of the forfeiture of rewards which are currently available to the client and these may not be the reinforcing contingencies that maintain the problem. For example, in a play group, aggressive behaviour which is maintained by adult attention might be extinguished by ignoring the aggression, whereas a response cost procedure might consist of removing the aggressive child from the group so that he forfeits the rewards of social play. Often, it is not possible to institute an extinction programme because of the difficulties mentioned above or identifying and controlling the rewards that maintain the problem, and in these circumstances it may be especially appropriate to check problems with response cost procedures while more acceptable alternative behaviour is promoted. As in the case of extinction, it is advisable to include such promotion in the treatment plan, in order to prevent one problem being replaced by others, as well as to mitigate any adverse emotional reactions to the cessation of reinforcement, although these are likely to be less than when punishment consists of presenting aversive stimuli.

'Time out from reinforcement' is a response cost procedure in which the client is removed from a rewarding situation, and it has been used by Tyler and Brown (1967) in an institution for delinquent boys aged between thirteen and fifteen years. Their very disruptive and troublesome behaviour around a billiard table was selected by the school staff for intervention. This consisted of immediately removing an offender to a time-out room in the cottage for a period of fifteen minutes, without any warnings, discussion or second chances and in a matter-of-fact way. Over a seven-week period, this regime was accompanied by a marked decline in the disruptive behaviour. To test the causal nature of this relationship as well as the persistence of the improvement, the time-out procedure was then discontinued and the staff reverted to verbally reprimanding offenders. This was followed by a rapid increase in the disruptive behaviour over a period of thirteen and a half weeks, until the time-out procedure was reinstituted and again disruption decreased. Thus, the problem appears to have been checked by the time-out regime but this outcome did not persist when the procedure was discontinued during the second stage of the study. The authors comment that the improvement might have been more enduring if the positive reinforcement of desirable alternative behaviour had been included in the treatment programme.

The same authors have published a paper entitled 'Time Out From Reinforcement: A Technique for Dethroning the "Duke" of An Institutionalized Delinquent Group' (Brown and Tyler 1968). The subject was a sixteen-year-old boy named John, who severely bullied smaller boys and directed his followers to do likewise. This intimidating–aggressive behaviour paid off in that it was followed by compliance and submission from his peers. The staff found it difficult to detect and interrupt the process because the threats were often quite subtle. For instance, John had only to walk towards the television for the occupant of a choice seat to vacate it in his favour. The essence of the time-out programme was that 'when there is any reason to *suspect* that any kid is being threatened, bullied or subtly intimidated, either directly or indirectly, by John *or his clique* John is to be taken immediately to isolation.' (p. 206), and this was expounded to the staff in some detail. After the regime had been in effect for six weeks they reported an appreciable decrease in John's aggressive behaviour. During the following months, the daily log included entries concerning him such as 'He is a real pleasant kid to have around', 'Couldn't ask for a better boy', and 'a model child'. The cottage supervisor commented that '... the programme did put the staff back in control of the cottage and removed a large percentage of the threat the kids were having to live with...' (p. 208). The authors suggest a number of ways in which the time-out procedure might have contributed to this change, but no follow-up data is presented.

A final illustration (Wetzel 1966) of a response cost regime is the treatment of compulsive stealing in a ten-year-old boy named Mike. After a long history of uncontrollability and stealing he was placed in a Home for mildly disturbed children, where his behaviour improved except in respect of stealing and bedwetting. It was thought that he might be stealing to obtain affection and an attempt was made to provide 'a loving maternal figure' by placing him in a foster family described as 'exceptionally warm'. His behaviour deteriorated, and five months later he was admitted to the Children's Home. The frequency of stealing appeared worse than ever before; it occurred almost every day in the home, school or shops, and had a deleterious effect on Mike's relationships with the other children and the staff. An extinction regime was not feasible because the stealing attracted a great deal of attention from many people and it was not possible to control this situation. As noted above, in such circumstances a response cost procedure is often most suitable. There were some indications of a potentially good relationship between Mike and Maria, a cook in the home, who co-operated in creating opportunities for this to be strengthened into a potent source of social reinforcement for the boy. When this was achieved, it was arranged that Maria would be told whenever Mike was found to have stolen something, and as soon as possible she would then say to him 'I'm sorry you took so-and-so's blank because now I can't let you come home with me tonight' (p. 370), but would not enter into any further discussion of the matter with him. In the later stages of the programme a positive reinforcement component for non-stealing was added, and Mike began to reduce his visits to Maria in favour of engaging in activities with other children. According to the records kept, after three and a half months on the regime, stealing had stopped completely and this continued during another two months of systematic follow-up. A suggestion that the cessation of stealing might have been accompanied by an increase in wetting was found to be without foundation.

Differential Reinforcement

As mentioned above, positive reinforcement, response cost and extinction procedures are most commonly combined into differential reinforcement treatment programmes, aimed at the promotion of desired behaviour and the reduction of problematic responses. Several reasons for the possible superiority of combination over the separate use of each type of procedure are indicated in the preceding discussion, and some examples of differential reinforcement are now considered.

There is a good deal of evidence (Salzinger 1969) that therapists influence the behaviour of their clients in interviews through differential reinforcement contingencies, which may be communicated by words, gestures, postural changes, facial expressions and other expressive acts. This occurs even when the therapist tries deliberately not to exercise such influence. Murray (1956) has reported a case

treated by a Rogerian non-directive therapist, whose whole philosophy, theoretical orientation and training was against influencing his client. It was demonstrated that in various subtle ways the therapist approved of statements indicating independent behaviour by the client and that these increased during therapy,
while he disapproved of statements relating to dependence, sex and intellectual
defences, all of which decreased. Recordings of a series of treatment sessions with
a single client, conducted by Carl Rogers himself, have been analysed by Truax
(1966). Three reinforcers were identified: empathy, non-possessive warmth or
acceptance, and directiveness. If Rogers had succeeded in being completely
non-directive, then these reinforcers would have been distributed equally over all
nine classes of client behaviour used in Truax's analysis of the data. In fact,
Rogers selectively reinforced five of these nine classes to a significant degree, and
the behaviour in four of these five increased during therapy, while behaviour in
three of the four non-reinforced classes did not vary. Thus the client's behaviour
was consistent with predictions from Rogers' pattern of reinforcement in seven
out of nine classes. In a further study of the group treatment of thirty patients,
Truax (1967) found a significant relationship between therapist reinforcement
(empathy, warmth and genuineness) for self-exploration by the patients, and their
actual level of self-exploratory behaviour. Moreover, the therapeutic outcome for
patients in groups in which self-exploration was highly reinforced was better
than for patients in groups where this was not the case.

The last finding bears upon the important issue of the generalization of
changes in patients' behaviour within interviews to their real life situations
outside. This is reported to occur in some studies (Lovaas 1961, 1964, Thoresen
and Krumboltz 1967, Ullman et al 1961) but not in others (Rogers 1960,
Ullman et al 1964, Williams 1959b) and the evidence must be regarded as
contradictory and inadequate, despite widespread reliance on therapeutic
interviewing as a means of producing generalized changes in behaviour.

Many of the studies reviewed below have the merit of circumventing this
difficulty by the application of differential reinforcement to actual behaviour in
the natural environment, rather than to verbal representations of it in interviews. The basic assumption, as discussed in Chapter 1, is that many forms of
deviant behaviour are influenced in some degree by their social consequences.
If these are rewarding or reinforcing, then the problem behaviour is likely to
be strengthened; in other conditions it will be weakened. It follows that the
contemporary environment plays an important role in the development and
maintenance of many forms of deviant behaviour, and more specifically, that
this is a function of the reinforcement patterns in operation. For instance, a
child's parents may complain about his problem behaviour, while at the same
time maintaining it by inappropriate positive reinforcement. This sort of
situation is illustrated in Chapter 1, and is referred to by Patterson (1969) as an
'irrational social system'. Therapeutically, the implication is that if the parental
reinforcement practices can be changed, then the child's problems might be
ameliorated. Therefore, the focus of intervention is on 'reprogramming the
social system' (Patterson 1969).

We have noted that an important criterion of the efficacy of any therapeutic approach is the generalization and persistence of beneficial change after the specific intervention ends, and in the approach being described, there are several ways in which this might be facilitated. In the first place the specific intervention might strengthen social skills or reduce social inhibitions so that the child has greater access to sources of reinforcement in his environment, which will then maintain the changes in his behaviour. An example of this is the treatment of an extremely withdrawn girl reported by Allen et al (1964), and introduced in Chapter 1. It was observed that her teachers gave her a great deal of attention when she isolated herself from other children. This situation was altered so that the teachers made their attention contingent upon the girl playing with other children. Consequently her social play increased and her enjoyment of it became sufficient to maintain the change in her behaviour after the teacher's special attention during play was discontinued. Thus a specific intervention may help a child to utilize existing sources of reinforcement which will then maintain the changes in behaviour after the intervention ends.

However, where sources of reinforcement for desired behaviour changes are not available in the environment, it may be necessary to arrange such reinforcement in order to maintain these changes. Several methods of training parents to provide appropriate reinforcement have been employed. In an illustrative case described below (Hawkins et al. 1966), the experimenters supervised the mother's initial attempts to change her reinforcement practices and used a system of signals to guide her reactions to the child's behaviour. Other methods used have included detailed and specific advice, the modelling of appropriate reinforcement practices by professionals or other parents, discussion of parental observations of their children's behaviour and their own ways of handling it or of video or audio taped interactions in the home, and formal instruction in the principles of reinforcement, sometimes including the use of a specially prepared programmed text.

Such training methods may be successful in initiating changes in parental reinforcement practices, but the maintenance of these changes is likely to be influenced by their consequences for the parents. Where a child's problem behaviour is aversive to them, any amelioration which follows their adoption of new reinforcement practices is likely to strengthen and maintain these practices. In other cases a child's problem may be rewarding rather than aversive to his parents, or they may have participated in the programme unwillingly under pressure from a court or school, or they may be so little concerned about their child that any improvement in his behaviour is not reinforcing to them. In circumstances such as these the parents are only likely to continue the new reinforcement contingencies for the child if they themselves are reinforced for doing so. During treatment the therapist might provide social and perhaps material reinforcement for the parents, but in the longer term the necessary reinforcement must become available in the natural environment and this may be difficult to ensure. In certain cases quite small improvements in the child's behaviour will have what Patterson et al. (1967) have called an 'avalanche effect'.

The improvement in his behaviour may make him more rewarding to his parents, or lead to a better atmosphere in the home with beneficial consequences for the relationships between husband and wife. It is clear, however, that much remains to be done in finding and developing ways of increasing the amount of mutual reinforcement in families, so that beneficial changes in the behaviour of parents and children are maintained after a specific treatment intervention ends.

So far we have considered two ways of facilitating the generalization and persistence of therapeutic change, first by enabling the child to benefit from existing sources of reinforcement in his environment, and second by creating and maintaining such environmental sources where they do not exist. A third way involves self-reinforcement rather than environmental reinforcement. There is evidence (Bandura 1969) that self-regulatory mechanisms can be established that render behaviour partially independent of its environmental consequences; persons do persist in behaviour that receives little or no social support. More particularly, behaviour may be strongly controlled by its self-evaluative consequences. People adopt certain standards of behaviour and reward or punish themselves according to how well they conform to their own standards. Furthermore, Bandura and his co-workers have shown that such self-evaluative and self-reinforcing patterns can be established by children observing the operation of similar standards and rewarding or punishing consequences in adult models. Thus in operating new reinforcement practices, parents might provide models from which children will develop self-regulatory mechanisms, and these may assist in the generalization and persistence of therapeutic change after the specific intervention ends.

A fourth way in which this may be facilitated in the approach has already been mentioned and it arises from the fact that the intervention focuses on real problem behaviour occurring in the natural environment, rather than verbal representations of it in an interview setting. This latter more traditional approach presents considerable problems in transferring beneficial changes from treatment situations to life situations, and these difficulties may be reduced if the focus of intervention in treatment is the life situation itself.

Finally, the generalization and persistence of change may be aided if the parents apply their training in analysing and managing current problems to any further difficulties which might arise in future. If this happens, then the approach may have a preventive as well as an ameliorative effect.

Before considering some examples of the modification of reinforcement contingencies in the natural environment, some further limitations and possible advantages of this therapeutic approach are discussed. Although some success has been reported in a wide variety of individual cases, it is not yet possible to assess the efficacy of the approach adequately. One reason for this is the lack of studies using a no-treatment control group. In most of the work reported so far, each client has acted as his own control, being assessed before and after the intervention. Such designs provide useful correlational support for an association between the intervention and the outcome, especially if the reinforcement contingencies are reversed in an intrasubject replication design (Chapter 3). However, they cannot establish cause–effect relationships, because of the absence of control over factors other than the specific intervention which might have contributed to the outcome. A second major deficiency in the current evidence is the lack of adequate follow-up data. There is insufficient information available about the persistence of therapeutic changes in children and the continued use of the new reinforcement practices by their parents. However, it seems certain that ways of facilitating the persistence of beneficial changes will need to be developed further.

There do seem to be certain advantages in using parents as therapeutic agents. In the first place, the shortage of professional staff both now and in the foreseeable future means that there is little prospect of providing adequate help on a one-to-one basis for the number of children who present with behaviour problems. Instead of concentrating on direct service, it may be desirable to maximize the impact of professionals by using them to train and supervise parents in the home environment. Furthermore, parents are likely to be therapeutically powerful because of their emotional significance to their children and the sheer amount of time they spend with them compared to a professional therapist. Finally, as we have seen, children's behaviour is influenced by environmental conditions which are under the control of their parents and to ameliorate behaviour problems it may be necessary for the parents to change these conditions. On the other hand, there are certain problems to be overcome in using parents as therapists, for example in obtaining their cooperation and if necessary increasing their reinforcement value to the children. Although this discussion is restricted to the treatment of behaviour disordered children, the approach described does seem to have wider applications and this is reflected in some of the following illustrations.

One example is the treatment of Peter, the four-year-old child whose problem behaviour was being reinforced by his mother, as described in Chapter 1 (Hawkins et al. 1966). Treatment was divided into five stages: the first baseline period, the first experimental period, the second baseline period, the second experimental period and a follow-up period. During the first baseline period, Peter and his mother interacted in their usual way and this was observed and recorded by the experimenters. Prior to the first experimental period, the mother was informed of the nine objectionable behaviours which would be treated. She was shown three gestural signals which indicated how she was to behave towards Peter. Signal 'A' meant she was to tell Peter to stop whatever objectionable behaviour he was emitting. Signal 'B' indicated she was immediately to place Peter in his room and lock the door. When signal 'C' was presented, she was to give him attention, praise, and affectionate physical contact. Thus, every time Peter behaved objectionably, Mrs S. was either signalled to tell him to stop or to put him in his room. When the experimenter noticed that Peter was playing in a particularly desirable way, signal 'C' was given and his mother responded to him with attention and approval. When placed in his room Peter was required to remain there a minimum of five minutes. In addition, he had to be quiet for a short period before he was allowed to come out. Since all objects likely to serve

as playthings had been previously removed from the room, he had little opportunity to amuse himself.

During the second baseline period, Mrs S. was told to interact with Peter just
as she had during the first baseline period, and in the second experimental period
the experimental procedure was reintroduced. For twenty-four days after the
second experimental period there was no contact between the experimenters and
the family. Mrs S. was given complete freedom to use any techniques with Peter
that she felt were warranted, including 'time out', but she was given no specific
instructions. After this twenty-four-day interval a three-session, post-treatment
check was made to determine whether the improvements effected during treatment were still evident. These one-hour follow-up sessions were comparable to
earlier baseline periods in that Mrs S. was instructed to behave in her usual
manner towards Peter.

Turning now to the results of the experiment (Figure 3), the rate of objectionable behaviour during the first baseline period varied between eighteen and one
hundred and thirteen per session. A sharp decrease occurred during the first
experimental period, the rate ranging from one to eight per session. During the
second baseline period, the rate varied between two and twenty-four per session.
Although this was an increase over the previous experimental period, the
frequency of response did not match that of the first baseline period. This failure

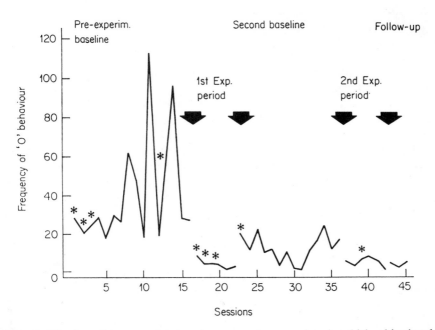

Figure 3. Number of ten-second intervals, per one-hour session, in which objectionable
behaviour occurred. Asterisks indicate sessions in which reliability was tested
(Hawkins et al. 1966).

to return to earlier levels may have occurred for several reasons. For example, midway through the second baseline, Mrs S. reported considerable difficulty in responding to Peter as she had during the first baseline period. She stated that she felt more 'sure of herself' and could not remember how she had previously behaved towards her son. It was apparent that Mrs S. now gave Peter firm commands when she wanted him to do something and did not 'give in' after denying him a request. The rate of objectionable behaviour in the second experimental period was comparable to that of the first experimental period, from two to eight per session. Data obtained during the follow-up period show that Peter's objectionable behaviour remained low in rate after the passage of a twenty-four-day interval. Mrs S. reported that Peter was well behaved and much less demanding than he had previously been. She stated that she had been using the 'time out' procedure approximately once a week. In summary, it seems that modification of the mother's reinforcement practices was accompanied by improvement in the child's behaviour, and that this persisted for at least twenty-four days after the specific treatment intervention ended.

A second example of a differential reinforcement programme in the natural environment is the treatment of Valerie, an eight-year-old school refuser (Ayllon et al. 1970). In a little over a year her attendance had dropped from 95% to 10%, and at the time of intervention she had been absent continuously for forty-one days (Figure 4). When her mother attempted to take Val to school she reacted with violent temper tantrums, screaming and crying, so that it was nearly impossible to move her from the house. On the basis of observational data it was postulated that Val's refusal to go to school was being maintained by its rewarding consequences. It enabled her to have an hour alone with her mother after the other children left for school and before the mother went to work; from then on Val spent a pleasant and undemanding day playing in a neighbour's apartment. Initially, Val was taken to school by one of the therapists who gradually withdrew as the child remained for longer periods. This procedure demonstrated that Val could go to school and stay all day without running away or displaying any sign of undue fear or panic, but it did not succeed in getting her to attend unaccompanied. The next step in treatment was to remove the reward of the hour alone with her mother by arranging for the mother to leave for work early, at the same time as the children went to school. Val still did not attend voluntarily and continued to spend the day in the neighbour's apartment. The third stage comprised a differential reinforcement procedure in which 'a large chart with each child's name and the days of the week was given to the mother. She announced that a star would signify one day of going to school on a voluntary basis and was to be placed on the appropriate spot by each child at the end of each day. Five stars would equal perfect attendance and would result in a special treat or trip on the weekend. In addition to the above, each child who went to school on a voluntary basis would receive, each day, three pieces of a favourite candy. If anyone had to be taken to school (non-voluntary attendance), the reward was only one piece of candy. It was felt to be important to attach some reward value to the school attendance even if, in the beginning, attendance was not voluntary. The occasion of putting up stars, handing out rewards and verbal praise was to be made into a special event each evening when the mother returned home. When Valerie did not leave with the other children to go to school in the morning, the mother was to leave the house fifteen minutes later taking Valerie with her to school. No excuses were to be tolerated with the exception of sickness. Since previously Valerie had used the excuse of being sick, this time the mother was given a thermometer and taught to use it to decide whether or not Valerie was ill.' (p. 133). This procedure also resulted in Valerie attending school when she was taken but not on her own, and although this was an improvement on her earlier refusal to accompany her mother the aim was still to obtain voluntary attendance. It was thought that this might be impeded by the reward of the mother taking Valerie to school. Consequently the differential reinforcement procedure was varied to include the removal of this possible reinforcement contingency, by arranging for the mother to leave home before the children and to meet them at the school where she would dispense candy on their arrival. If Valerie did not appear within fifteen minutes the mother was to return home and fetch her. This entailed a mild aversive consequence for the mother in that it required her to walk three miles between home and school, and the authors suggest that this increased her commitment to the treatment. On the first and third days after the modified differential reinforcement procedure was instituted, Valerie had to be taken to school by her mother, but thereafter she attended on her own and this continued during a nine-month follow-up (Figure 4).

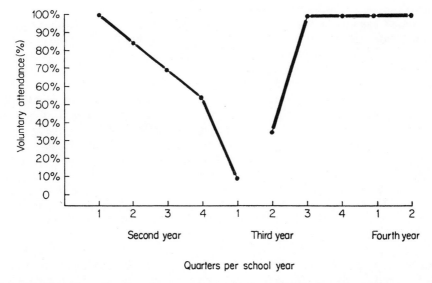

Figure 4. Each dot represents the percentage of voluntary attendance per school quarter (forty-five days). The behavioural intervention was initiated during the second quarter of the third year at school (Ayllon et al. 1970).

Much improvement was reported in her academic progress and social adjustment to school and home, without indication of possible 'symptom substitution'.

Differential reinforcement programmes in the natural environment have been used also with delinquents and predelinquents. Tharp and Wetzel (1969) report a two-year programme with such subjects of both sexes aged six to sixteen years. Reasonable records were kept for seventy-seven subjects in respect of one hundred and thirty-five problem behaviours. These were categorized as refusal or failure to perform chores in the home, poor academic work, disruptive behaviour, defiance, fighting, truancy and lateness, property destruction, encopresis, enuresis, and stealing. The authors summarize their results as a reduction to at least fifty per cent of the pre-intervention rate for one hundred and twenty of the one hundred and thirty-five problem behaviours. They comment that '. . . The social significance of a particular change depends upon the behaviour in question and the setting in which it occurs. Occasionally, as in property destruction, a response rate of zero is important. Most commonly, among the behaviours considered in the present project, a reduction to less than half the baseline rate was considered socially desirable by both project staff and persons in the natural environment of the child. Defiance, for example, is most appropriate when it occurs from time to time rather than always or never. But some may dispute this value judgement; for that reason, we have used the arbitrary fifty per cent point as the categorical division regardless of the behaviour. The reader may judge "success". There is no doubt, however, that much change in specific behaviour did in fact occur during intervention' (p. 166). However, the extent to which this improvement was sustained after the intervention ended is largely unknown as very limited follow-up data was obtained.

Another example is some work with the unclubbable type of hardcore delinquent (Schwitzgebel and Kolb 1964). A laboratory was set up in an old shop in a delinquency area and delinquent boys were invited to serve as subjects. Whenever a boy first put in an appearance this was at once reinforced with food, sweets and cigarettes—and immediately after talking into a tape recorder he was paid in cash. There was then opportunity for him to participate in other reinforcing activities such as learning to drive, building electronic equipment and listening to music. When his attendance became regular the method of successive approximation to the desired goal was used to shape punctual attendance, by paying him more or giving unexpected bonuses the nearer to the correct time he arrived. Within fifteen to thirty meetings attendance usually became regular and punctual, the boys' anti-work attitude changed, and their delinquent and gang activities decreased. It was possible to shift from material to social reinforcement as attendance increased. Three years after the study ended for the first twenty boys, a follow-up showed that they had been arrested less and incarcerated for shorter periods than a matched pair control group, in each case to a statistically significant degree. Thus the frequency and severity of offences appeared to have been reduced in the treated group, although there were no significant differences between groups in the number of subjects who returned to prison or reformatory.

A final illustration of the use of differential reinforcement with delinquents is provided by Thorne et al. (1967) from an American probation setting. One of their many cases is that of Loren aged sixteen years who was referred by the Juvenile Court following complaints of assault, uncontrollability and habitual truancy. His stepfather and mother tried to deal with these problems by withdrawing privileges, abusing him verbally and threatening to call the police, but with no effect. Exactly what was expected of Loren and how he could regain his privileges were not clear to him. The treatment plan was based on a contract between Loren and his parents which would allow him to earn money for conforming to certain requirements such as being in at a prescribed time at night, whilst entailing losses of money and deprivation of the family car for failures to observe these requirements. In the first thirty-five days after this plan was instituted, Loren was rewarded an average of eighty-one per cent in respect of the specified tasks, compared to an estimated nought to ten per cent before intervention. Despite this progress, the stepfather was refusing to pay for the renewal of Loren's driving insurance, and a new contract was negotiated whereby he could earn a maximum of fifty points each week towards the two hundred and fifty needed for his insurance to be renewed. In the first week he earned twenty-two points, followed by the full fifty points in each week thereafter. Loren re-entered high school where he performed satisfactorily and did not truant for a period of twenty-four days. The parents felt he was doing so well that the treatment plan should be abandoned. The project staff thought this premature and strongly discouraged the parents, but they insisted on ending the contract. Loren truanted for the next seven days and was arrested for burglary eleven days later. The authors conclude that the case indicates that problem behaviour can be changed by altering environmental consequences, while demonstrating the difficulty of achieving this with uncooperative parents.

Liberman (1970) has reported on his use of differential reinforcement in family therapy. In one of his illustrative cases, the wife, Mrs D., aged thirty-five years, had for fifteen years suffered from severe headaches of a migraine type. No neurological basis for these was revealed and they had not been alleviated by intensive, psychodynamically oriented, individual psycho-therapy over a period of eighteen months. She obtained relief only by going to bed for up to a week, with the use of narcotics. Mr D. was an active man who spent much of his time at home doing things about the house and he found it difficult to sit down and talk with his wife. It seemed that the only times she gained his undivided attention was when she developed a headache and had to retire to bed. He was then very solicitous, stayed home to look after the children and called the doctor. On the assumption that the headaches were maintained by Mr D.'s attention and care, the treatment plan was to transfer these reinforcing contingencies to Mrs D.'s satisfactory performance of the roles of housewife and mother. Liberman discussed his assessment of the situation with the couple and encouraged them to implement the plan, with the result that '... Mr D. worked hard to give his wife attention and approval for her day-to-day efforts as a mother and housewife. When he came home from work ... he enquired about the day at home and discussed with his wife problems concerning the children. He occasionally rewarded his wife's homemaking efforts by taking her out to a movie or to dinner (something they had not done for years). While watching TV he had his wife sit close to him or on his lap. In return, Mrs D. was taught to reward her husband's new efforts at intimacy with affection and appreciation. She let him know how much she liked to talk with him about the day's events. She prepared special dishes for him and kissed him warmly when he took initiative in expressing affection towards her. On the other hand, Mr D. was instructed to pay minimal attention to his wife's headaches. He was reassured that in so doing, he would be helping her decrease their frequency and severity. He was no longer to give her medication, cater to her when she was ill, or call the doctor for her. If she got a headache, she was to help herself and he was to carry on with his regular routine insofar as possible. I emphasized that *he should not, overall, decrease his attentiveness to his wife, but rather change the timing and direction of his attentiveness.* Thus the behavioural contingencies of Mr D.'s attention changed from headaches to housework, from invalidism to active coping and functioning as a mother and wife.' (p. 112). At the end of ten sessions each of forty-five minutes' duration, both partners were deeply committed to this new approach to each other, their marriage was mutually more satisfying, they had transferred the principles involved to the handling of their children with beneficial results, and Mrs D. had obtained a job she enjoyed. She still had headaches, but they were much less severe and chronic, and she coped with them herself rather than depending on Mr D. or her doctor. These changes were maintained over a one-year follow-up period, during which Mrs D. had occasional headaches but without having to go to bed or enter hospital.

Another interesting application of differential reinforcement procedures are the recently developed token economy systems, aimed at modifying the behaviour of client groups in institutions like psychiatric hospitals and penal establishments. The performance of specified desired behaviour is followed by the presentation of a token which is exchangeable subsequently for a variety of 'back up' reinforcers, such as sweets, cigarettes, leisure activities or privileges. The token functions as a discriminative stimulus signifying the likelihood of reward, and reinforcement value becomes attached to the token so that it can maintain desired behaviour with only intermittent recourse to the back up reinforcers. This entails several advantages. It facilitates presentation in that it is simpler to hand out something like a plastic disc for exchange later than to have a whole range of rewards constantly available. Furthermore, the wider the range offered the greater chance there is of at least one reward being reinforcing for each client. Finally, tokens can be used to maintain responses during the interval when a client is 'saving' for a single powerful reward, such as a bicycle. A limitation of token economies is that they serve to maintain desired behaviour within the institution, and further measures are required to ensure that this function is taken over by the reinforcing contingencies operating in the client's natural environment. Clearly, this limitation does not apply to the use of token economies with permanently institutionalized clients, and such systems are valuable means of initiating behaviour in other clients which can then be maintained more naturally.

Token economy programmes in a variety of settings are reviewed elsewhere (Davison 1969a, Krasner 1968, 1970) and they may be illustrated by the work of Ayllon and Azrin (1968) on psychiatric wards. The back up reinforcers for which tokens could be exchanged included facilities for privacy, freedom to leave the ward and hospital premises, interviews with the hospital staff, recreational opportunities and a choice of articles obtainable through the hospital shop. In one experiment some chronic female patients were first given tokens for the satisfactory performance of the work they preferred, the reinforcement was then switched to non-preferred work, and finally restored to the preferred tasks. The institution of the token system was followed by a marked improvement in the punctuality and regularity of the patients' attendance at work, even though they could take time off whenever they wished. Further, the importance of the reinforcement being contingent upon certain work was demonstrated by the patients changing to their previously non-preferred work when it was rewarded, despite being told that they could continue with the work they preferred although it would no longer earn tokens (Figure 5). This point is emphasized by the results of a subsequent experiment. Initially, the distribution of tokens was not made contingent upon satisfactory work performance, and within a week the patients had stopped working. They resumed work when tokens were again made contingent upon them doing so (Figure 6). Finally, it was shown that there was a marked decline in the patients' level of activity on the ward when the token system was

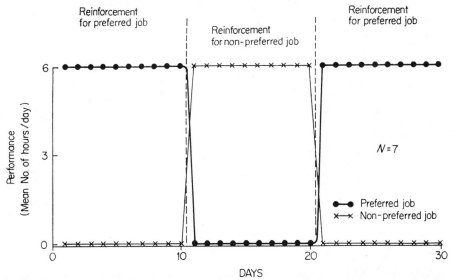

Figure 5. Mean number of hours of performance by seven patients (Ayllon and Azrin 1968).

discontinued and the back up reinforcers became freely available according to usual hospital practice (Figure 7).

Atthowe and Krasner (1968) conducted another important token economy project in a ward containing eighty-six chronic schizophrenic patients, for whom the median length of hospitalization was twenty-four years with a range of four to forty-nine years. They were a severely institutionalized group, living an apathetic, isolated and dependent existence. In an attempt to reverse this, tokens were presented to the patients for a range of behaviour including caring for themselves, acting responsibly, and participating in social and occupational activities. On the other hand, token fines and other sanctions were imposed for serious disruptive behaviour or stealing tokens. Additionally, banking, budgeting, credit card and bonus systems were employed to more

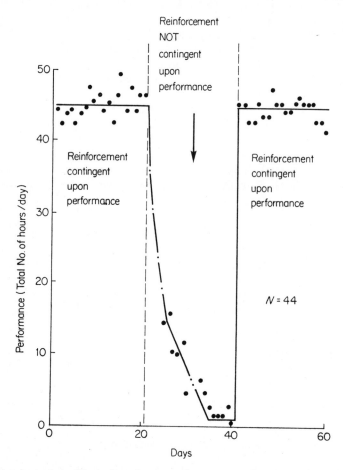

Figure 6. Total number of hours' performance by a group of patients (Ayllon and Azrin 1968).

nearly replicate economic life outside the hospital. The authors present substantial evidence for improvements in the patients' self-care, social participation and discharge rates, following the institution of the token economy.

With the aim of reducing the need to re-admit patients to hospital, Fairweather (1964) attempted to promote their problem-solving and self-directing capacities prior to discharge. They were matched and randomly assigned to a control or experimental group. During two hours in each day, the controls worked individually and had recreation, while the experimental patients worked as a group and had a decision-making session. This involved assessing the behaviour of group members and allocating them to an appropriate point on a four-step programme of increasing rewards and privileges. The staff did not share in this process except to provide information and resources, but they could approve or alter the group decision, and either raise

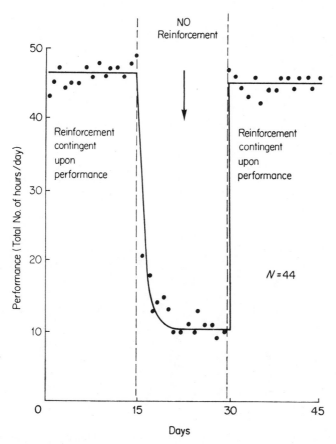

Figure 7. Total number of hours' performance by a group of patients (Ayllon and Azrin 1968).

48

or lower the reward stages of all its members according to the staff evaluation of the decisions made. Thus, the aim was to give the experimental patients a considerable degree of responsibility for their own lives, while the controls remained more dependent on the hospital staff. The results indicated that compared to the controls, the experimental group developed greater mutual interest, help and responsibility. In particular, they assisted each other vocationally and educationally. They also exhibited enhanced interpersonal responsiveness and communication, more positive attitudes to each other, to their treatment and to their future lives, and less bizarre behaviour. On follow-up, it was found that the experimental patients had spent shorter periods in hospital, were more frequently gainfully employed and engaged in more social interaction and communication. However, despite these beneficial changes in the experimental patients they still had to be re-admitted to hospital as frequently as the controls. Fairweather and his co-workers (1969), in a second project, then tried moving a successful group into the community where they could continue to support each other. An established group of chronic patients was transferred to a lodge in the hospital grounds where they ran their own

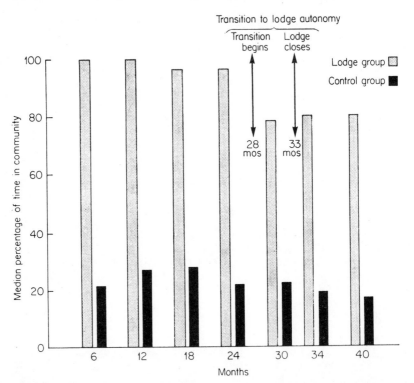

Figure 8. Percentage of time that patients in the lodge and hospital programmes spent in the community for forty months of follow-up. The lodge programme was discontinued after thirty-three months (Fairweather et al. 1969).

lives successfully and even conducted a business. Compared to a control group which received traditional hospital care and out-patient follow-up treatment, the experimental group remained in the community (Figure 8) and in gainful employment (Figure 9) for longer periods.

Token economy programmes have been established also in institutions for delinquents or pre-delinquents. One example is a project conducted at Camp Butler in North Carolina and reported by Burchard (1967) with a critique by Lachenmeyer (1969) and a reply to this by Burchard (1969). The subjects were anti-social delinquents, aged ten to twenty years, with intelligence quotients in the fifty to seventy range. Among the behaviour reinforced was maintaining a job, staying in school, budgeting money, buying and caring for clothes, buying food and meals, and cooperating with peers and adults. To reduce stealing, the tokens were stamped with the resident's number and they were exchangeable for a range of articles in a shop, recreatiohal activities and bus tickets for visits to town or home. In addition to this positive reinforcement, the programme included a response cost component. For mild offences, a resident was charged four tokens and required to sit in a row of chairs for

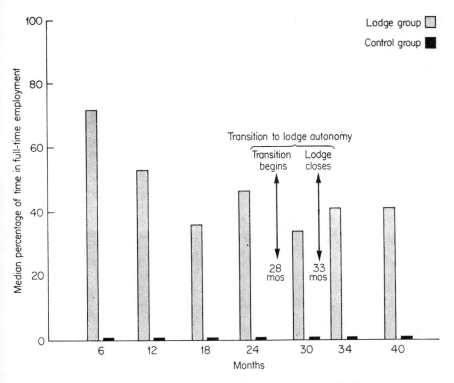

Figure 9. Percentage of time that patients in the lodge and hospital programmes were employed full time for forty months of follow-up (Fairweather et al. 1969).

a few minutes until his behaviour became appropriate. For more serious offences, a charge of fifteen tokens was made and the resident was secluded in an empty room until he was quiet for thirty minutes. If he went to the room and stayed there in an orderly manner for the minimum period possible, then he was rewarded with five tokens at the end of that time. Failure to repay all tokens owed by the end of each day resulted in the loss of a 'behaviour credit', and carried the penalty of having to pay more tokens for the back up reinforcers. In contrast, possession of the maximum possible number of behaviour credits entitled the resident to free access to the yard, and to the facilities of purchasing a trip to town for ninety tokens or recreation time with female residents at fifteen tokens an hour. Within this programme, Burchard conducted some experimental studies. In one of these, tokens were first distributed for satisfactory attendance and performance at school or work, then the same number of tokens were given non-contingently without the residents having to earn them in this way, and finally the first stage was reinstituted. Figures 10 and 11 show that school and work performance fluctuated according to the contingencies of reinforcement in operation at the time.

Cohen and his co-workers (Cohen 1968, Cohen et al. 1966, 1968) used token economy principles in the National Training School for Boys, an institution for young prisoners in Washington, D.C. In an attempt to promote the skills necessary to achieve status and possessions by legitimate rather than deviant means, the project was aimed at improving educational performance and

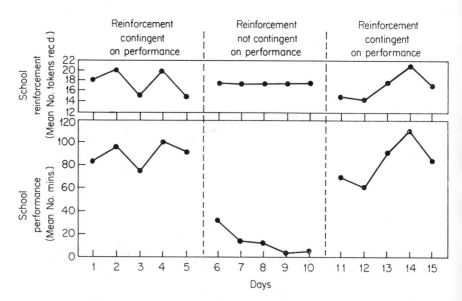

Figure 10. Mean number of minutes of school performance by nine residents (Burchard 1967).

attitudes. All the boys in the project were school drop-outs and had little interest in academic matters. In the project, when a boy studied satisfactorily and completed a course of programmed instruction with a score of ninety per cent, he could take a test which could earn him token reinforcement in the form of points. These were exchangeable for a range of back up reinforcers including a choice of meals, a private room, entry to recreational activities in a lounge with his friends, registration for a new course of instruction, library time or the loan of books. The boys had a good deal of freedom to organize their own lives in matters such as daily routines, leisure activities, visiting facilities and they could choose not to participate in any educational activities, but if their points dropped below a certain level they were placed 'on relief' which entailed loss of private room, ordinary institutional meals and no extra luxuries. Only very infrequently was it necessary to implement this sanction. In the second stage of the project, a special physical environment was built to enhance the probability of the desired educational behaviour. The results of the project show that the boys studied conscientiously and gained two grade levels on standard achievement tests over a period of eight months. There were accompanying favourable changes in problems of discipline and destructiveness, although no direct attempt was made to modify these in the project.

A final example of the application of token economy principles is the report by Phillips (1968) of a project he conducted as the housefather in a small Children's Home for pre-delinquent boys. They came from poor families, had histories of truancy and academic failure, and had been committed to the Home by the court after minor offences in an attempt to prevent them progressing to more serious

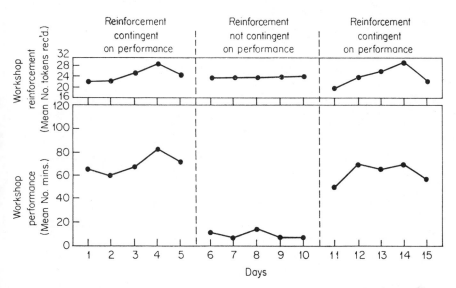

Figure 11. Mean number of minutes of workshop performance by eight residents (Burchard 1967).

52

crime. The subjects in the project were three boys, aged twelve, thirteen and fourteen years respectively. Tokens were earned for specified self-care, social and educational behaviour, while specified contrary behaviour incurred token fines. At the end of each week the tokens could be exchanged for rewards and privileges in the following week, including pocket money, access to a bicycle, television and other recreational facilities, and permission to go to town, stay up after bedtime and come home late from school. Within this programme certain experiments were conducted. One of these concerned the modification of verbal aggression by the boys. It seemed that they were often labelled 'aggressive' on the basis of their frequent use of statements such as 'I'll kill you', and if this could be reduced then they might be perceived and treated rather more favourably. To obtain a baseline measure of the frequency of such statements they were recorded over a three-hour period. Next, the boys were told what an aggressive statement was and that they were not to use them. When they did so the houseparents simply corrected them. Without prior warning to the boys, fines of twenty tokens were then imposed for transgressions. This contingency was removed in the next stage, during which the houseparents occasionally threatened to take away points

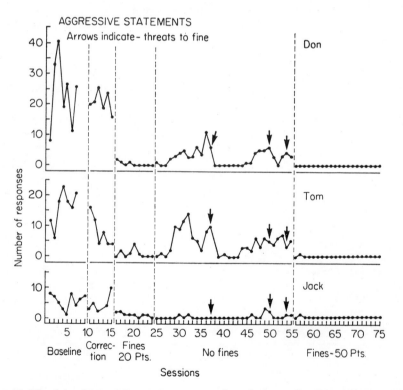

Figure 12. Number of aggressive statements per three-hour session for each youth under each condition (Phillips 1968).

for verbal aggression without in fact doing so. Finally the fining contingency was reinstituted, this time at the level of fifty points. Figure 12 shows that correction reduced the verbal aggression of only one boy (Tom), while fining reduced it in all three boys. The return to the 'no-fines' condition was accompanied by a gradual increase in aggressive statements and the threat to deduct points appeared to have a suppressive effect only on the first occasion it was used.

Another experiment in the project concerned punctuality in returning from school or errands and on going to bed. Initially, unpunctuality was reprimanded by the houseparents, and then the boys were fined twenty points for every minute they were late. Figure 13 shows that fining increased the punctuality of all the boys in the areas where this had been a problem. Other experiments are reported by Phillips and he concludes that the conduct of a token economy by the houseparents in a Children's Home is a practicable and effective proposition.

This ends the discussion of positive reinforcement, extinction, response cost and differential reinforcement as examples of therapeutic procedures containing an important element of outcome control. They have been applied to a wide range of conditions including children's disorders, delinquency, marital disharmony and psychotic behaviour. Much remains to be done in assessing their efficacy, for the bulk of the evidence consists of individual case reports, although some of these include an intrasubject replication design (Chapter 3) and there are a few studies employing a no-treatment control group. Additionally, more adequate follow-up data is needed on the persistence of beneficial changes in clients and their social environments after the specific intervention ends. Some potential difficulties in using extinction and response cost procedures are mentioned in the relevant sections, but certain problems are common to outcome generally. It may be difficult to find reinforcers, either those which are maintaining problems and need to be discontinued, or others which can be presented or removed to modify behaviour by positive reinforcement or response cost procedures. Sometimes it may be necessary to create or strengthen such reinforcers. This occurs in several of the cases described above; Wetzel (1966) strengthened Mike's relationship with the cook Maria, Patterson et al. (1967b) shaped up the reinforcement values of their five-year-old client and his parents for each other, and Stuart (1969a,b,) promoted mutual reinforcement between spouses. Secondly, it may be difficult to obtain sufficient control over the reinforcement contingencies attaching to the client's behaviour, and more is said about this below in discussing the use of these procedures by parents and other nonprofessionals. Thirdly, there is the constant problem of ensuring that beneficial changes in treatment situations are generalized and persist in the client's life situation. The inadequacy of the evidence for generalization from interviews and the need to provide specifically for the extension of changes obtained within institutions to the client's natural environment are noted above. This problem may be at least partially circumvented by intervening directly in the natural environment, although the task remains of ensuring the persistence of changes after treatment ends.

In addition to facilitating the generalization and persistence of changes, there

54

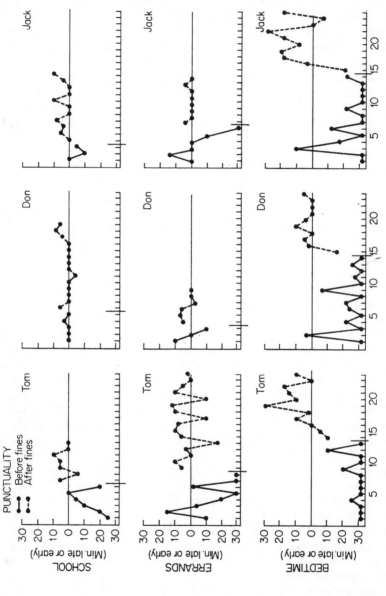

Figure 13. Number of minutes early or late before and after the application of point contingencies. Each youth's punctuality was measured for school, errands, and bedtime (Phillips 1968).

may be several other advantages in treatment being conducted by parents or other people in the client's environment. They are likely to be powerful sources of reinforcement because of their emotional significance and the amount of contact they have with the client and they may be the only people who can make the necessary changes in the reinforcement contingencies they control. Moreover, this treatment approach may serve to maximize the impact of scarce professional resources. It does however entail the problems of obtaining the efficient co-operation of parents and others in implementing the treatment plan, and of maintaining the changes in their behaviour towards the client after the intervention ends. There is some discussion of these issues above and Tharp and Wetzel (1969) present an interesting analysis of the 'resistances' they encountered in using the approach in Arizona. It is clear that much remains to be done in evolving ways of resolving these important therapeutic problems.

SELF-CONTROL PROCEDURES

So far we have considered some procedures involving the direct or indirect provision by social workers of conditions for therapeutic control. As an alternative these conditions may be provided by clients, either symbolically in their cognitive processes or externally in their environments. To the extent that this happens the clients may be said to exercise self-control and perhaps to be their own social workers.

The therapeutic manipulation of external controlling conditions is essentially the same whether undertaken by social worker or client and it is discussed extensively above. In this section therefore, some emphasis is placed upon procedures which involve an important element of symbolic self-control. We see in Chapter 1 that the sources of antecedent and outcome control may be in a person's own symbolic processes rather than his physiological changes or external environment, and here we are concerned with the manipulation of these symbolic sources of control for therapeutic purposes.

Self-Control of Antecedent Conditions

In Chapter 1 it is noted that aversive thoughts and images may serve as eliciting or reinforcing stimuli for problematic emotional responses, such as anxiety. Many clients recognize their own disturbing cognitions as irrational and unrealistic. They know, for example, that there is no real need to fear spiders or that compulsive handwashing does not really keep harm at bay, although this knowledge does not affect their phobic or compulsive behaviour. With such clients, treatment is aimed at the modification of the emotional and motor components of their problems. There are however other clients who believe their disturbing cognitions to be true. For example, some neurotics are convinced that they are becoming insane and the hypochondriac is sure that she is seriously ill. If such false beliefs can be corrected then the associated anxiety may be reduced

(Hart 1966, Lazarus et al. 1962, Schacter and Singer 1962, Valins and Ray 1967). Occasionally this is achieved by simple explanation, but more often some further steps are necessary. These may consist of the social worker attempting to modify the emotional and motor components of the client's problem behaviour with certain of the procedures described above, and any changes in these components may then be accompanied by corresponding changes in the false cognitions. Thus an overt shift from sick to healthy behaviour may entail some reduction in hypochondriacal ideas, or entry into a previously feared situation may mean that it is no longer perceived as dangerous. An alternative to this indirect modification of false beliefs is for the social worker to press his direct attack on them in a more systematic and rigorous way based upon relevant findings in experimental psychology. This possible alternative approach is relatively neglected in behavioural treatment to date, but there does seem to be an unexploited source of therapeutic procedures in the considerable literature on opinion and attitude change (Goldstein et al. 1966). A further task for future research is to determine the relative efficacy of the indirect correction of false beliefs through the modification of emotional and motor responses, and their direct correction by cognitive procedures. Each approach might be more effective with particular types of problem or their combination may be desirable.

Covert processes may serve also as eliciting stimuli for problematic approach responses, such as aggression, sexual deviance, drug addiction or alcoholism. In a procedure reported by Bergin (1969) these eliciting stimuli are ascertained and the client is trained to disrupt their evocation of the problem behaviour. One of his illustrative cases is a man aged twenty-four years with a ten-year history of compulsive homosexuality. This client's intense fear of heterosexual intimacy was treated by positive counter-conditioning, but his homosexuality remained unaffected. Careful and detailed assessment revealed a number of consistent stimuli (S)→response (R) sequences in the build-up of homosexual impulses, to the point where they were impossible for the client to control. One such sequence Bergin describes as follows: 'S (male person in a public place)→R (glance towards person)—S (return of glance)→R (mild emotion and fantasy plus additional glance)—S (establishment of visual contact)→R (intensified emotion and fantasy plus movement towards person)—S (physical proximity)→R (heightened desire)—S (heightened desire)→R (verbal exchange)—S (verbal exchange) →R (interpersonal engagement)—S (interpersonal engagement)→R (intense feelings, memories and fantasies)—S (feelings, memories and fantasies)→R (physical involvement)—S (body contact)→R (consummatory behaviour)' (p. 144).

Having identified such sequences, the client was instructed to attend closely to their onset and to interrupt them by switching to other thoughts or activities at this early stage before the impulse chain reached an uncontrollable level. With practice, it became increasingly easy for the client to do this and therapy was terminated. There was no relapse during a two-year follow-up, and he had contracted an apparently successful marriage one year after treatment ended. As the self-control procedure was only part of the therapy it is not possible to distinguish its specific contribution to the outcome, neither can its crucial therapeutic ingredients be identified in case studies of this kind.

A third symbolic antecedent control procedure is a form of positive counter-conditioning called 'emotive imagery' and employed by Lazarus and Abramovitz (1962) in the treatment of children's fears. The images used are assumed to arouse in the child feelings of self assertion, pride, affection, mirth and similar fear-inhibiting responses. A list is made of all the situations which frighten the child and these are ranked from the least to the most disturbing item. The child's wishes and heroes are ascertained also, and he is assisted to imagine vividly a sequence of events involving his wishes and heroes. When he is sufficiently emotionally aroused by this sequence, some references to the least disturbing situation are slipped in, until they no longer cause fear. The whole list of frightening situations is worked through in this way. An example of this method is the treatment of a fourteen-year-old boy who was extremely afraid of dogs. He was helped to imagine his wish to own an Alpha Romeo car and to race it at Indianapolis. During the description of a racing sequence a reference was made to a small dog at the side of the track as the boy sped past. Later an item higher in the list was introduced as a large boxer sniffing at the boy's heels while a crowd of people admired and enthused over his car. This treatment was accompanied by the rapid elimination of the boy's dog phobia. Another boy, aged ten years, was extremely afraid of the dark. His heroes were 'Superman' and 'Captain Silver', and in the sequences he was appointed their agent and directed by them to undertake tasks which involved entry into situations of gradually-increasing darkness, until his fear of doing so was removed. A final example is the treatment of an eight-year-old girl who was afraid of going to school. The sequence involved the character of 'Noddy' as a child who truanted and feared school. The little girl played the role of his protector, by reassurance and setting a good example. Her school phobia was eliminated.

The reverse of emotive imagery is the symbolic aversive counterconditioning technique called 'covert sensitization' (Cautela 1967) and used in the treatment of problematic approach behaviour, such as alcoholism (Anant 1967, Ashem and Donner 1968) and sexual deviation (Anant 1968, Barlow, Leitenberg and Agras 1969, Davison 1968). The patient is relaxed and asked to imagine a sequence of scenes leading up to the performance of the problem behaviour: for example, looking at a glass containing his favourite alcoholic drink, holding the glass in his hand and bringing it to his lips. At this point he signals and the therapist tells the patient to imagine that he begins to feel sick and is vomiting in his drink and all over himself and his companions. He is then asked to visualize the whole sequence and final scene by himself, and to actually feel nauseous as he prepares to drink. Alternate scenes are presented in which the patient imagines himself abstaining from drinking and then 'rushing out into the fresh clean air', or 'home to a clean invigorating shower'. The presentation of such relief scenes constitutes an escape and avoidance training component in the procedure. After several trials with the therapist, the patient is instructed to repeat the whole procedure on his own at home and immediately to imagine the vomiting scene whenever he is tempted to drink alcohol.

Davison (1968a) has used a similar procedure as part of the treatment of a twenty-one-year-old unmarried man who was extremely disturbed by his sadistic fantasies. Initially the treatment was concerned with changing the patient's masturbatory practices. He was accustomed to masturbating with sadistic fantasies, and instead he was advised to do so while looking at pictures of nude women. Only if he began to lose his erection was he to revert to sadistic fantasies, and these were to be abandoned in favour of the more normal sexual stimuli as soon as erection was regained. This part of the programme produced some improvement in the patient's fantasy and masturbatory activity, and at this point covert sensitization was introduced in the following manner. 'With his eyes closed (the patient) was instructed to imagine a typical sadistic scene, a pretty girl tied to stakes on the ground and struggling tearfully to extricate herself. While looking at the girl, he was told to imagine someone bringing a branding iron towards his eyes, ultimately searing his eyebrows. A second image was attempted when this proved abortive, namely, being kicked in the groin by a ferocious-looking karate expert. When he reported himself indifferent to this image as well, the therapist depicted to him a large bowl of "soup", composed of steaming urine with reeking fecal boli bobbing around on top. His grimaces, contortions, and groans indicated that an effective image had been found and the following five minutes were spent portraying his drinking from the bowl with accompanying nausea, at all times while peering over the floating debris at the struggling girl. After opening his eyes at the end of the imaginal ordeal, he reported spontaneously that he felt quite nauseated, and some time was spent in casual conversation in order to dispel the mood' (p. 86). After a total of eight sessions, no sadistic fantasies had occurred for more than a month, and follow-up for a further month showed that there had been no reappearance. Prior to treatment these fantasies had been present for ten years.

Anant (1968) has reported his use of covert sensitization to modify promiscuous behaviour in a twenty-year-old subnormal girl. She had a long history of promiscuity and had given birth to an illegitimate child when she was aged fifteen years. At the time of treatment she was losing every job almost immediately because she would seduce and disappear with the first available man. Treatment took place during ten sessions, each of an hour's duration, over a period of two weeks. The aversive scenes used were based upon the risk of pregnancy with the accompanying embarrassment for the patient, the contraction and consequences of syphilis, and the danger of being murdered by a sex offender. A typical scene in the last category is described as follows: 'Imagine that you meet a stranger in a bar where you are working. You agree to go out with him after your work. He drives you to a deserted place, far removed from the main road. There, he has sexual relations with you in a very aggressive way. You become a little bit scared. After the intercourse, he takes out a rope from the car and, before you realize what he is doing, he ties your hands and feet. Then he gags you and tells you that he would kill you. You are very much scared. You can't even scream for help. Now, he takes a knife out of his pocket and opens it. It is a very big and shining knife. He approaches you with the knife. You are scared to hell, but are quite helpless. You start feeling sorry that you came with him. Imagine that the knife is just one inch away from your throat and you are already anticipating your death. Now, stop and relax again.' (p. 796). After ten sessions the patient took another job, which she retained without exhibiting her previous promiscuous behaviour during an eight-month follow-up period.

There is some evidence to suggest that this apparently simple technique of covert sensitization may be surprisingly effective. Anant (1967) treated twenty-six alcoholic patients in about six sessions and obtained almost 100% success rate on follow-up eight to fifteen months later. Ashem and Donner (1968) compared the outcome for a group of fifteen alcoholics given nine sessions of covert sensitiz-ation with a no-treatment control group. Forty per cent of the treatment group were abstinent on follow-up six months later, while none of the controls were abstinent. Thus the results of covert sensitization with the notoriously intractable condition of alcoholism appear encouraging, especially in view of the relative brevity of the treatment given. It remains to replicate this work with alcoholics and to extend it to other conditions.

So far in this section we have considered some antecedent control procedures for reducing those stimuli in a client's psychological processes which are eliciting problem responses. Another aspect of antecedent self-control is the reduction by the client of any conditions in his environment which are evoking such responses. Thus a client may be helped to produce beneficial changes in the behaviour of others towards him, or to obtain for himself some needed resources or opportun-ity. Such reduction of excessive environmental stresses, whether achieved through the client or by the social worker, are a well recognized feature of casework and need not be further exemplified in this discussion.

Let us turn now to antecedent self-control procedures involving the manipu-lation of discriminative rather than eliciting or reinforcing stimuli. Attempts to bring instrumental responses under appropriate stimulus control are implicit in many forms of treatment, but little explicit use is made of relevant experimental findings on discrimination training, either within the behavioural approach or in other therapeutic systems. A social worker might try to modify a client's symbolic stimulus discrimination processes by helping him to see that he is over-generalizing responses learned in relation to his parents in childhood to his adult life. For example, hostility towards parents may be generalized to later authority figures, and the client may be helped to recognize that resentment of a perfectly reasonable boss is quite inappropriate. Sexual inhibition in childhood might be extended to marital relationships, and the social worker may try to help the client to distinguish the two situations. Dependence on parents might be generalized to the client's wife and children, so that he needs to recognize that overdependence on other people is inappropriate in a mature adult with a family dependent on him. Such therapeutic tasks are common to many forms of treatment, and the specific contribution of a behavioural approach should be the deliberate exploitation of knowledge about discrimination training, but this has hardly begun.

There are a few examples of clients manipulating the discriminative stimuli in their environments in order to ameliorate problem behaviour. In one of several cases reported by Goldiamond (1965), the subject was a girl who had difficulty in studying, and it was 'decided that her desk was to control study behaviour. If she wished to write a letter, she should do so, but in the dining room; if she wished to read comic books, she should do so, but in the kitchen; if she wished to day-dream, she should do so, but was to go to another room; at her desk she was to engage in her school work and her school work only.'

This girl had previously had a course in behavioural analysis and said 'I know what you're up to. You want that desk to assume stimulus control over me. I'm not going to let any piece of wood run my life for me.'

'On the contrary' (Goldiamond) said, 'you want that desk to run you. It is you who decides when you put yourself under the control of your desk. It is like having a sharpened knife in a drawer. You decide when to use it; but when you want it, it is ready.' (p. 854).

At the end of a week on this programme the girl reported that she had only spent ten minutes at her desk, but that she had studied during this period. The goal of doubling the time spent studying at the desk was set for the next week and within a few weeks she was studying regularly for three hours a day and using her desk for this purpose only. Goldiamond considered that satisfactory examination performance functioned as the reinforcer maintaining this study behaviour, for as we saw in Chapter 1, it is necessary to ensure suitable reinforcement when responses are emitted under appropriate stimulus control in order to establish and maintain this.

In summary, antecedent self-control procedures may involve the manipulation of those eliciting, reinforcing or discriminative stimuli in the client's symbolic processes which exercise some influence on his problem behaviour. Alternatively, the client himself may modify the operation of such stimuli in his environment. With the possible exception of the application of covert sensitization to the treatment of alcoholism, there is little systematic examination of these procedures and relevant experimental findings remain largely unexploited.

Self-Control of Outcome Conditions

In Chapter 1 we see that the probability of certain responses occurring in future may be influenced by their symbolic consequences of self-reward or self-punishment. This has important implications for human functioning. It enables people to maintain or modify their own behaviour by means which are relatively independent of environmental contingencies. For treatment purposes, desirable responses may be strengthened and maintained by the client symbolically reinforcing himself, even if he is not rewarded in his current environment. Similarly, problematic responses may be suppressed by symbolic self-punishment, although there are no environmental aversive consequences. Furthermore, such self-rewards and punishments can be administered as an immediate consequence of a response and are therefore likely to be more effective than an environmental contingency which is long delayed. External reinforcers are often remote in time from a response, for example, the award of a university degree may follow years after some of the studying required to obtain it. In the interim, responses may to some extent be maintained by symbolic self-reward. Similarly, the aversive consequences of, for example, smoking or overeating may be long delayed, and if they can be moved nearer in symbolic form then their suppressive effect may be greater.

Cautela (1970) has described a symbolic self-reward procedure called 'covert reinforcement'. First several scenes are identified which the patient finds pleasurable and that he can imagine clearly and quickly. The subsequent use of these scenes as reinforcers is illustrated by Cautela in the case of a man whose homosexual urges had been reduced by covert sensitization, but who still found it difficult to make heterosexual approaches such as asking a girl for a date. The patient was told, '. . . As soon as I say the word "reinforcement" try to imagine the reinforcing scene we practised before—the one about your swimming on a hot day, feeling the refreshing water, and feeling wonderful. As soon as the reinforcing scene is clear, raise your right index finger . . . I want you to imagine that you are home in the kitchen and you say to yourself, "I think I'll call Jane for a date". When you have that scene clearly, raise your finger. (As soon as he raises his finger to signal clear imagery, the experimenter says, "Reinforcement".). . . After you've decided to call Jane, you walk towards the phone and start dialling. Raise your finger when this is clear. ("Reinforcement.") All right, now you have finished dialling. Jane answers. You say "Hello" and ask her if she is free Saturday night and tell her that you would like to take her out. Raise your finger when this is clear. ("Reinforcement.") Now do the whole procedure yourself. Imagine you decide to call. Deliver a reinforcement to yourself. Then imagine you are asking for a date and again deliver a reinforcement to yourself . . .' (p. 38). After each treatment session, the patient is instructed to carry out the procedure on his own at home and is urged to actually make the call and to reward himself as he does so. To date, there is no systematic evidence on the therapeutic efficacy of this covert reinforcement procedure.

However, Rehm and Marston (1968) have conducted a controlled study of another treatment programme involving a symbolic self-reinforcement component. The subjects were college students experiencing difficulty in dating behaviour. They were screened to eliminate any with serious emotional problems, and those remaining were allocated to an experimental self-reinforcement group or to one of two control groups given respectively either non-directive or supportive psychotherapy. Each subject in the self-reinforcement group ranked thirty standard heterosexual situations, ranging from sitting next to a girl in class to kissing a girl, according to the degree of discomfort he would experience in the situation. He was then assigned to work his way through this hierarchy in steps by actually getting himself into the situations concerned, and to reward himself with self-approval for each successful attempt. On a number of measures, the self-reinforcement group showed the greatest pre-to-post-treatment improvement, although the study does not enable the specific contribution of the self-reward component in the treatment package to be distinguished.

Homme (1965) has evolved a treatment procedure called 'contingency management' which involves the self-administration of external reinforcers. These are selected according to Premack's (1959) differential probability hypothesis that 'For any pair of responses, the more probable one will reinforce the less probable one.' (p. 132). Thus in order to increase desired behaviour the therapist identifies a high probability response and makes it contingent upon the performance of the desired behaviour. For example, events which have a low probability of occurrence in certain clients, such as housework or thinking 'I am a worthwhile person', may be strengthened by making contingent upon them certain high probability events like drinking coffee or shopping. Similarly, problematic approach responses like smoking may be reduced by the self-reinforcement of antagonistic thoughts such as 'If I smoke, I'll get lung cancer', which are inserted at an early stage to interrupt the sequence of smoking behaviour. At present the only evidence on the efficacy of Homme's contingency management procedure consists of individual case reports, and its employment is reviewed by Mahoney (1970).

Turning now to self-punishment procedures, a possible illustration of their use in symbolic form is provided by Davison (1969b) as part of his treatment of an eleven-year-old boy who was extremely rebellious at home, but not school or a summer camp. He attributed his good behaviour in the latter two situations to the immediacy and severity of punishment for bad behaviour. In contrast, his misbehaviour was generally ignored in the home unless the father was angry or in a sour mood. At such times the boy never crossed his father and was obedient to him. The therapist instructed the patient to note when he might misbehave and then to imagine a sour and angry father. It was explained to him that if he could create an imaginal angry father as a consequence of possible misbehaviour then he might be able to avoid having to face an actual angry father. At the next session, nine days later, the patient reported that he had used the 'little trick' about ten to twenty-five times, and Davison says that there appeared to have been notable improvements in the home situation and in the relationship between the boy and his father.

An example of a self-imposed response cost procedure involving the removal of environmental reinforcers is reported by Nolan (1968). The subject wished to reduce smoking and the treatment consisted of the restriction of this behaviour to a special chair, which was sited so that conversation, television viewing, reading, and drinking coffee or alcohol were very difficult to engage in. Thus, smoking entailed the self-administered aversive consequence of losing these reinforcers. There was a gradual decline in cigarette smoking over a period of one month.

To summarize this discussion of some therapeutic procedures involving the self-control of outcome conditions, it does seem that clients may be able to modify or maintain their own behaviour by administering rewards and punishments to themselves in a contingent manner. These consequences may occur either in the clients' symbolic processes or in their environments. To date, the evidence on the efficacy of such procedures consists almost entirely of case reports.

Problem-solving

The components of the problem-solving process were described in Chapter 1 as attending to and perceiving the relevant elements in a situation, storing these in short-term memory and recalling other essential information, conceptualizing the data into appropriate categories and manipulating these by inductive reasoning to yield hypotheses, rules or principles which solve the presenting problem and others of a similar nature. In social work treatment, this problem-solving process may be facilitated by assisting clients to identify and focus their problem behaviour and to recognize the antecedent and outcome conditions which control it, so that the whole situation is presented in a manner most likely to lead to a solution.

The client's observation of his own behaviour in relation to particular situations may be improved by self-monitoring procedures. Lindsley (1966), among others, requires patients to record the frequency of occurrence of symptoms, together with their consequences and the antecedent events under which they occur. This data is used to show patients the relationships between the symptoms and their controlling conditions. In some cases, the data collection process itself seems to be accompanied by therapeutic change. In the next chapter, this procedure is considered further in the context of assessment. Another technique is to expose patients to audio-, or video-, tape recordings of themselves in situations such as therapeutic interviews or groups, and there is some evidence supporting the efficacy of these self-confrontations in producing beneficial change (Bailey and Sowder 1970, Boyd and Sisney 1967, Gallup 1968, Stoller 1968).

Another possible way of helping clients to perceive the relationships between their problems, the conditions controlling them and the means of solution is for the social worker to give information, advice or instructions. This may facilitate problem-solving and behavioural change, providing that the desired responses exist in the client's repertoire and that their performance is reinforced. Social workers will attest to the frequent inefficacy of advice or instruction alone, and there is some systematic evidence which accords with this impression (Ayllon and Azrin 1964, O'Leary et al. 1969, Phillips 1968). Especially interesting are the studies by Ayllon and Azrin. They attempted to get psychotic patients to pick up cutlery instead of following their usual practice of eating with their hands. After a baseline period of observation, one group of patients was reinforced with extra food or cigarettes for picking up the utensils, but no explanation was given to them. In the next phase, the attendants added the following instruction: 'Please pick up your knife, fork and spoon, and you have a choice of extra milk, coffee,

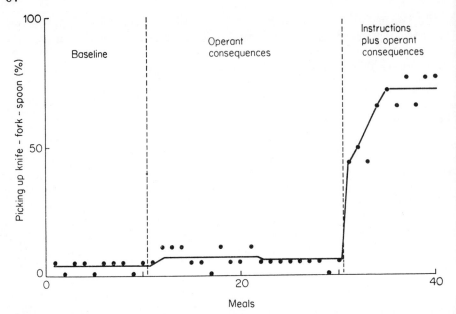

Figure 14. Percentage of patients who picked up cutlery during the baseline period, the reinforcement period when correct responses were rewarded and during a final period when instructions were combined with reinforcement (Ayllon and Azrin 1964).*

cigarettes or candy.' Figure 14 shows that the reinforcement procedure alone produced no improvement in the patients' behaviour, perhaps because few of them made the response necessary to obtain reinforcement, and even these few did not seem to recognize the connection. In contrast, the addition of the instruction was followed by a dramatic increase in the number of patients who picked up the cutlery. To distinguish the effect of instruction alone, a second group of subjects was asked to pick up the utensils, without any differential reinforcement contingencies being implemented. Figure 15 shows that this condition was accompanied by the appearance of the desired behaviour in about half the patients, but this proportion declined subsequently in the absence of contingent reinforcement. When this was introduced in combination with the instruction, then almost all the patients picked up the utensils.

Some writers advocate the communication and establishment of therapeutic response contingencies by means of a 'behavioural contract' between a client and those administering the contingencies. These contracts set out the goals of treatment, the means of achieving them and their consequences for the client, in very explicit terms. The process of negotiating the contract involves the clarification of these factors with the client, as well as laying the basis for appropriate reinforcement by the other parties. Tharp and Wetzel (1969) provide an example

*Additional information and related research can be found in *The Token Economy: A Motivational System for Therapy and Rehabilitation* by T. Ayllon and H. H. Azrin, published by Appleton-Century-Crofts 1968.

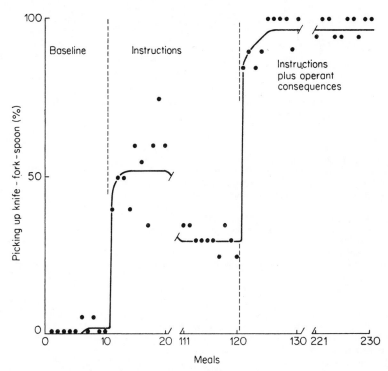

Figure 15. Percentage of patients who picked up cutlery during the baseline, instruction and combined instruction—reinforcement periods (Ayllon and Azrin 1964).*

of the use of such a contract in the treatment of Salvador, a sixteen-year-old-boy who was unmanageable at home, to the extent of chasing his stepfather with a butcher's knife on one occasion. Sal was buying an old car from his stepfather with money earned in part-time jobs, and they both agreed that these payments would be made in the form of acceptable behaviour by the boy. This arrangement was negotiated in detail and embodied in the contract which is reproduced in Figure 16. Stuart (1971) also discusses and illustrates the use of behavioural contracts in the families of delinquents.

Training certain patients in behavioural analysis so that they recognize the functional relationships between their problematic responses and the antecedent and outcome conditions which control them is advocated by Goldiamond (1965) among others. He suggests that the Greek maxim 'Know thyself' might be translated into 'Know thy behaviours, know thy environment, and know the functional relationships between the two'. This approach requires the patient to observe his own behaviour and its environmental conditions, to recognize the relationships between them, and to treat himself by manipulating these conditions. To this end, he is given formal instruction in the principles of be-

*See footnote to Figure 14, page 64 opposite.

CONTRACT

English Ford Automobile

Section I

Sal R. is buying a $400.00 English Ford from his stepfather at the rate of $5.00 per week. This money is to be earned in the following way:

Item	*Value*
1. Remaining home or bringing in the car keys on Sunday through Thursday nights by 9:30 and giving them to his stepfather or placing them in an agreed upon place.	40¢ per night
2. Remaining home or bringing in the car keys on Friday and Saturday nights by 12:00 and giving them to his stepfather or placing them in an agreed upon place.	60¢ per night
3. Mowing front and/or back lawn once a week on day and at time of Sal's choosing. This task must be completed within one day.	60¢ per week
4. Feed dog daily prior to evening meal. (Monday through Friday)	10¢ per feeding
5. Arrive for evening meal at 6:30 or at time specified by mother in the morning. Mother shall indicate any changes prior to the 6:30 meal.	5¢ per meal
6. Straighten room each morning before leaving house or by noon. Mother and Sal are to decide what straightening up room means.	5¢ per day

Total possible—$5.00

Section II

A. Penalty for failure to make car payments.
  1. The penalty for payment failure shall be computed at the rate of 15 minutes of restricted car use the following week for each $.05 under the required $5.00 per week payment.
  2. These restrictions will be imposed by the current car owner, Mr. G.
  3. Failure to make any car payment at all will result in restriction of car privilege for the following week.
B. Payments are to be computed on Sunday evenings.
C. Additional car payments may be made if purchaser acquires a job and has access to additional money.

This contract can be rewritten or in other ways changed by either Sal or Mr. G. at their request and at anytime. All changes must be made in consultation with Mr. Douglass.

Signed:

_____
Mr. Sal R., Purchaser   Date

_____
Mr. Paul G., Owner   Date

Figure 16. Sample behavioural contract (Tharp and Wetzel 1969).

havioural analysis and their application to his own problems is discussed with the therapist until the patient can assume complete responsibility himself. This procedure is likely to be restricted to intelligent, educated and highly motivated patients, but for them it may be especially suitable.

It is suggested above that the procedures of self-monitoring, instruction, or training in behavioural analysis may enhance a client's awareness of the relationships between his problems, their controlling conditions, and the means of solution. It remains to consider the possible contribution of such awareness or insight to therapeutic change. This issue is discussed fully in Chapter 5, and at this point we merely draw attention to some relevant findings in experimental psychology. After reviewing the evidence, Bandura (1969) concludes that: 'In studies of both instrumental and classical conditioning persons who discern the contingencies governing the administration of rewards and punishments typically display significant increments in learning or performance, whereas unaware subjects generally show few or no conditioning effects. . . . The overall findings seem to indicate that awareness is a powerful facilitative factor, but it may not be a necessary and certainly is not a sufficient condition for behavioural change. Awareness in itself is unlikely to produce response changes unless persons possess the necessary performance skills and unless adequate incentives are provided to elicit and to sustain appropriate responsiveness.' (pp. 622-3). Other sources of evidence on the role of awareness include Duncan's (1959) review of research on problem-solving, in which he concludes that it is facilitated by appropriate anticipatory sets or preliminary structuring procedures. Similarly, in the field of verbal learning, Ausubel (1963) considers that 'an individual's organization, stability, and clarity of knowledge in a particular subject-matter field' (p. 26) is an important influence on the learning and retention of meaningful new material. Finally, Locke et al. (1968) have reviewed a large body of evidence indicating the contribution of knowledge of results to efficient learning and performance. We may conclude the present discussion on the role of awareness by suggesting the probable relevance for treatment purposes of knowledge available in experimental psychology, although to date this is largely unexplored. It is exemplified by Bandura (1969) who comments that '. . . the most rapid and enduring changes in instrumental behaviour are achieved when knowledge of contingencies is supplemented with appropriate reinforcing consequences. In interview approaches interpretations of probable contingencies and suggestions for preferable courses of action are offered repeatedly, but favourable outcomes are rarely arranged. On the other hand, practitioners utilizing reinforcement procedures carefully plan the necessary behavioural consequences, but often fail to specify the basis for the reinforcement. It is apparent from the influential role played by cognitive variables in change processes that in an optimal treatment programme change agents should designate the conditions of reinforcement in addition to arranging the requisite response consequences.' (p. 585).

Conclusion

Therapeutic procedures which are under the control of clients appear to have several advantages. These include the possibility of clients maintaining or modifying certain aspects of their own behaviour by symbolic rewards or punishments, which are relatively independent of the contingencies operating in their current environments. This is especially valuable when appropriate environmental consequences are lacking, delayed or beyond the control of the social worker, and it is likely to be an important means of achieving the generalization and persistence of therapeutic changes. Moreover, there is evidence to suggest that such changes might be facilitated if the client sees them as produced by himself rather than by the social worker or anyone else. This suggestive evidence almost entirely relates to the facilitative effect of the subject perceiving himself as having some choice in attempts to change his attitudes (Brehm and Cohen 1962, Goldstein et al. 1966, Winett 1970), and its implications for treatment are still to be ascertained, although Davison and Valins (1969) reported an analogue study. Another possible merit of therapeutic self-control is that it may be applied by the client in future conditions of stress. This is an important goal of treatment, for as Skinner (1953) says, 'Since the therapist cannot foresee all the circumstances in which the patient will find himself, he must also set up a repertoire of self-control through which the patient will be able to adjust to circumstances as they arise . . .' (p. 380). Many therapeutic systems have this preventive aim of reducing susceptibility to future breakdown, as well as the amelioration of current problems, and the introduction of self-control procedures appears to strengthen the behavioural approach in this respect. These procedures also permit therapeutic intervention into certain aspects of a client's behaviour which may not be accessible to the social worker directly. Among these aspects are the client's covert psychological processes which only he can observe, as well as some overt activities, like sexual behaviour, which it is undesirable or impracticable for the social worker to monitor.

This leads to a major limitation in using self-control procedures, that is their restriction to motivated and cooperative clients who are capable of monitoring, reporting and manipulating their own behaviour and the situations in which it occurs. Another limitation at the present time is the lack of adequate data on the efficacy of these procedures, as indicated earlier in this section.

NON-SPECIFIC FACTORS IN
TREATMENT

So far in this chapter we have considered some therapeutic procedures which are relatively specific to a behavioural approach. Certain other factors operate not only in this approach but also in most other forms of treatment. These non-specific factors, including placebo influences and the therapeutic relationship, are not denied or disregarded in behavioural treatment. Instead, the aim is to investigate them systematically as a basis for deliberately enhancing their contribution to the effectiveness of such treatment.

The placebo reaction is defined by Shapiro (1960) as the 'psychological, physiological, or psychophysiological effect of any medication or procedure given with therapeutic intent, which is independent of or minimally related to the pharmacological effect of the medication or the specific effects of the procedure, and which operates through a psychological mechanism' (p. 110). Thus, in the context of this discussion, the term placebo reaction refers to any effects of administering a behavioural procedure which are not attributable specifically to that procedure.

Placebos have a long history in medicine, indeed until this century they were its major therapeutic resource (Shapiro 1960), and their potency is well demonstrated. Volgyesi (1954) has reported a study of patients who were hospitalized with bleeding peptic ulcers. One group were given an injection of distilled water by a doctor who assured them that it was a new medicine which would cure them. A second group received the same injection from a nurse with the information that it was an experimental treatment of unknown effectiveness. In the first group, 70% of the patients showed excellent results lasting over one year, while only 25% of the second group responded favourably. According to Frank (1961), painting warts with a highly coloured but inert dye and telling the patient that the wart will be gone by the time the colour wears off is as effective as any other form of treatment including surgical excision. In a study of the efficacy of vaccines for the common cold, of those injected with the vaccine some 50% had fewer colds compared to 61% of subjects who received inert injections of saline solution (Dhiel et al. 1940). Chronic headaches were relieved by placebos in 60% of cases (Jellinek 1946). Similarly, severe pain was relieved in one-third of cases (Lasagna et al. 1954). Uhlenhuth et al. (1959) have demonstrated the efficacy of placebos in reducing anxiety symptoms, and this effect persists even if the patients are told that the pills are inactive (Park and Covi 1965). Finally, Beecher (1955) has reviewed fifteen investigations involving a total of one thousand and eighty-two patients. He concludes that placebos were effective in approximately 32% of cases, and comments that many drugs have been extolled on the basis of clinical impression when their only power was that of a placebo.

The placebo influences associated with both medical and psychological procedures are commonly conceptualized in terms of explanation and expectancy. For example, Wolberg (1967) writes that 'Assignment of the illness to its responsible determinants tends to alleviate fear of the unknown. It matters little whether the identified source is factual or not. So long as the patient believes it, his catastrophic sense of helplessness is palliated. The healer may diagnose the condition as due to infestation with evil spirits, or regression to an anachronistic psychosexual level of development, or operations of unconscious conflict, or to a disrupted biochemical balance within the body. If the patient accepts the diagnosis, his very focusing on a presumed source of mischief opens up new possibilities of action. . . . Rituals to exorcise offended spirits or to destroy them;

free associations to liberate unconscious foci of conflict; medicaments to reinstate the biochemical balances; conditioning to restore the individual to healthy habit patterns; whatever the theory of etiology, pertinent measures are executed to resolve the problem source. If the patient has faith in the healer, he will believe in the virtue of his methods, whether these be anomalous or scientific . . . The feeling that one is not alone, that a curative agency is at work, subdues anxiety and diverts the individual from self-defeating defences, towards more realistic dealings with existing problem situations. The disruptive physiological effects of anxiety are brought under control, and restoration of self-confidence and assertiveness ensues . . .' (p. 27). These benefits are likely to accrue in behavioural treatment for it is customary to offer an explanation of the client's problem in terms of the system outlined in Chapter 1, as well as some account of the rationale and efficacy of the proposed treatment procedures.

Such an account may promote the expectation of effective help in the client, and there is a considerable body of evidence supporting the therapeutic value of expectancies of this kind (Frank 1968, Goldstein 1962). For example, Friedman (1963) asked psychiatric patients before their initial interview to complete a symptom check list describing how they felt at that time, and then to complete the list again saying how they expected to feel after having six months' treatment of their own choice. The difference between these two scores gave a measure of expected improvement. After the initial interview they again filled in the check list, and the difference between this score and that on the first administration was taken as a measure of symptom reduction. A significant positive correlation was found between the measures of expected improvement and symptom reduction. A second possible example of the relationship between patient prognostic expectancies and therapeutic outcome is provided by Frank et al. (1959). They randomly assigned neurotic patients to one of three types of treatment: group therapy for one and a half hours a week; individual therapy for one hour a week; or individual 'minimal contact' therapy for half an hour every two weeks. After six months' treatment, there was a significant reduction of symptoms in all three groups, but no significant differences between groups in this respect. Furthermore, those patients who had dropped out of treatment within a month improved as much as those who completed six months' treatment. Thus, symptom relief was unrelated to the type or duration of therapy and seemed to occur quite promptly. The investigators sought, therefore, an explanatory factor which was common to all the patients, and suggested that this might be the expectation of help aroused in their initial contact with a therapist.

The therapeutic relationship is another non-specific factor, which is closely related to placebo influences. It is discussed extensively in Chapter 6, and at this point we need note only that in a behavioural approach the importance of the relationship is in no way devalued, and an attempt is made to conceptualize it more adequately and to identify the mechanisms by which it produces change. The social worker is conceived as a source of eliciting, discriminative and reinforcing stimulation which may serve to modify the problem behaviour of clients. Some of the ways in which this may occur are described earlier. Positive reinforcers such as attention, approval and praise may be dispensed or withheld in order respectively to strengthen desirable or weaken problematic responses. Aversive conditions such as disapproval, criticism or punishment may be withheld so that anxiety and similar negative feelings are extinguished. The social worker's warmth, sympathy, attention, interest, concern and professional discretion and competence may elicit positive feelings in clients such as confidence, trust, optimism and self-regard, which may countercondition certain problem responses including anxiety, guilt and self-devaluation. Observational learning procedures depend upon the social worker exhibiting appropriate behaviour for the client to imitate, and the extent to which he will do this is known to be influenced by the warmth, nurturance, expertise and prestige of the model. Cognitive learning calls upon the social worker's knowledge, intelligence, and ability to analyse problem situations in conjunction with clients. Thus the role of the social worker in a behavioural approach is by no means an impersonal one, and it involves an attempt to exploit deliberately any mechanisms by which the casework relationship achieves its effect so that this is maximal.

Some systematic evidence is available on the operation of non-specific factors in behavioural treatment. Explaining it to subjects in ways which arouse their expectations of a favourable outcome has been shown to enhance the efficacy of systematic desensitization (McGlynn et al. 1969, Oliveau et al. 1969). There are also several studies in which the therapeutic relationship is identified as a variable associated with differences in outcome between patients (Crisp 1966, Koenig and Masters 1965, Schmidt et al. 1965). However, this evidence on the contribution of non-specific factors does not imply that they constitute sufficient conditions for the success of behavioural treatment. As Bandura (1969) says, 'It is widely believed that noncontingent "relationship" experiences are the primary determinants of behavioural change, and consequently that the specific methods employed are of secondary importance. In a "therapeutic" atmosphere in which the therapist exhibits permissive non-judgemental and unconditionally positive attitudes, it is contended, a variety of methods, within certain broad limits, will produce essentially similar changes in behaviour.

'This view—which is somewhat analogous to relying on "bedside manner" rather than on specific therapeutic interventions in the alleviation of physical disorders—can be seriously questioned. . . . Let us assume that two children have been referred for treatment, one passive and nonaggressive, the second exhibiting a hyperaggressive pattern of behaviour. Since the goal is to increase assertiveness in the passive child and to decrease the domineering tendencies of the hyperaggressive child, should the therapist employ the same methods? Clearly, the answer is in the negative. Based on established principles of behaviour change, procedures aimed at reducing inhibitions . . ., the provision of assertive models . . . and the reinforcement of assertive response patterns . . . are most appropriate and effective for promoting increased assertiveness. These methods, however, would be clearly inappropriate in the treatment of the hyperaggressive child since they would simply strengthen the already persistent deviant behaviour. Withdrawal of rewards for aggression ... combined with modelling and positive reinforcement of nonaggressive frustration responses ... is highly effective for decreasing aggressiveness. Although in both these hypothetical cases warmth, interest, understanding and other relationship factors would apply equally, it is unrealistic to expect these general factors to increase aggressiveness in one child and to reduce it in the other. Nevertheless therapists often adhere to a single set of therapeutic conditions, disregarding the nature of the client's deviant behaviour ...' (pp. 76-77). Thus Bandura regards nonspecific factors as facilitative rather than sufficient conditions for the production of therapeutic change by behavioural treatment. This view accords with the material presented throughout this chapter, although the only evidence from adequately controlled trials to date is in respect of the use of modelling or systematic desensitization with certain phobic disorders. The evidence concerning modelling is reviewed above and in several trials systematic desensitization is shown to achieve better results than placebos or other forms of treatment (Davison 1968b, Gelder and Marks 1968, Gelder et al. 1967, Lang et al. 1965, Marks and Gelder 1965, Paul 1966, 1967). These consistent findings provide strong support for the effective operation of specific factors in the modelling or systematic desensitization treatment of certain phobic disorders, in addition to the non-specific factors which are common to these procedures and to the others studied in the trials. A similar conclusion remains to be demonstrated for the use of modelling or systematic desensitization with other disorders, as well as for those behavioural procedures which currently lack controlled trials. It may well be that the relative therapeutic importance of specific and non-specific factors varies both between procedures and between types of problem.

To conclude, in a behavioural approach non-specific factors are regarded as facilitative rather than sufficient conditions for therapeutic change, and the aim is to investigate them systematically so that their effectiveness can be enhanced. The corollary is that specific behavioural procedures are implemented in the broad context of social work treatment, rather than as an alternative to it. An appropriate analogy might be the employment of specific medical or surgical procedures within the total care and concern for the patient.

SUMMARY

The procedures described in this chapter represent an attempt to apply systematically certain principles from experimental psychology to the modification of problem behaviour. These procedures are categorized according to whether they appear to operate primarily through antecedent, outcome or self-control, although it is stressed that more than one form of control may contribute to a particular procedure. Contemporary antecedent events are manipulated for therapeutic purposes in the procedures of reducing environmental stresses, positive counterconditioning and observational learning. Among the outcome control procedures used to alter the future probability of instrumental responses are positive reinforcement, extinction, response cost and differential reinforcement. In the third category of self-control procedures, the therapeutic conditions are provided by the client either in his cognitive processes or externally in his environment, and they may involve antecedent, outcome or problem-solving processes. Finally, consideration is given to the operation in behavioural treatment of non-specific factors, such as placebo influences and the therapeutic relationship. In the following chapter we discuss certain necessary preliminaries to the implementation of behavioural treatment.

3

Assessment and Planning Treatment

Before treatment is attempted it is necessary to identify and specify the client's problems and the conditions controlling them, to ascertain the resources available, to select and specify therapeutic goals, and to plan a treatment programme. This is subject to continual revision in the light of the assessment of progress and outcome throughout the treatment and follow-up periods. The kind of information needed at each stage is considered below, followed by some discussion of the methods used to collect the data.

Identification and Specification of Problem Behaviour

Initially, preliminary information is gathered about all aspects of a client's behaviour which are considered to be problematic by the client, the social worker or any other person or agency. Kanfer and Saslow (1969) suggest that these problems might be categorized into behavioural excesses or behavioural deficits. Behaviour may be excessive in frequency, intensity, duration or because it occurs when this is inappropriate to the circumstances. Alternatively, it may be deficient in any of these respects. Examples of excesses are compulsive handwashing, temper tantrums, manic episodes or sexual exhibitionism, while among the conditions involving behavioural deficits are social withdrawal, lack of assertiveness, prolonged depression or impotence. A certain arbitrariness is recognized in this allocation; for instance, any of the examples of excesses given above might be regarded as deficiencies in self-control. Nevertheless, the classification may provide a useful starting point for treatment decisions, as we shall see later.

Behavioural assessment procedures involve the specification of problems in terms of objectively observable responses which are accessible to the social worker as well as the client, in contrast to subjectively observable responses accessible only to the latter. Examples of objectively observable responses are a client's physical avoidance of a feared situation and his verbal description of the fear it arouses in him. Both the physical act and the verbal statement are 'public events' in that they are open to observation by the client, the social worker and anyone else who may be present. The importance of the public nature of objectively observable responses is that it admits the possibility of their consensual validation by more than one observer.

Subjectively observable responses, such as thinking and feeling, are 'private events' in that they are not accessible to observation by the social worker or other outside observers. In varying degree, these events are open to observation by the client, who may report on them verbally. The problem is of course that both the observations and the verbal descriptions may be impaired or distorted by inattention, repression or suppression, and because of the private nature of the events there is no means of reliably ascertaining the accuracy of the client's report. All the social worker can do is to check the internal consistency of such reports. This may be done by repeated observations over time, as in a series of interviews, or by checking verbal reports against other concurrent responses, thus a client's denial of anxiety may not correspond with his profuse sweating, flushing, stammering and agitated movements. The problem of validating a client's verbal descriptions of his subjective experiences does not render such reports valueless, but it does entail recognition that they may or may not be accurate and that the social worker cannot certainly determine this. In summary, a client's subjectively observable responses can never be directly ascertained by the social worker, and must remain a matter of *inference* from the client's objectively observable responses, including his verbal descriptions of his own 'private events'.

As an example we might consider how a social worker can assess the emotions or feelings being experienced by his client. These may be judged from certain objectively observable reponses, including:

1. Motor responses—restlessness, facial expressions, gestures, nail biting, running away, or attacking.

2. Physiological responses—sweating, deep or rapid breathing, blushing or blanching, or pupil dilation.

3. The sequence of the client's behaviour and the related environmental events—for example, 'anger' is in part inferred from the client being in a frustrating situation and subsequently attacking the person frustrating him.

4. Verbal reports by the client of (1), (2) and (3), and of certain subjectively observable responses, including:

(*a*) proprioceptive responses from the striped muscles, tendons, and joints of the body—for example, sensations of tension,

(*b*) interoceptive responses from autonomic, smooth muscle, and glandular activities—for example, palpitations, dry mouth and throat or gastrointestinal sensations.

Because of his language training, the client will often report various patterns of objectively and subjectively observable emotional responses in terms of rather vague and global labels, such as fear, anxiety, guilt, depression, or unhappiness. These labels may be used to refer to very different sets of responses, both by the same client on various occasions and by different clients. The social worker attempts to specify what objectively observable responses the client is referring to when he uses such labels, so that a more precise and publically verifiable assessment can be made of his emotional state at any time. More generally, these same considerations underline the specification of all aspects of a client's problem behaviour in objectively observable terms for the purposes of behavioural assessment.

Identification of the Conditions Controlling the Problem Behaviour

This second aspect of assessment reflects the approach to the explanation of problem behaviour presented in Chapter 1. It is regarded as a function of somatic factors, previous learning experiences and contemporary events. The assessment of these events is directed towards the precise identification of the antecedent, outcome and symbolic conditions which control the problem behaviour, as exemplified in the earlier chapter. First, certain antecedent conditions may be eliciting or reinforcing problem responses, especially those of an emotional kind, while other such conditions may involve some lack of appropriate discriminative stimulus control over the client's instrumental responses. Second, there may be outcome conditions which either reinforce problem behaviour, or punish or extinguish desirable responses. Finally, any of these inappropriate forms of antecedent or outcome control may be operating in the client's symbolic processes, rather than in his external environment or physiological changes, or there may be an impairment of his problem-solving capacity.

Such an impairment might arise from some organic pathology, and this is one example of the need to identify any contribution by somatic factors to the client's problems. His behaviour may be limited or distorted by a physical handicap, subnormality or an organic psychiatric disorder. These conditions may produce the problem behaviour directly, or they may contribute to it indirectly through the reactions of the client or others to his disability so that his life pattern or self-perception is adversely affected.

The identification of the somatic factors or contemporary events which are controlling a client's problem behaviour may be assisted by information about his life history. This will include particulars of any earlier somatic disorder and of the reaction to it by the client and others. The history will cover also any previous learning experiences which might have contributed to the current problem. Certain experiences may have resulted in the classical conditioning of responses to inappropriate antecedent conditions, or in the extension of these by higher order conditioning or stimulus generalization. There may have been inappropriate reward or avoidance training, or the observational learning opportunities available to the client might have been conducive to problem behaviour. Finally, problems may not have been presented to him in ways most likely to facilitate their solution. The possible contribution to problem behaviour of all these types of previous learning experiences is illustrated in Chapter 1, where it is stressed also that it is often difficult to trace current problems to specific learning experiences with any degree of confidence. This is one reason for an emphasis on the identification of contemporary controlling conditions in behavioural assessment, as well as because it is these conditions that are manipulated for treatment purposes. Thus, information about the client's life history is gathered primarily as a source of clues to the contemporary conditions controlling his problem behaviour, rather than for the more specifically therapeutic aims of insight giving or working through.

Assessment of the Resources for Treatment

This aspect of assessment concerns the therapeutic potentialities and limitations of the client and his environment, as well as those possessed by the social worker and his agency. First, it is necessary to consider the extent to which the client's environment might facilitate or impede the implementation of any possible treatment procedures. The feasibility of reducing certain stresses which are eliciting or reinforcing problematic responses may require examination. Counterconditioning procedures are facilitated if there are environmental conditions for the elicitation of responses which are incompatible with the problem responses. In contrast, these procedures are difficult to implement effectively if the problem responses are being reinforced concurrently in the client's environment. For example, it is difficult to countercondition phobias if the client cannot avoid any feared situations not yet dealt with in treatment. Consideration may need to be given also to the availability of appropriate models in the client's environment, as this may determine the use of observational learning procedures in treatment.

Turning now from the environmental conditions for antecedent control procedures to those for outcome control, it is necessary to ascertain the resources available for the reinforcement, punishment or extinction of the client's behaviour. In particular, to discover what is rewarding to him in his environment, as well as the feasibility of presenting these rewards to strengthen desired behaviour or of withdrawing them to reduce problem behaviour. Conversely, there is the question of what environmental aversive stimuli might be withdrawn or presented in order to produce similar changes in the client's behaviour. The feasibility of the social worker obtaining sufficient control over the administration of rewards or punishments is an especially important point, as discussed in the previous chapter.

Several advantages of using parents as therapeutic agents are noted in that chapter also, and the assessment process includes some evaluation of the potential of people in the client's natural situation for this role. In addition, consideration is given to the availability of environmental resources for the enhancement of this potential in possible agents. Such resources might comprise any of these mentioned in the previous two paragraphs; for example, suitable rewards for dispensation to agents contingent upon their performance of the therapeutic role. Again, it is important to assess the feasibility of the social worker being able to control the administration of such resources, in this case to the agent rather than the client.

The second major area in the assessment of resources concerns the client's personal potentialities and limitations for treatment. Important among these is his capacity for self-control. This will affect decisions about treatment involving the correction of false beliefs which are eliciting problematic emotional responses, or the disruption of covert processes eliciting problematic approach responses. Similarly, the client's imaginal capacity may determine the use of procedures such as emotive imagery or covert sensitization. Thirdly, it may be necessary to assess his ability to assume personal responsibility for the reduction of excessive stresses in his environment. Finally, as far as antecedent self-control is concerned, it is necessary to ascertain the client's capacity for discrimination learning and the therapeutic manipulation of discriminative stimuli in his environment. Turning to the self-control of outcome conditions, the social worker will want to know the extent to which the client can administer symbolic rewards or punishments to himself in an appropriate manner, as well as his capacity for arranging such contingencies in his environment. The final aspects of self-control requiring assessment is the efficacy of the client's problem-solving processes, as described in Chapters 1 and 2.

The client's degree of motivation for treatment is likely to influence his cooperation and persistence, and it is therefore another important personal factor requiring assessment. In part this is based upon the client's behaviour, for example his appointment keeping and verbal comments, but the attendant circumstances are also useful sources of information. He may have sought help on his own initiative or because of pressure or encouragement from other people or agencies. It may be useful to assess the adverse effect on his future life if treatment were withheld or unsuccessful. Conversely, the problem behaviour may entail rewards or secondary gains for the client or others in his environment, and if treatment were successful these might be lost, as in the case of the reformed criminal who loses the material rewards of crime as well as the companionship and esteem of his associates, and whose family may also suffer some decline in their standard of living. Successful treatment may entail clear benefits but also some new problems, such as the former homosexual client's enhanced self-esteem but also his need to develop heterosexual skills. All these attendant circumstances together with the social worker's observations of the client's behaviour may provide clues to his degree of motivation.

Self-control and motivation are discussed as examples of personal factors assessed as theraputic resources. They are not the only such factors; others include any somatic conditions that might limit or influence the client's participation in treatment, as well as any skills or competencies which could be exploited for treatment purposes. For example, the treatment of an agoraphobic client who is a skilled musician might involve attendance at musical events as a stage towards a fuller range of public activities.

The third and final area of treatment resources to be assessed concerns those possessed by the social worker or his agency. They include the procedures available for the treatment of a client's particular problems, and the facilities necessary for their implementation, including the social worker's time and any material or social aid she requires. The factors to be assessed in this group are considered at greater length in the sections following.

Selection and Specification of Treatment Goal

Traditionally, casework theorists have emphasized a 'medical' model of problem behaviour, by which it is seen as resulting from underlying causes such as internal motives or conflicts. These processes are regarded as analogous to the germs, viruses, lesions and other factors foreign to the normal working of the organism, which lead to the production of symptoms in physical medicine. An important implication of the utilization of this model is that the direct modification of the symptomatic problem behaviour without removal of its underlying causes is likely to be followed either by the return of the same behaviour or by the substitution of other problem behaviour in its place. It follows that the modification of the presumed underlying causes of problem behaviour is a commonly stated goal of casework, just as an attack on the disease process rather than the symptom is often but not always preferred in physical medicine. This and other implications of adopting a medical model in casework are considered at much greater length in Chapter 5.

When discussing the explanation of problem behaviour within a behavioural approach, we saw that it is regarded as a function of somatic factors, previous learning experiences and contemporary events. This is an alternative to conceiving hypothetical internal motives or conflicts as underlying causes of problem behaviour. It leads also to an alternative approach in casework treatment, that is instead of attempting to remove these presumed underlying causes, one may aim at the direct modification of the client's problematic responses to his current conditions. Thus in a behavioural approach casework goals are framed in terms of the prevention or reduction of problematic responses, and the acquisition and maintenance of appropriate responses. As these two ways of responding are not distinguished according to the presence or absence of an underlying 'disease' process, this distinction must be made by other criteria and these are the subject of Chapter 4.

The behavioural attempt to modify problems directly is often held to entail the risk of symptom return or substitution, but several authoritative psychodynamic writers do not accept this as an inevitable consequence of any symptomatic treatment. They include Alexander and French (1946), Fenichel (1945) and Wolberg (1967) who writes: 'Amongst the most solecistic of legends is the notion that elimination of symptoms is wicked if not worthless. This notion stems from the steam engine model of psychodynamics that conceives of energy in a closed system, bound down by symptomatic defences, which, when removed, release devils that need new chains. This in spite of the fact that physicians from the time of Hippocrates have applied themselves to symptom removal in both organic and functional ailments with little or no baneful consequence. Yet legends, possessing perpetuity, survive from one generation to the next. The presumed dangers of symptom removal are now as threatening to the younger therapists as they were to their teachers. Little proof is offered of a causal relationship between the fact of symptom relief or removal and any pathological sequelae. The evidence persuades that supposedly precipitated disasters are either coincidental or the product of inept therapeutic interventions. . . . The complaint, then, that symptom removal is an arbitrary, incomplete, irrational and unsatisfactory approach in psychotherapy is apocryphal. Symptom relief or removal is an essential goal in any useful psychotherapeutic approach.' (p. 102).

Furthermore, there are indications that substitution is infrequent following the direct modification of problem behaviour, but when it does occur this does not necessarily entail support for the medical model, for it may be accounted for within a behavioural approach as Cahoon (1968) has shown. In the first place the client may be subjected to fresh stresses which evoke fresh problem responses. There is no more reason to regard this as arising from continuing underlying causes than the case of a person who twice breaks his leg while skiing; it is a new problem rather than a return of the original one. Second, all relevant problem responses may not have been modified; for example, if avoidance responses are removed but the stress they serve to reduce is left untouched, then fresh avoidance responses may appear. Third, problem responses may not have been modified to all relevant stimuli; for example, anxiety and avoidance responses need to be eliminated in relation to all the phobic situations which elicit them. Fourth, correcting a deficit in behaviour means adding responses to the client's repertoire, which may in turn be either acceptable or problematic. An example of the latter occurred in the treatment of an autistic child described by Wolf et al. (1965). This involved training him to wear spectacles, but when this was accomplished by positive reinforcement, he began throwing the spectacles away with great frequency, so that this new problem required modification. Clearly the correction of the original problem was a necessary pre-condition for the appearance of the second one. Fifth, where problem behaviour has obtained reinforcement for the client, removal of his behaviour may be followed by other means of gaining reinforcement which may in turn be either acceptable or problematic. Goldiamond (1965) has described the case of a woman who assumed a foetal posture for three days after an argument with her husband. She was restored to mobility in two hours by direct treatment, but Goldiamond comments that new childish means of influencing her husband are likely to appear unless she learns more appropriate ways of doing so. Finally, potential responses may be arranged in a hierarchy according to their respective probabilities in occurrence. The removal of one problem response high in a hierarchy may facilitate the appearance of others which in turn will require extinction. An example of this is cited by Ullmann and Krasner (1965). A boy at a summer camp exhibited a series of problem responses, including self-punishing behaviour, tantrums, taking his clothes off in public, stealing food, smearing faeces and finally mixing up all the children's shoes in one pile. Each of these responses had to be extinguished in turn. In conclusion, this discussion of problem substitution highlights the need for accurate and comprehensive assessment of the problems and their controlling conditions as a necessary basis for the selection of goals and planning of treatment.

It is mentioned above that a behavioural formulation of the goals of casework includes the prevention as well as the amelioration of problems. The latter is exemplified in Chapter 2, and Poser (1970) has proposed a preventive role for behavioural procedures. He reviews evidence suggesting that stress reactions can be mitigated by appropriate prior exposure to the stressful conditions, while problematic approach responses may be blocked by previously associating them with aversive stimulation. For instance, clients might be inoculated against stressful events like separation from parents or surgery by appropriate counter-conditioning, while addictive or anti-social behaviour might be prevented by differential reinforcement programmes. In fact, most people are exposed to such preventive experiences in the normal course of upbringing, and the role of behavioural prophylaxis may be to correct any deficiency in this respect. Finally, we may reiterate the point made in the previous chapter on the importance of the therapeutic enhancement of client self-control as a means of reducing suscepti-bility to future stresses.

Turning now from the nature to the selection of treatment goals, this is influenced by several groups of factors. In the first place there are the wishes and values of the client, the social worker and perhaps other people or institutions. Their respective rights, responsibilities and influences in selecting goals are discussed in Chapter 7. Then there is the degree of distress or incapacity that the problem entails for the client or others, together with the beneficial or detrimental consequences expected from treatment. Thirdly, the selection of goals is influenced by the availability of the environmental, personal and therapeutic resources discussed in the previous section. In particular, consideration is given to the availability and efficacy of procedures for the treatment of particular kinds of problem. The efficacy of some procedures with certain problems is noted in Chapter 2, and a few more general comments are added here.

A behavioural approach may have the advantage of being applicable with certain categories of client who may be difficult to help with the more traditional approach. These might include the less verbal and well-educated clients, who might profit from the more direct modification of their problems with less reliance on their understanding and verbalization to mediate change. Similarly, because of the great use of material controlling stimuli in a behavioural approach, it may be useful with clients who are little influenced by social stimuli, including some psychotics or psychopaths. Some such clients may become more susceptible to social motivation and reinforcement, following the use initially of material controlling stimuli. Conversely, it is often difficult at present to see how to apply a behavioural approach to certain types of problem which are hard to analyse into particular dysfunctional behaviour, however broadly defined. These conditions might include so-called 'existential problems' such as general unhappiness or lack of meaning or purpose in life. They may be more appropriately conceptualized as problems of meaning rather than functioning, and although it is theoretically possible to see how certain aspects of experimental psychology, such as cognitive learning or attitude change, might provide suitable treatment approaches, this has not been much explored to date. The scope of a behavioural approach is limited also to the extent that a client is unable to learn because of any somatic constraining factor, or where problems are not under recognizable controlling conditions: for example, in certain cases of pervasive anxiety, depression or psychopathic disorder.

The next group of factors taken into account in selecting goals concerns the range and interrelationships of the problems presented by the client. A number of these may constitute a single theme. For instance, various specific phobias of particular social situations may have the common element of fear of failure, and treatment might be directed towards this rather than the specific situational phobias. On the other hand, clients may exhibit several problems with no ascertainable connection between them. An attempt might be made to treat them all concurrently, but it may be more practicable to concentrate on a very small number at a time, and this could entail certain other advantages. It is likely to focus the treatment efforts of the client and social worker, and to maintain these by expediting some beneficial outcome from treatment. Furthermore, it may avoid unnecessary treatment, for the improvement of one problem is sometimes accompanied by beneficial changes in others. Thus, the successful treatment of a condition such as enuresis may be associated with a general improvement in family relationships. Similarly, the reduction of social anxiety may enable a client to obtain a more responsible and remunerative job and thereby improve his self-esteem and financial situation. However, it may not be easy for the social worker either to establish common themes linking particular problems, or to identify any key problems for which immediate treatment is likely to produce more widespread beneficial effects. There does not appear to be any clear guide lines for these tasks up to the present time, and pragmatic decisions must be made.

Having selected the goals of treatment it is necessary to specify them very precisely in terms of the responses to be produced and the conditions under which these should occur. This specification forms an essential basis for the planning, execution and assessment of treatment. It serves to clarify the objectives for both client and social worker, to guide the choice of precedures, and to facilitate the assessment of progress and outcome so that treatment programmes can be improved both for the individual client and in the approach generally.

For the reasons discussed in the earlier section on the specification of problem behaviour, the goals of treatment are also specified as objectively observable responses rather than global, abstract and inferred states such as self-esteem, self-fulfilment or self-knowledge. This does not imply that these states are not desirable, only that they are more usefully conceptualized in terms of the behaviour from which they are inferred. For instance self-fulfilment might be inferred from certain vocational or interpersonal achievements which accord with the client's verbal descriptions of his level of aspiration in these areas. Both the achievements and the descriptions are potentially accessible to observation by the social worker or others, so that reliable assessment is possible. In contrast, the abstract state of self-fulfilment cannot be publically verified and its meaning is poorly defined and open to dispute. Consequently, in a behavioural approach an attempt is made to specify the goals of treatment as the performance in defined circumstances of certain objectively observable responses at given levels of frequency, intensity and duration.

It does not follow necessarily that behavioural goals are unduly narrow or limited. Not only might their achievement be of significant value in itself, but it may be accompanied by more widespread beneficial repercussions. This 'avalanche effect' (Patterson 1967b) is noted and illustrated in Chapter 2. Furthermore, Bandura (1969) considers that: 'Greatest progress will be made in the successful treatment of so-called complex disorders when they are conceptualized, not as nebulous general states, but as psychological conditions involving multiple-problems with varying degrees of interdependence. From this perspective, altering complex behavioural dysfunctions does not require radically different methods from those applied to the modification of single disorders . . . : A child may have developed satisfactory academic skills in all areas except mathematics. Another child is grossly deficient in mathematics and in other academic skills, lacks social behaviour skills that would enable him to maintain satisfying interpersonal relationships, and has not developed motor competencies required for play activities. There exists no single non-specific treatment that can simultaneously create competencies in intellectual, linguistic, social and motoric areas of functioning. Separate programmes would have to be devised for each type of problem. But the procedures used to develop arithmetic competencies would be essentially the same in the single-problem and multiple-problem case . . . The developments in behavioural therapy in some respects parallel those in medicine, where global all-purpose treatments of limited efficacy were eventually replaced by powerful specific procedures for treating particular physical disorders' (pp. 89—90). We return to this point in the following section.

Planning Treatment

Decisions are required concerning the agent and setting of treatment, the procedures to be employed in certain combinations and sequences, and the measures necessary to promote the maintenance of beneficial changes after the intervention ends.

Several considerations enter into the choice of agent and setting of treatment. Its conduct by the social worker in office interviews entails the problem discussed in Chapter 2 of achieving the generalization of therapeutic change to the client's natural environment. Some important considerations in deciding whether to attempt treatment in this way include the client's degree of motivation and capacity for self-control, the availability in his repertoire of the behaviour it is desired to produce, and the existence in his environment of suitable conditions for its control. One alternative, also discussed in Chapter 2, is to arrange for parents or other people to conduct the treatment in the natural environment. This circumvents the task of generalizing change from interviews, and the agents are likely to be therapeutically potent because of their emotional significance and the amount of contact they have with the client. They may also be the only people who can make the necessary changes in the conditions controlling the problem behaviour. An additional merit of this approach is that it may maximize the impact of scarce social worker resources. However, there remain the problems of obtaining the cooperation of the agents concerned, and of ensuring the persistence of beneficial changes in their behaviour as well as that of the client after the social work intervention ends. In certain circumstances, the selection of agent and setting may relate to the client's entry into a residential institution. For example, he might be committed to a penal establishment, or admitted to hospital because his environment lacks the resources necessary for treatment or contains stresses likely to impede it.

Turning now to the choice of procedures; one group of factors influencing this are the wishes and values of the client, the social worker and perhaps other people or institutions. Their respective rights, responsibilities and influences in choosing procedures are discussed in Chapter 7. Next, there is the issue of whether to alter the client's responses to his environment without deliberately changing the latter, or to change the environment as a means of modifying his problem behaviour. These two general strategies are exemplified in Chapter 2, and attention is drawn to the appropriateness whenever feasible of reducing excessive stress rather than attempting to modify the client's reactions to it. In many cases of course, both strategies are employed.

Thirdly, the choice of procedures is influenced by the kind of behaviour to be modified, together with the nature and sources of its controlling conditions. Thus, relatively involuntary reflexes and responses mediated by the autonomic nervous system, including those involved in emotional behaviour, are primarily under antecedent control and it may be appropriate to use procedures containing an important element of this. They include the reduction of stressful conditions in the client's environment by himself or the social worker, positive counterconditioning, observational learning, the correction of false beliefs or disruption of problematic approach responses, emotive imagery, covert sensitization, discrimination learning or problem-solving. In contrast, voluntary responses mediated by the central nervous system, including speech and skeletal movement, are subject mainly to outcome control, and procedures in which this is important may be chosen. These include positive reinforcement, extinction, response cost, differential reinforcement, covert reinforcement, contingency management, self-punishment or problem-solving procedures. Within the categories of antecedent or outcome control, a further decision must be made between environmental or self-control procedures, and some advantages and limitations of the latter are considered in the relevant section of Chapter 2. The total treatment programme may of course include various combinations of antecedent and outcome procedures, as well as both environmental and self-control.

Another criterion for selecting procedures is whether the problem is conceptualized as an excess or deficit in behaviour, as discussed at the beginning of this chapter. Among the procedures available to correct excesses are positive counterconditioning, emotive imagery, disruption of problematic approach responses, extinction, response cost, covert sensitization or self-punishment, while deficits may be remedied by procedures such as positive reinforcement or covert reinforcement. Certain other procedures might be used to correct either excesses or deficits. These procedures include the reduction of excessive stresses or correction of false beliefs, observational learning, differential reinforcement, contingency management, discrimination learning or problem-solving. Some arbitrariness is recognized in conceptualizing problems as excesses or deficits, and elements of each may occur in the same problem or client, therefore it is quite common to employ combined or dual-purpose procedures.

Three further factors to be taken into account when selecting procedures are their feasibility, efficacy and efficiency. The judgement of feasibility depends upon the assessment of resources for treatment. Some evaluation of efficacy is included in the review of certain procedures in Chapter 2 and more generally in the present chapter. Finally, consideration is given to the relative efficiency of possible procedures in terms of the resources required for their implementation.

It is emphasized that a behavioural approach does not entail the routine application of particular procedures to certain problems. Instead an individualized treatment programme is evolved to suit the difficulties and goals of each client, bearing in mind the factors discussed in this section. Usually some combination of procedures is required to meet the range of a client's problem behaviour, and they may be associated with other forms of intervention such as physical treatments.

Having selected the procedures to be implemented, it is necessary to plan the sequence of treatment. Often, an important aspect of this is the arrangement of a series of intermediate steps to the ultimate goal. Situations which arouse problematic emotional responses may be introduced into treatment in a graded manner from the least to the most disturbing, so that the client is not overwhelmed or precipitated into escape or avoidance reactions. Similarly, while an ultimate goal is beyond a client's current capacity, then the achievement of a series of intermediate goals will minimize his experience of failure and optimize the frequency and scheduling of reinforcement. Finally, it may be necessary for the client to first acquire the component parts of a complex pattern of behaviour which is the final goal of treatment.

The last aspect of treatment planning discussed here concerns the maintenance of therapeutic change after the specific intervention ends. It is not always necessary to arrange special measures for this purpose; the intervention may strengthen skills or remove inhibitions so that the client gains access to existing sources of reinforcement, or it might reduce the aversiveness of his behaviour for himself or others and thus entail reinforcing consequences. In other circumstances it may be desirable to plan for the maintenance of change, and the following are some ways of approaching this task.

Stimulus and response generalization (Jehu 1967) may be facilitated by making the treatment setting as similar as possible to the client's natural environment. The term 'stimulus generalization' refers to the observation that similar situations tend to elicit the same behaviour, and the more alike the situations are the greater is this tendency. On the response side the comparable phenomenon is that a situation which elicits one response is likely to elicit similar responses, and there is also a gradient of response generalization according to the degree of similarity between responses. The therapeutic exploitation of these principles is illustrated in the case of Tessa (Sluckin and Jehu 1969), among others described in Chapter 2.

Secondly, one can reinforce behaviour in treatment in ways which are likely to promote its persistence afterwards. For instance, an intermittent schedule of reinforcement might be used, as behaviour which has been reinforced in this way then requires fewer reinforcements to maintain it, and it takes longer to extinguish after reinforcement ceases (Jehu 1967). Similarly, as treatment proceeds, artificial reinforcers such as tokens or material rewards might be replaced by others like social attention and approval which are more likely to apply after treatment ends.

Third, one might fade out special discriminative stimuli used in the therapeutic situation, so that the desired behaviour is emitted under the control of appropriate cues which will exist in the client's natural environment. An example of the therapeutic employment and subsequent fading of special discriminative stimuli is the signal system used to guide the mother's handling of Peter, as reported by Hawkins et al. (1966) and cited in Chapter 2.

Another approach is to help the client to acquire any new skills he needs to function satisfactorily after treatment ends. For instance, the former homosexual might need to acquire the social skills necessary to establish and maintain heterosexual relationships, or the reformed criminal might be enabled to obtain material and social reinforcement without further recourse to delinquent acts or associates. Two final ways of promoting the persistence of beneficial changes are the creation and maintenance of sources of reinforcement in the client's natural environment or the enhancement of his self-control processes, and each is discussed in the previous chapter.

Assessing Treatment

Having formulated and implemented a plan, its outcome is assessed throughout the treatment and follow-up periods. This provides feedback to the client on his progress and there is evidence to suggest that such information may have beneficial effects (Locke et al. 1968). It may also enhance the social worker's conduct of the treatment (Locke et al. 1968), and reveal any necessity for a revision of the programme. In the longer term, the assessment of treatment outcome for individual clients provides the data for evaluating the general efficacy of the procedures concerned, so that they can be continued, improved or abandoned. More specifically, it may permit identification of the crucial therapeutic ingredients in a procedure, thus providing a basis for its future refinement. As we saw earlier, the reliable assessment of the efficacy of procedures is facilitated in a behavioural approach by specification of the problem behaviour and the goals of treatment in terms of objectively observable responses, rather than as global, abstract and inferred states. Finally, the efficacy of treatment procedures and their ingredients can be established only by systematic investigation, and commitment to this in a behavioural approach is perhaps one of its most valuable derivatives from experimental psychology, for it contains the promise of cumulative improvement in the help given to clients.

Any post-intervention changes in a client's problem behaviour might be the result of treatment or of certain other factors (Campbell and Stanley 1966). Among these are extra-therapeutic events in his life, such as marriage, re-employment, a new house or help from a relative or friend. Then there are maturational changes, which might, for example, account for the resolution of adolescent problems. Next, the means by which clients are assessed might change during treatment or follow-up; perhaps an interviewer will become more skilled or more bored and this will influence his later assessments. Fourth, post-intervention changes might arise from statistical regression. Among clients seeking social work help will be some whose problems are to some extent due to chance factors of a temporary kind. Since chance seldom operates twice in the same way, it follows that some such clients are likely to have improved when they are re-assessed on a later occasion, and this improvement may be wrongly attributed to treatment. A fifth possible explanation of post-intervention change may operate whenever clients are not assigned randomly to treatment or control groups. It is then possible for selection biases to occur so that the two groups are different in certain respects before the treatment begins, and these initial differences are a possible explanation of any post-treatment variation between the groups. For instance, there may be pressure to offer help immediately to clients who press their plight, while the less assertive are left on the waiting list as controls. When the first group has been treated, any differences between it and the controls might be attributable either to treatment or to their initial differences. Another possible source of post-treatment differences between treatment and control groups is variation in their respective rates of drop-out. Clients may drop out of treatment because they do not like it, because they improve and lose their motivation, or because their problems worsen and have to be dealt with in some other way. They may drop out of control groups because they seek help elsewhere, because their problems are resolved without treatment, or because the agency loses contact with them. These sorts of factors operating in treatment or control groups may lead to differences between them which are wrongly attributed to treatment. Finally, if clients know that they are participating in a therapeutic experiment, this knowledge may influence their reactions. For instance, they may respond as they think the investigator wants them to, or the special interest and attention they attract may boost their morale. Any such effects of being experimental subjects might be incorrectly attributed to treatment.

Awareness of these and other alternative explanations to treatment as the source of changes in behaviour leads to the attempt to design investigations so as to eliminate the maximum number of such alternatives. This is done by controlling for their possible operation, while applying the treatment and assessing the outcome. In this way, one can test for cause–effect relationships between treatment and outcome, and so evaluate the efficacy of the procedures used.

In the 'own control' type of experimental design, each subject experiences both the treatment and control conditions and thus acts as his own control. The simplest design of this kind consists of assessing an individual client before and after he receives treatment, and many of the case studies in Chapter 2 are examples of it. However, this individual pre-test–post-test design has serious limitations, for one cannot be sure that any changes in the client's behaviour are due to treatment rather than to one or more of the possible alternative factors discussed above. Furthermore, this design does not permit identification of the active therapeutic ingredients in the whole treatment package.

A more rigorous form of own control is the intrasubject replication design, which often involves the repeated reversal of treatment and control conditions. First, the problem behaviour is assessed to establish a baseline for predicting what the behaviour would have been in future if the treatment had not been instituted. The second stage consists of applying the treatment and of assessing the client's behaviour during it. In the third stage the treatment is discontinued, and if the problem behaviour returns to the original baseline level this supports the prediction of the continuance of the behaviour at that level if the treatment had not been introduced. The fourth stage consists of reinstituting the treatment and if this is followed by another improvement in the problem behaviour, it suggests that it is the treatment which is causing the changes in the behaviour. Examples of this type of design are the cases of the withdrawn nursery school child (Allen et al. 1964) described and illustrated (Figure 1) in Chapter 1, and the treatment of Peter (Hawkins et al. 1966) described and illustrated (Figure 3) in Chapter 2.

A limitation of this type of intrasubject replication design is that the aim of treatment is to produce beneficial changes in behaviour which persist after the intervention ends. If this is done successfully then it will not be possible to recover the original baseline behaviour by withdrawing treatment in the third stage. An example of this occurred in the treatment of Peter (Hawkins et al. 1966) when his mother reported considerable difficulty in responding to him as she had during the first baseline period, because she felt more 'sure of herself' and could not remember how she had previously behaved towards her son. Sometimes when it is not possible to recover the original baseline in a reversal intrasubject replication design, it may be appropriate to use a variant of it called a multiple baseline or sequential analysis design.

Intrasubject replication designs can be used also to ascertain the active ingredients in a whole treatment package. For example, it would be possible to distinguish the contribution of the 'time-out' component in the treatment of Peter (Hawkins et al. 1966) by systematically varying it while keeping constant the positive reinforcement and other components.

The major limitation of the intrasubject designs is that one cannot be certain that any changes in the problem behaviour accompanying the application and withdrawal of the treatment are in fact a function of this treatment. The changes may be due to the operation of other factors which happen to co-vary with the treatment conditions. If the investigation is conducted over a lengthy period, the other factor concerned might operate in the client's life situation, such as a cycle of unemployment, employment, unemployment and employment, which happens to coincide with the baseline, treatment, withdrawal and re-treatment periods. Over shorter periods, this sort of coincidence is much less likely. Perhaps the greater risk in interpreting intrasubject replication designs lies in mistaking the active ingredients in a treatment package. For instance, by assuming that it is some specific factor such as reinforcement that produces the fluctuations in the problem behaviour, when non-specific factors such as the therapeutic relationship which may co-vary with the specific factor remain uncontrolled and may contribute to an unknown extent. However, as mentioned earlier, it is possible to distinguish the respective contributions of particular treatment components by appropriate use of intrasubject replication designs.

A third form of own control is the non-factorial single group design. Essentially it is a collection of case studies using the individual pre-test–post-test or intrasubject replication designs. Consequently all the merits and limitations of these designs apply also to the non-factorial single group design, except that the latter renders less plausible certain of the alternatives to treatment as the source of change. For example, it is less likely that extra-therapeutic alternatives, such as marriage, will apply to a number of subjects. To the extent that such rival alternatives are eliminated the case for treatment as the source of change is strengthened. An example from Chapter 2 of a non-factorial single group study using an individual pre-test–post-test design is the report by Wolpe and Lazarus (1966) on their treatment of a group of impotent men. Another example, using an intrasubject replication design, is the report of a token economy programme in a Children's Home by Phillips (1968), which is described and illustrated (Figures 12, 13) in Chapter 2.

Turning from own control to control group designs, in the latter the treatment and control conditions are applied to separate groups of subjects, rather than to the same subjects as in the own control designs. The major problem is to ensure that the treatment and control groups are equivalent in all respects other than the experience of treatment, and this may be tackled by eliminating or holding constant certain factors, matching, randomization, blocking or statistical control (Campbell and Stanley 1966).

Taking non-factorial control group designs first, one of the simplest of these is the pre-test–post-test control group design. The subjects are randomly assigned to the treatment or control group, their pretreatment behaviour is assessed, treatment is applied to one group but not to the other, and the behaviour of both groups is then assessed again. This design controls all the alternatives to treatment as the source of any post-treatment differences between the groups, since they have both been exposed equally to these alternatives. Examples of this design in Chapter 2 include the modelling treatments of isolated children by O'Connor (1969), and of aggressive reactions by Chittenden (1942). Its most serious limitation is that it does not permit identification of the active ingredients in the treatment given, or the influence on outcome of other factors such as the severity of the client's problems.

This limitation can be met by using a factorial control group design. To take a simple example, one might attempt to distinguish the respective effects of specific and non-specific factors in a treatment package by randomly assigning subjects to a treatment group, an attention-placebo group, or an untreated control group. The aim is for the attention-placebo group to have the same experience of contact with the social worker, and the same expectation of help, as the treatment group; the only difference being the withholding of the presumed specific components in the treatment from the attention-placebo group. It is of course possible to complicate this design much more by adding other forms of treatment or other components of treatment packages, as well as by factorizing other conditions such as the severity of the clients' problems. Thus, these factorial control group designs are very potent. They may be exemplified in Chapter 2 by the series of studies of the treatment of animal phobias by Bandura and his co-workers (Bandura et al. 1967, 1968, Bandura and Menlove 1968).

Particular types of design may vary in their usefulness according to the stage reached in the development of a treatment procedure. Own control designs are most useful in the early stages when they may serve as sources of ideas or hypotheses, to sharpen or demonstrate procedures, and, in the case of intrasubject replication designs, to provide *correlational* evidence of an association between a procedure and a change in the client's problem behaviour. However, as we have seen, *cause–effect* relationships between procedures and changes cannot be established by intrasubject replication designs because of the absence of control over possible alternative sources of influence on outcome. Non-factorial control group designs do enable cause–effect relationships to be established between procedures and changes in problem behaviour. Effective procedures can then be implemented in general social work practice, while ineffective procedures are dropped or modified. Furthermore, the effective procedures can be subjected to additional investigation in order to identify their active ingredients as well as the influence on outcome of various other factors such as client characteristics. This sort of additional investigation is especially appropriate for the employment of a factorial control group design. These yield the maximum information but also require the most resources, and are therefore perhaps only worth undertaking at a fairly advanced stage in the development of a treatment, when the package as a whole has been shown to be of some value.

So far in this discussion of the systematic investigation of treatment outcome we have been concerned with designing investigations so that the effect of the treatment can be distinguished from that of possible alternative factors. A second important matter concerns the generalization of findings from a particular investigation to other client groups or treatment situations, and in certain circumstances it may not be valid to make such generalizations (Campbell and Stanley 1966). In the first place, when subjects selected for treatment are those most likely to respond to it there is a selection–treatment interaction, and findings can only be generalized to other clients exhibiting the specific characteristics which led to the selection of the experimental subjects. For instance, if highly motivated and cooperative clients are selected for an experiment, then its results can only safely be generalized to other clients exhibiting these characteristics. Second, the possible reactions of subjects to being in an investigation is mentioned earlier, and it may restrict the generalization of findings from experiments to non-experimental treatment situations. A third threat to the validity of generalization is a multiple treatment effect which may occur when several different treatments are administered to the same subjects. In these circumstances, exposure to the first treatment may influence the client's reactions to the second, and so on. Therefore, the findings can only be generalized to other clients who also experience the treatments in the same order.

Prima facie, laying the basis for valid generalization is a problem of sampling to ensure the representativeness of the experimental group and treatment situation. However, in practice, sampling is usually directed to the selection of a representative group of clients, and the sampling of factors in the treatment situation is often neglected. For instance, treatment is often conducted by a single social worker or a small group of social workers, who may be quite unrepresentative of those who might use the treatment in general practice. Social workers in an investigation may be highly motivated, perhaps because their research degree or career advancement depends upon it, or they may be used because they are highly skilled, and less committed or less skilled social workers may not be able to make the treatment work as well. It is quite legitimate to optimize a treatment in such ways, but caution must be exercised in generalizing the results. Similarly, the administration of a treatment procedure in an investigation may be unrepresentative of general practice. In order to control procedural variation, it may be administered in a standard way throughout the investigation, perhaps by visits being at the same intervals or interviews of a certain length, and this may make the experimental treatment less and less like its ordinary use, and thus increase the risk of invalid generalization.

In conclusion, the crux of experimental investigations into the outcome of treatment is the control of other factors, the application of the treatment, and the assessment of change in the client's problem behaviour. This permits the establishment of causal relationships between the treatment and the change in behaviour. For, if the application of treatment while other possible sources of change are controlled is followed by such change, then it is possible to infer a causal relationship with some confidence. In contrast, the lack of control in non-experimental investigations, such as individual pre-test–post-test case studies, means that one cannot be equally sure that one has identified correctly the actual source of change out of several possible alternatives, including the common ones discussed earlier. The major possible limitation of experiments in this context occurs if the experimental treatment is too artificial and unrepresentative of the treatment as it may be conducted in general social work practice, so that findings cannot safely be generalized. This limitation can be reduced or avoided by careful attention to the common threats to valid generalization and the sampling considerations discussed above.

Methods of Data Collection

Traditionally, casework theorists have adopted a psychodynamic model of assessment with an emphasis on underlying internal states of an inferred and hypothetical kind. They include structural concepts like the id, ego and super-ego, as well as dynamic concepts such as drives, conflicts, defences and complexes. These personality constructs are presumed to have a general and persistent casual influence on all aspects of the client's behaviour, so that it remains more or less stable regardless of the particular situation. It follows, that objectively observable responses to particular situations are of relatively little interest, except as signs of the underlying states which are considered to be the most valid indicators of the client's future behaviour in any situation. However, the available evidence does not appear to support this contention. After a comprehensive review, Mishel (1968) concludes that 'With the possible exception of intelligence, highly generalized behavioural consistencies have not been demonstrated, and the concept of personality traits as broad response predispositions is thus untenable'. (p. 146). It seems that behaviour is much more specific to particular situations than the psychodynamic model suggests. For this reason as well as others discussed earlier, there is an emphasis in a behavioural approach on the client's responses to specific situations. Data about this may be collected from the client himself, from other informants or through direct observation by the social worker.

Data may be collected from clients by means of interviews, questionnaires or records. An interview guide has been developed by Kanfer and Saslow (1969) and a summary of it (Kanfer and Phillips 1970) is reproduced as Figure 17. Three specimen interviews have been published by Wolpe, one with a depressed woman (1970a), one with a man suffering from hypochondriacal anxiety (1970b), and one with an agoraphobic patient (1970c). Among the questionnaires available are some to obtain reports from clients about their fear responses to certain situations (Geer 1965, Wolpe and Lang 1964), their sexual reactions (Bentler 1968a, 1968b), and the conditions they find rewarding (Cautela and Kastenbaum 1967, Tharp and Wetzel 1969). Lastly, clients may be asked to record the frequency of occurrence of problem responses together with the conditions preceding and following each occurrence (Kanfer 1970, Lindsley 1966). One use of this method with an asthmatic patient revealed that attacks

1. Analysis of a Problem Situation.

The patient's major complaints are categorised into classes of behavioural excesses and deficits. For each excess or deficit the dimensions of frequency, intensity, duration, appropriateness of form, and stimulus conditions are described. In content, the response classes represent the major targets of the therapeutic intervention. As an additional indispensable feature, the behavioural assets of the patient are listed for utilisation in a therapy programme.

2. Clarification of the Problem Situation.

Here we consider the people and circumstances that tend to maintain the problem behaviours, and the consequences of these behaviours to the patient and to others in his environment. Attention is given also to the consequences of changes in these behaviours that may result from psychiatric intervention.

3. Motivational Analysis.

Since reinforcing stimuli are idiosyncratic and depend for their effect on a number of unique parameters for each person, a hierarchy of particular persons, events, and objects that serve as reinforcers is established for each patient. Included in this hierarchy are those reinforcing events that facilitate avoidance responses. The purpose of obtaining this information is to lay plans for utilisation of various reinforcers in prescription of a specific behaviour therapy programme for the patient, and to permit utilisation of appropriate reinforcing behaviours by the therapist and significant others in the patient's social environment.

4. Developmental Analysis.

Questions are asked about the patient's biological equipment, his sociocultural experiences, and his characteristic behaviour development. They are phrased in such a way as (a) to evoke descriptions of his habitual behaviour at various chronological stages of his life, (b) to relate specific new stimulus conditions to noticeable changes from his habitual behaviour, and (c) to relate such altered behaviour and other residuals of biological and sociocultural events to the present problems.

5. Analysis of Self-Control.

This section examines both the methods and the degree of self-control exercised by the patient in his daily life. Persons, events, or institutions that have successfully reinforced self-controlled behaviours are considered. The deficits or excesses of self-control are evaluated in relation to their importance as therapeutic targets and to their utilisation in a therapeutic programme.

6. Analysis of Social Relationships.

Examination of the patient's social network is carried out to evaluate the significance of people in the patient's environment who have some influence over the problematic behaviours, or who in turn are influenced by the patient for his own satisfactions. These interpersonal relationships are reviewed in order to plan the potential participation of significant others in a treatment programme, based on the principles of behaviour modification. The review also helps the therapist to consider the range of actual social relationships in which the patient needs to function.

7. Analysis of the Social-Cultural-Physical Environment.

In this section the preceding analysis of the patient's behaviour as an individual is extended by consideration of the norms in his natural environment. Agreements and discrepancies between the patient's idiosyncratic life patterns and the norms in his environment are defined so that the importance of these factors can be decided in formulating treatment goals that allow as explicitly for the patient's need as for the pressures of his social environment.

Figure 17. Interview guide (Kanfer and Saslow 1969, Kanfer and Phillips 1970).

almost always occurred when she met her mother in the home (Metcalfe 1956). Although this patient was well below normal intelligence, she was able to record the occurrence and circumstances of her attacks in a diary over a period of eighty-five days.

There is little to add on the methods of collecting data about a client's behaviour in certain situations, from other informants. Clearly, they may be interviewed or asked to keep records as described above, and interview guides for use with the parents of disturbed children have been published (Holland 1970, Wahler and Cormier 1970).

Especially characteristic of behavioural assessment is the collection of data by direct observation of the client's responses in specific situations. These may be in a special environment such as an office, institution, clinic or hospital, or in the client's natural environment. Furthermore, the social worker may deliberately vary the symbolic or real life conditions in the situations in order to observe the client's reactions to these changes. The following are a few examples of the use of direct observation in behavioural assessment. Pictures of nude males and females have been presented to assess reactions in cases of sexual deviation (Freund 1963, 1965, Solyom and Miller 1965). Beech (1969) has described how he asked a patient suffering from writer's cramp and stuttering to write and speak in the presence of people characterized by various degrees of authoritarianism, in order to ascertain if this was a condition controlling the problem behaviour. Fear reactions have been assessed by graded exposure to phobic situations (Bandura et al. 1967, Lang and Lazovick 1963, Lang et al. 1965, Lazarus 1961). The preferred activities of patients on psychiatric wards have been observed in order to identify back-up reinforcers for use in a token economy programme (Ayllon and Azrin 1968). Many other examples are cited in earlier chapters, including the papers by Allen et al. (1964), Hawkins et al. (1966), Johnson and Brown (1969) and Patterson et al. (1967b).

The observation and recording of problem behaviour and its attendant circumstances by the social worker, the client or others may be facilitated by suitable coding systems or by certain electro-mechanical devices. Systems have been developed for the coding of observations on the social interactions of disturbed children in their families (Patterson et al. 1969) or at school (Ray et al. 1968), and of depressed clients in their home environments (Lewinsohn 1968). The electro-mechanical devices available are reviewed by Schwitzgebel (1968), and audio-tape recorders are perhaps the commonest example in contemporary social work practice.

Direct observation by social workers may have the advantages of yielding more precise, accurate and unbiased data than the verbal reports of clients and others, and of not being dependent upon their observational and communicative skills, but it has also certain limitations. In the first place, only the client can observe and report on his thoughts, feelings and similar private events. Secondly, some public events may not be accessible to the social worker. In respect of historical events he must rely on the reports of the client or other informants. It may be impracticable for him to arrange to be present during the occurrence of very infrequent responses; and certain others, such as sexual difficulties, are usually considered too personal for professional observation, so that the reports of the participants are the only data available. Finally, although biases may be reduced by direct observation, they are unlikely to be eliminated. Clients are liable to conform to the 'demand characteristics' of the situation (Orne 1962), that is their responses are likely to be influenced by what they consider to be expected of them. Similarly, the observations and reports of clients, others and social workers may be biased by their respective preconceptions and personal attributes (Rosenthal 1966). These and other forms of bias may be reduced by suitable structuring of the assessment situation; whenever possible, by gathering data in objectively verifiable ways, including the appropriate use of electro-mechanical devices; and by checking data within and across sources.

SUMMARY

Assessment includes identification of the client's problem behaviour and its specification as objectively observable responses which admit the possibility of consensual validation. The contemporary conditions controlling the behaviour are conceptualized in terms of somatic factors or current events, and the identification of these may be assisted by information about the client's life history. Consideration is given to the environmental, personal and social work resources which are available for treatment. Its goals are framed in terms of the prevention or amelioration of problematic responses, and the acquisition and maintenance of appropriate responses. These goals are specified as the occurrence of certain objectively observable responses in given circumstances. The planning of treatment involves the choice of agent, setting and procedures to form an individualized programme for each client, often including intermediate steps to the ultimate goal as well as specific provision for the maintenance of beneficial changes. Outcome is assessed throughout treatment and follow-up, and commitment to the systematic investigation of the efficacy of treatment is emphasized. Similarly, stress is laid upon the assessment of the client's behaviour in specific situations, preferably through direct observation by the social worker, although other methods of data collection are also employed.

Part 2

Emergent Issues

4

Problem Definition: an Interactionist Approach

Much of the discussion of behaviour problems elsewhere in this book rests on an implicit assumption that the 'problem' is already defined as such. Thus, the existence of the 'problem' is taken for granted and discussion is restricted to its aetiology and treatment. In this chapter, it is the nature and process of problem definitions that is examined.

People exhibiting disorders such as anxiety states, sexual deviations, criminal or psychotic behaviour are often classified as objectively deviant on statistical, medical or legal grounds. When deviance is so defined, the questions we ask about the deviant person become relatively straightforward (Rubington and Weinberg 1968). For example, who is the deviant? how did he become deviant? why does he continue to be deviant despite controls brought to bear on him? what socio-cultural conditions are most likely to produce deviants? what are the best ways to control or change the deviant's behaviour? From such a perspective, the problems to be solved are fairly clear and direct. However, this approach may not be the most useful one for understanding deviance in complex societies.

The interactionist approach argues that deviance does not exist objectively in either people or situations; it is created in social relationships. Deviance is a status conferred on particular people in particular social situations. Thus, explanations of deviance must focus on people in deviance-conferring situations—conformists and deviants alike. This approach makes certain social-psychological assumptions about normal everyday social behaviour which we shall outline very briefly.

Firstly, human perception is complex, dynamic and constructive behaviour. Man does not passively receive or register external stimuli (McCall and Simmons 1966, Vernon 1962). The environment of objects, people and events is not objectively 'given' to him. He *selectively* perceives, interprets and imposes meanings on his environment. 'What is seen is as much a function of who is looking, how he is looking, and what he is looking for as it is of what is out there' (Worsley 1970, p. 342). Man's limited span of attention, sensation and memory forces him selectively to perceive, interpret, code and recode sensory inputs, otherwise he would not be able to create meanings in the world around him; he would be overwhelmed by stimuli and unable to behave meaningfully towards people and objects in his environment. Thus, in deviant and conforming situations, the 'deviance' and 'conformity' do not exist 'out there' in the environment; they are creatively perceived meanings attributed to particular people in particular situations. It is the factors which influence and determine these perceived meanings which must be explained.

Secondly, human perception is symbolic (Strauss 1965). 'Man lives in a symbolic as well as a physical environment and can be stimulated to act by symbols as well as by physical stimuli. A symbol is . . . a stimulus that has learned meaning and value for people, and man's response to a symbol is in terms of its meaning and value rather than in terms of its physical stimulation of his sense organs' (Rose 1962, p. 5). Thus, their intellectual and symbolic capacities enable people to classify, code and categorize stimuli by naming the labelling them. Once an object, person or situation has been labelled, then the labeller knows how to behave towards it. For example, he labels objects 'inedible' or 'edible' before deciding which of them to eat. He labels a person 'friend', 'foe', 'superior' or 'subordinate' in order to behave appropriately towards him. Situations are named and labelled 'economic', 'familial', 'political' or 'recreational' by participants so that they will know how they are expected to behave.

Thus, identifying, categorizing and labelling these things serve to release or inhibit certain reactions towards them. '. . . we do not know what to do with regard to another person until we have established his meaning for us and our meanings for him' (McCall and Simmons 1966, p. 126). Therefore, whenever someone is labelled a 'deviant', there are normal, symbolic perceptual mechanisms at work guiding the relationships between the people concerned. For instance, the label 'deviant' is applied to an individual in order to impose meanings on situations that are perceived to be ambiguous, and in order to justify changed behaviour, such as exclusion or stigmatization, towards him.

Thirdly, these assumptions have implications for our views about human personality. Personality and self-identity are not static entities with objective characteristics—deviant or otherwise (Brim 1960, Brim and Wheeler 1966, McCall and Simmons 1966). People are continually creating the meanings of themselves and others. Thus, self-identity emerges in social situations and must be continuously confirmed by other people as well as by ourselves. It follows that if other people change their definitions of our identities, then this has implications for our own behaviour. In particular, if we are defined and labelled 'deviant', then this label is likely to be incorporated into our own self-definition, with behavioural consequences.

Therefore, we do not view deviance as a characteristic of personality; deviance is a characteristic attributed to people, in order to name and place their behaviour, thereby conferring on them a deviant status. We are concerned with the consequences that a deviant label and status has for a person's self-conception. Does he begin to view himself a 'criminal' or 'mentally ill'? What changes in his personality occur as a result of learning to play a deviant role?

These assumptions about interpersonal perception and human personality suggest that the labels applied to people are neither identical with, nor an objective reflection of, their actual behaviour. The labels function to identify and code what would otherwise be overwhelming stimuli, to name and place a person's behaviour and to guide and legitimate subsequent behaviour towards him. Labels also influence the future behaviour of the labelled person. As Foote (1951, p. 17) sees it, 'A rose by any other name may smell as sweet, but a person by another name will act according to that other name'. The labelled person does not passively adjust to proffered labels. He may accept or reject the label, by agreeing or disagreeing with those who label him deviant. He may come to behave in ways expected of people with that label (self-fulfilling prophecy), for example the 'naughty' schoolboy begins to behave according to that label, thus confirming initial definitions made of him. People often incorporate deviant labels into their own self-conceptions; in this way deviant labelling is an important source of personality change.

The interactionist approach therefore leads us to ask a very different set of questions about deviance. Viewing deviance as a conferred status rather than an attribute of the individual turns our attention to the circumstances under which a person gets set apart, henceforth to be considered deviant. How are people cast into deviant social roles? What actions do others take on the basis of this redefinition of the person? How does the named deviant react to the label and adopt the profferred role? How is the deviant role incorporated into his self-conception and what changes in his group membership occur as a result?

The Interactionist Approach to Deviance

To be 'really mad' or to 'actually kill another person' is unquestionably deviant to those who would argue that deviance is objectively defined. In other words, the deviance lies in the behaviour and may even be construed as an intrinsic characteristic of the person. However, as soon as we look more closely at the meaning and prevalence of such behaviour, a rather different picture emerges. For example, even the 'maddest' of people conform most of the time, and their very 'madness' may be viewed as honourable in some societies or at certain times and places. Similarly, the act of killing another person will be defined differently by different people at different times and places. For example, the soldier who kills during wartime will not be labelled a murderer or a deviant; the policeman who kills in self-defence will not be seen as a murderer. Yet a killing by a drunkard during a street brawl or by a thief during a criminal act will be unquestionably seen as murder.

Fixed qualities tend to be imputed to people when in reality everyone's behaviour and personality are changing constantly. No one is 'mad', 'bad', 'smart' or 'angry' all the time. These names are used to identify particular behaviour in particular situations and should not be construed as intrinsic qualities or enduring characteristics of person.

In the same way, as Becker (1963, p. 9) indicates, ' ... deviance is *not* a quality of the act the person commits, but rather a consequence of the application by others of rules and sanctions to an "offender". The deviant is one to whom that label has successfully been applied; deviant behaviour is behaviour that people so label.' It is this conferred, negotiable characteristic of deviance which makes it subjectively problematic. Because of this, we need to examine the complicated sequence of events surrounding the labelled and the labeller in situations where a deviant status is conferred on someone. As much can be learned from the situation and the labeller as from examining the intrinsic qualities of either the person or his actions.

This process of labelling the deviant and conferring a deviant status on him is influenced by a variety of factors, such as norms, rules, differential enforcement of rules, context, attributes of behaviour, and the characteristics of both the labelled person and the labeller.

Norms

Norms refer to customary and appropriate ways of behaving in specified situations, for example norms relating to speech, dress, appearance and sexual behaviour. As Ullman and Krasner (1969) suggest, normal people are expected to act according to their age, be responsive to stimuli, show good judgment, work and enjoy others, and be understandable and predictable. These norms are not of course neutral or arbitrary because different societies and subcultures within societies will have different clusters of norms appropriate to their own cultures and patterns of social organization such as their kinship, economic, political and religious institutions. Mills (1943) and Erikson (1964) suggest that the dominant norms in Western industrialized societies tend to cluster around a middle-class, puritan, rural ethic; for example, they uphold the virtues of hard work, thrift, honesty, stability and adjustment.

It is this type of normative expectation which is often used when someone is labelled a deviant. In a very general way, the perceived appropriateness of a person's symbolic, affective or social responses to given situations becomes an important measure of deviance from the point of view of the labeller. A person may be labelled deviant, for example, because he does not work, he misinterprets cues and signals, he does not conform to group expectations, he is not heterosexual, he is *too* aggressive, he spends too much time washing his hands, he does not wash himself enough, or he is depressed.

Deviance cannot be inferred from the *degree* of departure from normative standards. For one thing, the 'degree' is culturally relative and a thing to be negotiated in the social group. Furthermore, as Bandura (1969, p. 3) points out, 'Departures from normative standards that do not inconvenience or interfere with the well-being of others are usually tolerated', and there would never be any technological inventions or scientific and artistic innovations if no one ever departed from the norms.

Norms guide social behaviour but norms themselves cannot be used as absolute or fixed criteria for measuring the emergence of deviance. Close scrutiny of any social situation will point to the tremendous variability in the type of norms which govern behaviour and in the ways in which normative standards are successfully applied in the naming of deviants.

Rules

Norms are frequently translated into rules which operate more specifically in formal and informal ways to guide and control behaviour. Becker (1963) points out that deviance is created by society in that social groups make rules whose infractions constitute deviance. Different societies and institutions within these societies will have different rules. Many of these rules will be embodied in the legal system, and there would seem to be universal rules which taboo murder, violence, theft and rape; what constitutes murder, violence, theft and rape will of course vary in different cultures, but generally there will be rules relating to these activities.

It is the enforcement of rules which creates deviance. For example, legitimacy rules relating to paternity within kinship systems are often broken; the fact that such rules exist and are enforced both formally and informally creates a group of deviants, i.e. illegitimate children.

No society, especially a complex one, has a homogeneous body of rules because there are different rules for different institutions and for different subcultures. For example, rules relating to property ownership and protection are different in the family and at work. Sometimes, following the rules of one group simultaneously involves breaking the rules of another group, and this occurs particularly in immigrant/host community relations. For example, the Sikh who wore his turban at work broke the rules of the Midlands bus company whilst he upheld the rules of his own culture.

Society's rules are not, however, static, but are changing in varying degrees. For example, the legal rules relating to homosexual and suicidal behaviour have been changed in Britain during the past decade; this has meant that consenting male adult homosexuals and people who commit or attempt suicide are no longer classed as legal deviants. However, rules are also enforced informally, and prevailing opinions, attitudes and social practices **may** continue to confer a status of social deviant on homosexuals and suicidal people.

Rule Enforcement

None of society's rules is enforced all the time and this is one of the major reasons why the definition of deviance is so variable. Much rule-breaking of all kinds is undetected, ignored, normalized or tolerated. This may be a 'healthy' feature of society for if human beings were so rigidly controlled that their every infraction was made the object of social control then no one would ever dare to be creative or innovative let alone criminal or mentally ill or just plain different.

'Imagine a society of saints, a perfect cloister of exemplary individuals. Crimes, properly so called, will there be unknown; but faults which appear venial to the layman will create there the same scandal that the ordinary offense does in ordinary consciousness.'

(Durkheim, 1938, p. 68.)

Technically, no society has sufficient resources to either enforce all its rules or confer deviant status on all its rule-breakers. If the policeman brought all the petty larcenists he sees to court, he might be neglecting his duties with regard to other rule-breakers such as professional criminals.

Thus, there is more deviant behaviour in every society than is ever subjected to rule-enforcement procedures and this is one point in the argument that deviance is a status conferred upon a person rather than being a quality of his behaviour or personality. If this is so, then it may be instructive to look at patterns of rule enforcement in a society as well as the psychological states and social characteristics of particular people.

Context

Behaviour finds its meaning in particular contexts. What appears on the surface to be bizarre and irrational behaviour often becomes more meaningful once the context in which it occurs is known. For example, the postures of someone 'at prayer' may appear bizarre without the meaning given to such behaviour by the social context; indeed, the same behaviour at another time and place would be perceived as bizarre.

The same behaviour may be therefore conforming in one context yet rule-breaking in another context. For example, promiscuity, vandalism and symbolic fantasies may be legitimated and even expected patterns of behaviour at parties, student 'rags' and religious ceremonies respectively. In fact, the people involved would not be labelled promiscuous or vandals in these situations, but they would often be given such deviant labels if they behaved in the same way in everyday life. Likewise, the same behaviour at home or at work, with friends or with superiors, in town or in village, will take on different meanings and be given different interpretations according to its context.

The context will also provide clues about the balance of power in a relationship; the power factor is very important in influencing who is able to label the behaviour of whom as deviant and to confer a deviant status on that person accordingly. For example, it is more likely that an employer will be able to define the behaviour of an employee as deviant than the other way round. The same factors will operate in parent–child, social worker–client relationships. For example, when children present problems, it is more likely that the child rather than the parent will be referred to the psychiatrist.

Attributes of Behaviour

Some people are labelled deviant even though they have broken no rules; for example, those who are falsely imprisoned, or admitted to psychiatric hospitals under false pretences. The same objective behaviour may be labelled differently in a variety of circumstances; for example 'aggressive' behaviour in children may be labelled 'normal', 'criminal' or 'disturbed' by different people in different situations. Sometimes, the same label may be applied to varieties of behaviour, for example, all types of adolescent behaviour patterns are labelled 'youth' problems.

Although definitions of deviance are not a *direct* outcome of a person's behaviour, his own behaviour is not always a completely neutral or fluid source of material upon which to base a deviant label. Bandura (1969, p. 5) argues that, '(Emotional) responses of high magnitude ... often produce unpleasant experiences for others; they are therefore more likely to be considered pathological manifestations than are responses of low or moderate intensities'. It is likely, therefore, that behaviour perceived to be grossly aggressive, manic, violent or psychotic will be more frequently labelled deviant in a variety of contexts by a variety of people than 'milder' forms of behaviour. Prevalence and incidence rates for serious psychoses seem to be far more consistent than corresponding rates for milder psychoses, neuroses and personality disorders (Mishler and Scotch 1963, Susser 1968). This would seem to be valid evidence that *some* attributes of a person's behaviour *some* of the time will invariably attract deviant definitions, and this may be so especially when there is an associated somatic disorder.

Characteristics of the Labelled Person

A person's age, sex, social class and race, and especially the social meanings attached to such personal attributes, are used as guidelines for understanding, predicting and judging the appropriateness of a person's behaviour. The same behaviour will be appropriate at one age and not at another, for example, bedwetting. In Western societies, dependent behaviour is expected of the adult female but not of the adult male. Conjugal role segregation (Bott 1957, Klein 1965) is probably more prevalent amongst working class couples than amongst middle class couples. The wearing of female apparel by males is unacceptable and frequently labelled deviant in Western societies, whilst it is (or was) acceptable behaviour among the Tchambuli (Mead 1935).

Characteristics of the Labeller

The willingness, ability and power of the labeller to confer deviant statuses on people are largely a function of his age, sex, social class, and social values. The social meanings of such personal attributes are more important than their intrinsic characteristics. For example, the client's perception of the 'superiority' of his social worker does not depend on the innate inferiority or superiority of either of them; it is a consequence of the social distance created between them by virtue of the different roles they are playing and the social meanings attached to personal attributes within these roles. These are often class based; Spohn (1960) provides evidence that therapists think that patients in similar class positions to themselves are the healthier ones. Susser (1968) found that the social class of the labeller is an influential factor; middle class parents detect and label subnormality in their children much sooner than do working class parents.

In the interactionist approach, deviance is viewed as a conferred status and a product of labelling. The deviance-making process is complex and dynamic, involving a large number of factors, including norms, rules, differential rule enforcement, context, behavioural attributes and the characteristics of the labeller and the labelled. The operation of the process is now considered in relation to certain illustrative problems.

Mental Illness

In Western societies, certain forms of behaviour, for example depression, incongruous affect, delusions and hallucinations are viewed as psychiatric symptoms, either caused by or indicative of an underlying illness or pathological state located within the individual. Psychiatric classification and treatment of mental illness tend to confirm the view that it is a condition which lies in the individual; it is seen as a quality of his behaviour, and social processes are given a subsidiary role in the dynamics of the illness.

From the interactionist viewpoint, mental illness is not a disease or symptom but a label applied to people displaying a wide variety of behaviour patterns in widely varying social situations. The application of such a label confers a deviant status on the person so labelled, and in this case accords to the labelled person the socially privileged rights and obligations of the sick role (Parsons 1951). For example, the sick role gives a person the right to shed some of his basic responsibilities, such as those at work and at home, and at the same time carries the obligation that the incumbent should seek all the possible aids his society provides to help him get 'better' and subsequently resume his normal responsibilities.

Although society provides a sick role for the mentally ill and views and treats them accordingly, it does not follow necessarily that their 'illness' is an objectively defined intrinsic state rather than a conferred status. It is the latter view which leads Scheff (1966, p. 29) to argue that '... the variables that afford the best understanding and prediction of the course of "mental illness" are not the refined aetiological and nosological features of the illness, but gross features of the community and legal and psychiatric procedures'. Thus, if we look at the social system instead of at the individual exclusively, we may find some clues as to the kinds of situation which produce mental illness. As we saw earlier, an examination of the norms, rules, enforcement patterns, context, characteristics of people in situations and the behaviour they display may help us to understand how and why such a deviant status is conferred.

Scheff proposes the following model in an attempt to bring together into some organized pattern the multitude of factors which seem to operate in the development of some forms of chronic mental illness. Most such illnesses are at least in part a social role; thus, the behaviour of the person in the role of the mentally ill is learned as a consequence of entry into that role. The reaction of other people is usually the most important determinant of entry rather than the intrinsic qualities of the person's behaviour per se. Thus his own and other people's definitions of the situation are important determinants of the outcome of events.

The symptoms of mental illness are violations of residual rules. As we saw earlier, rule-breaking and rule-enforcement are central to any understanding of deviance. In many situations, the rules are relatively clear, and labels are readily available for the rule-breakers—criminals, perverts or drunkards. However, there are many situations in which it is not appropriate or acceptable to apply this type of label; there is always a residue of the most diverse kinds of violations, for which the culture provides no explicit label. In situations where the violation is unnameable, it may be put into a residual category—in our society, 'mental illness'. Generically, then, mental illness is residual deviance, and Scheff advances the following propositions:

1. Residual rule-breaking arises from diverse sources: organic, psychological and environmental.

2. Relative to the rate of treated mental illness, the rate of unrecorded residual rule-breaking is extremely high. Evidence from one's own observations and the literature point to the numerous occasions in which such rule-breaking is ignored, tolerated and normalized.

3. Most residual rule-breaking is ignored and is of transitory significance. This being the case, it is necessary to determine the factors which distinguish transitory rule-breaking from stable deviance. It is likely that the pattern of societal reaction constitutes one of the major variables in determining whether or not a rule-breaker enters into a deviant status. The person whose deviance becomes stabilised is not subsequently 'putting on an act' in his status as mentally ill. The expected patterns of behaviour which go with such a status must be learned and internalized; the deviant undergoes a socialization process in his new role. 'Entry into a role may be complete when this role is part of the individual's expectations, and when these expectations are reaffirmed in social interaction.' (op. cit., p. 63). We need to know, therefore, where the mental patient gets his ideas about what it is to be mentally ill. Scheff suggests that:

4. Stereotyped imagery of mental disorder is learned in early childhood. Children pick up stereotypes about being 'crazy', 'mad', and develop fears about 'bogie men' during their early socialization, in particular in their peer groups.

5. These stereotypes are inadvertently and continually reaffirmed in ordinary social interaction, in ordinary conversation, through jokes and anecdotes. At the same time the mass media emit highly stereotyped views of mental illness,

and most people pick up some notion of what the symptoms of mental illness are supposed to be. In the crisis, when someone is being labelled mentally ill, it is these stereotypes which become the guiding imagery for both the labeller and the labelled. The stereotype and entry into the status of the mentally ill serve to structure what was previously amorphous, unstructured behaviour. 'The stabilization and uniformization of residual deviance are completed when the deviant accepts the role of the insane as the framework within which he organizes his own behaviour.' (op. cit., p. 84). But why does he accept the deviant role? The following three propositions attempt to answer this question.

6. Labelled deviants may be rewarded for playing the stereotyped deviant role. For example, patients who display 'insight' are rewarded by psychiatric personnel.. There are also pressures from other patients and the hospital staff to accept the role of the mentally ill as part of his self-conception. For example, if a patient asserts that he is not ill, his custodians may interpret this in itself as symptomatic of his illness; they may tell him that he would not be in hospital if he were not ill. It is difficult for anyone to get out of such a vicious circle!

7. Labelled deviants often are punished when they attempt to return to conventional roles; for example, stigmas may operate to block their complete acceptance and re-entry into their family, community and work environments.

8. In the crisis, when a residual rule-breaker is publicly labelled, he is highly suggestible; this may encourage him to accept the proffered role of the mentally ill as the only one open to him. For himself and for 'significant others', the offer and acceptance of the mentally ill role introduces some stability and predictability into a situation which is otherwise in many ways incomprehensible. The final proposition suggests that:

9. Among residual rule-breakers, labelling is the single most important cause of careers of residual deviance—or chronic mental illness. If labelling is then such an important factor in the production of stable mental illness, it is important to consider some of the factors which influence this labelling process As we saw in our earlier discussion, it is not actual behaviour which determines who is labelled what, but rather a variety of social contingencies. Generally, these can be summarized as: the nature of the rule-breaking, the person who breaks the rules and the community in which the rule-breaking occurs. The pattern of societal reaction will also be influenced by such factors as the degree, amount and visibility of the rule-breaking, the power of the rule-breaker and the social distance between him and those who label him, and finally the tolerance level in the community for this type of rule-breaking.

This social system perspective of mental illness oversimplifies in its own way the great complexity of psychiatric events. In particular, it fails to provide an adequate account of the variety of strategies available to those people who react to the residual rule-breaker; he is not invariably given the status of the mentally ill. Furthermore, though Scheff realizes this, the model may be more applicable to chronic mental illness in traditional psychiatric settings than to the current psychiatric picture of people experiencing more acute episodes of residual rule-breaking, which are not invariably stabilized into the role of the mentally ill; if they are, it is likely to be more of a revolving-door pattern than on the back ward of a mental hospital. In agreement, Scheff remarks that, 'the typical mental patient today has a much better chance of passing back into his nondeviant status than he would have fifty or even twenty-five years ago.' (op. cit., p. 195). Even so, there are still some significant groups of people who become chronically mentally ill, and it would be useful to know which factors operate to differentiate the acute and the chronic—are they social class, age, sex, race, pattern of illness or something else?

Scheff's approach to mental illness is a good example of the application of the labelling perspective. It well illustrates the very complicated nature of psychiatric referral procedures, and points out that a simple variable such as the person's behaviour does not go far enough in explaining the course of mental illness. His observations on the social contingencies governing the labelling process and pattern of societal reaction are confirmed in many other studies (Lawson 1966, Mountney et al. 1969, Susser 1968). All these studies report that social factors and a sort of informal referral system regulate the flow of cases into the psychiatric services. People's perception of what is psychiatric and their threshold for the sick role is a very variable thing, governed by many factors, including time, place, past experience and availability of treatment facilities. The labelling process is one of the major links between the rich variety of human behaviour and the types of roles and institutions through which such behaviour is processed.

In a recent article (1970), Gove has produced evidence that suggests that the societal reaction explanation of how and why persons enter into the mentally ill role is incorrect. He suggests that screening processes in mental illness, even if largely informal, are fairly rigorous and that most people who are hospitalized for mental illness are suffering from a serious disturbance. The labelling approach to mental illness has tended to overstate the degree to which secondary deviance is the major variable in mental hospitalization. Much more consideration needs to be given to the original behaviour (primary deviance) of people who are subsequently labelled mentally ill.

Crime

For decades, many criminologists and penologists have considered criminals and delinquents as 'natural social types' (Cicourel 1968, Matza 1969), that is, criminality exists as a thing which objectively exists either in the individual or in the social structure. Put this way, the problems to be explained are the factors which produce criminality in people or in situations. Consequently, criminality in individuals has been explained as a product of such factors as genetic abnormalities (Price 1969), faulty libidinal development (Friedlander 1947) or inappropriate social learning (Trasler 1962). Basically these explanations suggest that the individual criminal is inadequately socialized as far as the wider society is concerned.

Some sociologists have attributed criminality to the social structure rather than to individual personality factors. One of their theories suggests that it is contradictions in the social structure which give rise to crime (Cloward and Ohlin 1960, Durkheim 1938, Merton 1957). Not everyone in society can be successful in terms of society's goals, such as work advancement or successful marriage. When faced with such failure, certain significant social groups, such as adolescents or lower class males, may resort to a variety of criminal activities, which to them become symbolic of success. Thus, this view holds that crime arises because certain social groups do not have equal access to the means of achieving society's desired goals. Such criminal behaviour is transmitted through deviant subcultures (Shaw and McKay 1942), and like any other behaviour it is learned in interaction with other people (Sutherland 1947).

Such theories may explain why crime originates, how it is transmitted in society and how and why individuals learn criminal behaviour. However, these are necessary but not sufficient conditions for explaining the distribution of criminality in society. Two major factors force us to look elsewhere for our explanation of criminal patterns. The first is that there is ample evidence (Jones 1965, Kitsuse and Cicourel 1963, Merton 1957) that there is far more criminal rule-breaking than is ever detected and brought to the notice of law-enforcement agencies—the 'dark number'. The second is that the demographic characteristics of those individuals whose crimes are detected, and who are subsequently dealt with by the police, courts and probation service, display a definite social pattern —the *typical* criminal is male, working class and adolescent.

The criminals who are the subjects of psychological and sociological theories are not, therefore, a representative sample of the criminal population. However, they may be a representative sample of something else—the social organization of justice. If this is so, then comparisons of the criminal and the non-criminal may not be very useful because criminality does not exist as an intrinsic quality or condition of the person or social group—it is a status conferred on certain types and groups of people.

As with mental illness, differential rule-enforcement procedures, labelling and societal reactions to criminal behaviour are likely to be important variables in the emergence of crime. Social contingencies as well as the quality of a person's behaviour will influence who comes to be designated a criminal.

Cicourel's work on the 'Social Organization of Juvenile Justice' (1968) provides empirical evidence that criminal justice can only be understood by looking at the ways in which people come to be labelled suspects and victims, and labels are assigned to offenders in order that they can be processed through social control organizations. The accounts given of the situation in which an offence was committed, and the reports compiled about the offender, are less a depiction of what actually happened than of the means the agency is going to use to process the offender through the courts. Members of the community and official agents of social control reconstruct criminal events in terms of their views about the typical offence and the typical offender. Cicourel suggests that in the course of being processed, criminals are transformed in a way that produces familiar scenes and depictions of juveniles, their families and their activities. In this way, criminals can be evaluated and disposed of in a standardized way.

A variety of social contingencies at various stages of arrest, search, seizure, committal and sentence are influential factors in who is defined as criminal and into which criminal category he is put. At each successive stage of legal decision-making, his initial rule-breaking is transformed into a different object or event in order that it will fit in with the type of sentence to be negotiated in judicial undertakings.

Cicourel found that the police in the area he was studying felt that they had no control over the delinquent conduct of the middle class in their community because of the high social and economic standing of their families, and their willingness to cooperate with the police; middle class offenders are well-behaved and articulate and often their families make arrangements to send their offending children away for a time; in all these ways, the law-enforcement system is seen to be undermined.

If the typical criminal is young, male and working class, this has a great deal to do with the fact that such a type of person is seen to be a 'typical offender' by law-enforcement agents. Because of such lay theories about the causation of delinquency, certain juveniles are singled out for court appearance and treatment whereas others with similar records are excluded from these processes. There is much discretion, ethnic and class bias and bargaining in the administration of justice, and these are important factors to be taken into account in any discussion or explanation of crime.

Sudnow's (1965) work on 'normal crimes' such as petty theft, burglary, assault and rape, reiterates Cicourel's argument that the labelling and processing of criminal offenders depends very much upon police perceptions, ideologies and activities.

'In the course of routinely encountered persons charged with "petty theft", "burglary", "assault with a deadly weapon", "rape", "possession of marijuana", etc., the Public Defender gains knowledge of the typical manner in which offenses of given classes are committed, the social characteristics of the persons who regularly commit them, the features of the settings in which they occur, the types of victims often involved, and the like. He learns to speak knowledgeably of "burglars", ... etc., and to attribute to them personal biographies, modes of usual criminal activity, criminal histories, psychological characteristics, and social backgrounds.'

(Rubington and Weinberg, 1968, p. 162.)

In this way, the police build up their own picture of the pattern of offence and type of offender, in order to decide whether to charge offenders with a lesser offence in exchange for a guilty plea from them. Therefore, the link between the actual rule-breaking and the sentence outcome depends upon a variety of social contingencies, such as the way defendants are represented, the way the trial is conducted, the way interviews are carried out, the penal code employed and police interpretations.

However, the social organization of justice perspective is an important but inadequate explanation of crime and delinquency. Logically, it underestimates diversity in society. Criminal behaviour is not randomly distributed in the social structure. If fertility, mortality, kinship, economic and religious behaviour is socially patterned in different groups, then there is no reason to believe that criminal activities will not be socially patterned. This is not to argue that the official picture of criminal behaviour faithfully reflects actual criminal activities; the argument above is powerful evidence that criminality is a negotiable status. Empirically, there is evidence (Phillipson 1971, Power et al. 1967) that schools are an important structural source of delinquent behaviour—*independently of known variations in local police practices*. The culture and social organization of schools and the labelling that occurs within them produce significant variations in delinquency rates in different schools—thus streaming in secondary schools operates to produce delinquent subcultures in the system (Hargreaves 1967).

The contingency process influences the way a rule-breaker's problems are defined. It may be that psychiatric labels are attached to delinquent behaviour in some class groups more than in others. Labelling in basic social groups (family, neighbourhood, school) and official agencies of social control is a crucial variable in the aetiology of crime.

Phobias

Phobias may be viewed as excessive or unrealistic fear responses to certain objects or situations. In themselves such responses may not be problems. They only become problematic if, for a variety of social or psychological reasons, the patient or someone else labels them a problem. For example, if a person has a phobia for lifts, this may never be a problem for him unless he comes to work or lives at the top of a very high building, or otherwise needs to use a lift. His social functioning would then be radically impaired, and if this leads to the labelling of his fear as a problem requiring help, then a complex referral system may be set in motion.

Because Western society provides a psychiatric label for phobias, the psychiatric services may be used as a solution to the problem. Referral to the psychiatric services may run the risk of inducting the phobic into a chronic sick role. This is less likely these days, as the treatment provided for phobias is likely to avert such a stable deviant career commitment.

Thus, even in the case of such specific conditions as phobias, it is likely that social contingencies as well as the person's actual behaviour will determine whether the condition is labelled a problem, what type of label is provided, and what form of treatment is offered for its removal.

Homosexuality

Empirical evidence (Kinsey et al. 1948, Schofield 1965) indicates that a significant number of males in America and Britain have had some homosexual encounter during their lives. However, only a minority become self-confessed homosexuals or enter upon a stable homosexual career. For these and many other reasons (legal and psychiatric) homosexuality is '... commonly seen as a condition characterizing certain persons ... If homosexuality is a condition, then people either have it or do not have it'. (McIntosh 1968, p. 183.) Thus, the aetiology of homosexual conditions has been sought, and the 'condition' has been explained by some investigators as a product of inadequate male identifications (Whitener and Nikelly 1964).

However, homosexuality is socially learned behaviour, lies on a continuum with heterosexuality, and homosexuals play a social role rather than have a condition (McIntosh ibid). Not all societies have a role for homosexuals and homosexual behaviour is not monopolized by persons who play the role of the homosexual. In societies where the role is stigmatized, deviant labelling of homosexuals may expedite their entry into a sexually deviant career. Thus, homosexuality should be seen as a social category and label which is applied to and adopted by various people in particular situations. In itself, it is neither a medical nor a legal condition, though this is a status often conferred on homosexual behaviour, both by other people and the individual concerned.

Even so, a homosexual career need not be permanent; it may be specific to particular age statuses. For example, Reiss (1964) points out that homosexual prostitution is often a form of sex delinquency, confined to particular adolescent groups. The organized activity and culture of such groups operate in ways that keep the heterosexual self-definitions of their members intact and serve to avert stable commitments to homosexual careers for most of them.

For these reasons, homosexuality may be viewed as a status conferred upon certain people as a consequence of a variety of social contingencies, labelling in particular. Homosexuality per se may not be a problem to either the individual or others. However, once it becomes defined and labelled as the 'problem of homosexuality', then such labelling will have consequences for the stabilization of a sexually deviant career and for the homosexual's self-concept.

Adolescent Problems

Allen (1968) observes that, 'Young people in industrial societies share the common experience of being considered non-adult and are excluded from full participation in adult society. They are admitted into adult status by formal and informal processes, which can be abrupt or gradual and which in Britain take place at different ages in different areas of social activity.' (p. 1.) Thus, adolescents of different ages, races, social classes and sexes will experience the transition from childhood to adult status in many different ways. The problems experienced by the nineteen-year-old, middle class, male university student will be very different from those of the fifteen-year-old, working class, 'C' stream school-leaver starting work in a factory. Their 'problems' cannot be put under some generic label of 'adolescent' based simply on criteria of age and physiological changes.

Furthermore, it is not necessarily the youth who experiences the problem; it may be the social workers, educationalists and his parents who want him to act in certain approved ways, for example: stay on at school, take and hold a particular kind of job, reject delinquent peers, and behave 'responsibly'.

Some young people facing contradictory role expectations at home, work or club refuse to go to work or to continue at school, sit in their rooms all day long, neglect to wash or to subscribe to the norms of acceptable social behaviour with their family or friends. How do their relatives react to such incomprehensible and relatively unpredictable behaviour? Often they will tolerate such a situation for quite a long time, but eventually they will resort to some label as a means of understanding and dealing with the young person's behaviour. Often, they will use a psychiatric label because there is no other available to them; his behaviour is an example of residual rule-breaking.

However, the psychiatric label will not be applied automatically nor is it an inevitable outcome of the behaviour which the youth displays. Social contingencies are likely to influence the origin and direction of the labelling process. For example, if the family's circumstances change, perhaps by the rent being increased, the mother falling ill, the father losing his job or the siblings' refusal any longer to accept the differential treatment of their brother, then the family's tolerance level for the youth will change.

The offer of a psychiatric label to the youth in such a situation will serve to name and place his behaviour, to explain and justify it, and to rationalize the altered tolerance threshold of the relatives. Furthermore, the youth himself may in time be happy to accept the proffered label, because he may then be able to explain his own behaviour to himself; some kind of self-identity—albeit a psychiatric one—will be confirmed and his existence in the world validated.

The whole sequence of events will be a highly complicated one and not directly related to the youth's behaviour. If he adopts the role of the psychiatrically sick or perhaps engineers the role for himself, then the people around him must *validate* his entry into that role; they must give the youth certain expectations to live up to, providing him with clear notions as to the behaviour they consider appropriate for him in his new position. At the same time, the youth must *commit* himself to the sick role, adopting the styles of behaviour of the mentally ill as his own (Erikson 1959).

A complex set of social contingencies will therefore determine whether or not the youth's behaviour will be labelled a psychiatric problem, and whether he will accept or reject the psychiatric label when it is offered him. An alternative way out for him may be to accept a non-psychiatric status by becoming a 'hippy'.

The Social Functions of Labelling

Naming, categorizing and labelling are means by which human beings selectively perceive, interpret and create meanings in a highly complex social world of people and objects. We would not survive if we did not label incoming stimuli in our normal, everyday lives. Once we have found out the meaning of an object or a person for ourselves by naming it, then we know how to act towards it. Labelling a person's behaviour serves to name and place him, thereby reducing the degree of ambiguity and unpredictability in social situations.

When behaviour is labelled deviant, a meaning may be given to what may otherwise appear to be bizarre or incomprehensible behaviour; the labelled person has had a new status conferred on him and there are certain expected patterns of behaviour, rights and obligations attached to such a status. The labeller and the labelled subsequently have a different set of rules to guide their future encounters. For example, labelling someone's behaviour 'criminal' may legitimate his exclusion from the group; it certainly enables agents of social control to process him through their organization. Labelling someone 'mentally ill' provides a structure by which to comprehend, legitimate or tolerate his behaviour. The new status thereby provided for him may justify his exclusion from the group by sending him to a psychiatric hospital or it may enable him to re-enter the group, this time as the scapegoat, the village idiot or the sick, dependent partner. Thus, labelling operates as a mechanism of social control.

Erikson (1964) describes how deviant labelling performs important functions for the society as a whole. It used to be argued that deviance arose in individuals and society and *then* social control agencies and their personnel went into action to label behaviour as 'criminal' or 'mentally ill' so that they could then control and process people in prisons and mental hospitals. However, societies may be organized in such a way as to promote deviance as an important resource, because deviant labelling functions to promote social integration amongst those members of society who are not so labelled, to define society's boundary-limits with regard to acceptable behaviour and to give expression to the dominant values in society.

An examination of the kind of people or groups labelled deviant should indicate the tolerance levels of a particular society and its dominant value patterns. The culture and institutions of a society will influence the criteria used for directing traffic between the deviant and non-deviant areas. In Western societies, much approved behaviour is governed by norms which cluster around rural, protestant, middle class ethic—hard work, honesty, thrift and cleanness. Powerful groups in society acquire and uphold these dominant values because they represent their own interests. These interests will be preserved by enforcing certain rules relating to them through various social control agencies, such as courts, prisons, social welfare institutions, schools and mental hospitals. The consistent finding of an inverse relationship between social class and schizophrenia and crime respectively suggests that differential rule-enforcement practices do create a group of deviants who are seen to behave in ways which are unacceptable to dominant power groups or influential people in society, and these are the middle and upper classes in the West. As Becker indicates (1963), Social rules are the creation of specific social groups. Modern societies are not simple organizations in which everyone agrees on what the rules are and how they are to be applied in specific situations. They are, instead, highly differentiated along social class, ethnic, occupational and cultural lines'. (p. 15.)

Deviance is Normal and Endemic in Society

Some explanations of deviance suggest that it is a product of a disease process—either a personal or social pathology. From such a perspective, deviance is a condition produce by broken-down or 'disorganized' personalities or social structures. When the problem was defined thus, attempts were made to compare the mentally ill with the sane, the criminal with the non-criminal, and slums or difficult housing estates with 'healthy' social areas. It was thought that comparisons of their intrinsic differences would indicate the biological, psychological and social factors which caused the deviant conditions. As we have seen, however, deviance is behaviour that is so labelled and a conferred status; the difference between the deviant and non-deviant lies in different societal reactions to various groups, types of people and behaviour. If the typical criminal comes from a poor and broken home, has low intelligence and a bad educational record, is a member of 'too big a family', and lives in a bad neighbourhood (West 1967), this may tell us more about the typical patterns of societal reactions to crime than it does about the typical personal and social characteristics of the criminal.

The labelling approach to deviance suggests, therefore, that social and personal problems are governed by 'normal' organized psychological and social processes. Buckley (1967) suggests that, 'Both conformity and deviance ... are understandable in terms of similar principles of the social process ... This view does not require structures to "break down" though this can be a factor; it says that very hearty and tenacious structures, well supported from many sides, help to generate deviance in a continuous and ramifying stream, and that this deviance ... contains essential positive elements for the group'. (pp. 166-167).

Deviance is as much a product of organized society as is conformity. For example, the ways in which political, economic, educational, familial and legal institutions operate in complex societies may produce patterned contradictions in that system (Cloward and Ohlin 1960, Merton 1951). One such contradiction may be that everyone is expected to do well at school and get a job which has long-term prospects of advancement, yet the way the educational system is organized and the requirements of the economic system—which needs and has room for some of the poorly educated people the schools produce—ensure that specific groups of people will not be successful in society's terms. Some of these groups, for example lower class adolescents, may respond to these contradictions by organized group activities, which are to them a solution to the difficult situation which society has created for them. Deviant behaviour, which is learned in these groups, may be a pre-requisite for membership (Cloward and Ohlin 1960), or a secondary consequence of such group membership (Downes 1966).

Society (in particular people in power and those who uphold conventional standards) often responds to such group activities by labelling the behaviour of the members as criminal, whilst they would not necessarily label the behaviour of traffic offenders or tax evaders in the same way. This pattern of societal reaction may operate, through the way justice is socially organized, to confirm and even increase the deviant behaviour of those against whom they are reacting. The deviant self-images of members of such groups may be confirmed and the group may engage in further deviant behaviour to accord with their newly created self-image or because access to conventional groups has been closed to them.

The behaviour of both the labelled and labelling groups is a product of normal psychological and social processes. It is impossible to argue that this complicated series of actions, events and reactions represents a breakdown in the society or in the individual. Very complicated and organized mechanisms are at work in the production of the deviant, and these mechanisms are normal, basic and endemic in every society, despite wide cultural variations.

The Dynamic Complexity of Societal Reactions to Deviance

We shall now bring together some of the important factors underlying the labelling process.

Firstly, *the deviant status which is conferred on the individual* (criminal, mentally ill, homosexual) *has a different significance at different phases of his deviant career*. When the labelling first occurs, it merely gives a name to rule-breaking which has a variety of roots; it sets the sequence of the societal reaction, thereby influencing whether the deviant will be processed through penal, psychiatric or other agencies. When and if the rule-breaking becomes an issue, and is not ignored or rationalized away, labelling will create a social category; this category will guide the behaviour patterns expected of the person who is labelled, for example, the mentally ill will be expected to behave in a bizarre way, the criminal will be expected to err. Eventually, the deviant label may become internalized as a part of the individual's personality; he no longer 'goes through the motions' of the criminal role, but actively plays it, and uses the appropriate label as the guideline for his own self-image and future behaviour.

At any point in this complicated sequence, the process may be reversed, change direction or be further intensified. The labeller or the labelled may reject or change the label being proffered; the deviant may be offered and may accept a conforming status, for example, after an acute psychotic episode, or he may be sent through different deviant channels, perhaps a mental hospital instead of prison.

The labelling process is intensified when the 'primary deviant' takes on 'secondary deviant' (Lemert 1951, 1967) characteristics. For example, rule-breaking occurs for a variety of reasons: biological, psychological or social; such 'primary deviance' has minor consequences for the rule-breaker unless his behaviour is labelled deviant by himself or others. Once labelled, the person's behaviour takes on new characteristics. 'Secondary deviance' arises either because the labelled deviant, once labelled, breaks even more rules, or begins actively to play the role of the deviant. For example, drug addicts often engage in criminal activities in order to acquire their drugs (Schur 1965); people in prisons or mental hospitals (Goffman 1961) display behaviour which is not a symptom of their 'badness' or 'madness' (primary deviance) but is a strategy they use to cope with their envelopment in a 'total institution'; much of the 'withdrawal' behaviour of the psychotic can perhaps be seen as 'secondary deviance' rather than a symptom of some underlying pathology.

If labelling has a different significance at different phases of a person's deviant career, then the possibilities of delabelling and relabelling (Trice and Roman 1970) must also be examined. As we have seen, deviant labelling is often a relatively irreversible process, especially if it produces 'secondary deviance' or is associated with somatic changes. Despite the emphasis on community psychiatry and the rehabilitation of the former mental patient, '... successful "delabelling" or destigmatization of mental patients subsequent to treatment appears rare' (ibid. p. 538).

However, Trice and Roman (ibid.) suggest that there are three ways whereby delabelling may successfully occur. Firstly, organizations of deviants may develop which have the primary goal of changing the norms of the community or society so that their originally offending behaviour becomes acceptable, for example homosexual groups. Secondly, professionals who initially label deviant behaviour and process the deviant through 'treatment' may facilitate delabelling by making certain public pronouncements during the deviant's status-passage into the community. Thirdly, delabelling may operate through the development of mutual aid organizations which encourage their members to return to strict conformity to the norms of the community, as well as creating a stereotype which is socially acceptable. Trice and Roman suggest that Alcoholics Anonymous functions in this way; it brings alcoholics together in an effort to cease their disruptive and deviant drinking behaviour, prior to conforming to the wider society's occupational, marital and community norms and roles. This 'return to the community' is facilitated by offering the alcoholic a 'repentant' role.

Secondly, *the labelling process is socially structured*. Who generally labels whom deviant, and what kinds of label are offered, will be determined largely by the culture of the society and the distribution of power within it. If we consider the distribution of labelled deviants by social class, race, religion, occupation, sex and age, then the pattern we find will tell us something about the dominant power and interest groups in society. If the lower classes predominate in criminal statistics and in the incidence of schizophrenia, then the social situation of people in this class and the class basis of social control systems will influence this distribution. For example, neighbourhood organization, social isolation, family dynamics and socialization processes in lower class groups may produce certain forms of behavioural response to situations, which official agents of social control (who are predominantly middle class) will label deviant.

This should not be seen as a spurious association—in other societies, political or religious criteria may be used to process deviants (Field and Aronson 1964).

If we analyse the types of behaviour which lead to psychiatric labelling, then this will tell us something about the kinds of social problems which are processed through psychiatric institutions. For example, old people, teenagers and suburban housewives in Western societies may be labelled psychiatric deviants because mental hospitals can then provide for them or their relatives an asylum or refuge from 'intolerable' social circumstances. It is these factors which lead Szasz (1962) to argue that mental illness is not a 'disease' but rather a name we use for 'problems-in-living'.

Human behaviour is to a large degree culturally relative (Benedict 1934). For example, there will be no labelled malarial psychoses in societies where malaria is absent and there will be little senile psychosis in societies where the expectation of life is low. Infanticide is acceptable in some societies but not in Western societies (Weinberg 1967). What appears to the Westerner to be 'paranoid' behaviour is acceptable social behaviour amongst the Kwakiutl Indians (Weinberg 1967), whilst in the West it is frequently labelled a symptom of mental illness (Lemert 1967).

However, a completely culturally relative approach to deviance should not be adopted. Cultural norms will be related in complicated ways to social institutions and to different people at different times and places. For example, the types of psychoses detected will vary according to a society's political and economic institutions and its psychiatric facilities. Who will be labelled 'paranoid' will depend on many factors, such as the power balance between the labeller and the labelled.

Thirdly, *the labelling process is not completely independent of the individual whose behaviour is being labelled.* In the first place, there are some disease processes which affect behaviour, for example, senility, porphyria or brain damage. There will be little disagreement in these cases that the 'patient's' rule-breaking is real and that a psychiatric label is appropriate in the situation. In the second place, the evidence that certain psychoses are universal (Weinberg 1967) would indicate that some extra-cultural factors may be operative in things like schizophrenia. ' . . . the "blunting" or flattening of emotional responsiveness and the inappropriateness of associations, often accompanied by the use of language with private, symbolic meaning; and an inward orientation with marked indifference to, and uninvolvement with, the social environment' (Mishler and Scotch, 1963, p. 321) may be internal processes albeit subject to very varying cultural definitions. Cultural variations in content of and societal reactions to schizophrenic processes do produce tremendous differences in the incidence, prevalence and course of this psychosis. However, we should not leave out the behaviour of the person being labelled when we attempt to explain deviance.

Fourthly, *the individual is seldom a passive automaton in the labelling process.* Human beings do not merely react to or interact with people in their environment; they are active transactors in social situations (Zigler and Child 1969). They must be continually interpreting and creating meanings for themselves in the world around them. They are not neutral agents of either their environment or their own internal physiological, psychological and social stimuli. They constantly code, select, and interpret the stimuli around them and engineer the kind of responses they will make to them. These mechanisms are at work in determining whether a person accepts or rejects deviant labels applied to him. However, his acceptance or rejection of proffered labels will not depend upon static unitary personality traits, such as conformity and conditionability alone. The social contingencies which buttress the labelling process will be factors that will be taken into account by the labelled person; for example, the power balance between the labeller and labelled, the amount and visibility of the rule-breaking, community tolerance levels for deviance, the ways in which his behaviour is reinforced and his own 'commitments' (Becker 1956, 1960 and 1964a,b) elsewhere will be crucial determinants of the kind of transactions the individual makes with those who wish to confer upon him a deviant status.

The labelling process does not operate in just one direction. Many people 'engineer' situations in which they will be offered a deviant label. For example, those who want an 'asylum' from intolerable social situations may display bizarre behaviour in front of 'significant others', a police station or their own doctor. How successful their own 'engineering' will be, however, will depend not only upon their success in fabricating bizarre behaviour. The audience is as important as the actor in determining whether or not a deviant status is conferred and the kind of label offered and applied.

Fifthly, *community tolerance thresholds* will vitally influence the deviant outcome. Wilkins (1963) points out that different societies and subgroups within societies have different tolerance thresholds for deviance. General tolerance levels for different types of deviance will influence significantly the speed with which a deviant label is either applied to or successfully chosen by a particular rule-breaker. People's tolerance varies in different places. For example, rural communities seem to have a high tolerance for the proverbial 'village idiot' whilst urban communities have a reduced tolerance for such a person—probably because of differences in the amount and availability of background information about him. People in different social classes also have different tolerance thresholds. Tizard and Grad (1961) suggest that the middle class are most likely to request institutional care for adult defectives. This implies reduced tolerance thresholds for subnormals on the part of middle class families.

Community tolerance levels, affecting the speed of labelling processes, also change over time. Changes in fashion, in the amount of information available about certain classes of deviant, in community facilities for deviants and in mass media presentations of deviants combine to influence the general levels of tolerance for certain types of behaviour in any particular society or social group. For example, current theories, myths and ideologies about teenagers and mass media presentations of youths appear to be reducing British society's tolerance level for the leisure pursuits of some young people. They are labelled 'hooligans', police increase their efforts to control them, thereby producing the kind of behaviour which they are supposed to eradicate; their 'secondary deviance' then confirms society's preconceptions of the youths' deviance, tolerance thresholds decrease further, and the vicious circle starts again.

Tolerance levels for rule-breakers are also influenced by types of community care facilities provided for processing deviants. For example, the increasing stress on community care for the mentally ill since the 1959 Mental Health Act does mean that the community is expected to raise its tolerance thresholds for certain types of residual rule-breakers or people with mental disorders. The increasing use of drugs and out-patient treatment for schizophrenics (Freeman 1969) may mean that those who label someone schizophrenic will increasingly have to contain him within the community; the label 'schizophrenia' will not automatically legitimate entry into or containment within a psychiatric institution.

However, changing community mental health practices also operate in the opposite direction for some people; new labels may facilitate a person's acceptance within the group. For example, Training Centres provide a different status, role and label for subnormal people, thereby re-integrating them into the community. A 'subnormal' label no longer automatically legitimates admission into an institution. New social supports also buttress the altered label.

Improved mental health facilities and changed attitudes towards the mentally ill may be changing community tolerance thresholds for psychiatric problems generally. Psychiatric labels may be more willingly applied to a rule-breaker by himself and his audience for minor problems because they know that they may get help thereby and also that the 'psychiatric episode' need be stabilized neither into chronic mental illness nor stigmatized. For example, suicidal gestures and mild depression, once labelled, are increasingly becoming legitimate and acceptable reasons for seeking psychiatric help. The increasing use of parole and probation for criminal offenders may similarly influence tolerance levels for the criminal in the community.

In summary, labelling is a highly complex, dynamic process in which the outcome is always open and negotiable. It will have different consequences for the individual at different phases in the sequence, follows socially structured channels and does not operate independently of the individual's own behaviour. The individual is not a passive victim of community labels, rather he is a transactor in a complex social situation. The transactions he makes will also be greatly influenced by tolerance thresholds in the group and in the wider community, and these thresholds vary at different times and places and are constantly changing.

Labelling in Social Work Practice

If labelling is a normal, basic, ubiquitous social process, then the things we have said in this chapter will be as relevant to clients of the social services generally as they are to the specific 'problems' which we used as examples; crime, mental illness, phobias and homosexuality. Social work with clients necessitates the naming and placing of a person in respect of a particular problem, in order to create some meaning in a highly complex social and personal situation. Labels are applied to the client so that he can be processed through the 'appropriate' organization. This is often described as a process of 'social diagnosis' in relation to 'agency function'. For example, the client's 'presenting problem' in his initial contacts with social workers must be re-interpreted and relabelled so that his 'real problem' can be tackled, in social security, local authority or probation departments.

Social contingencies will influence what type of person, with what type of problem, arrives at what kind of agency to be helped by what form of social work. Ultimately, it will determine the label applied to his problem, and such a label will have consequences for his future behaviour and will influence the type of service provided. The social worker, like anyone else, would not be able to function socially without using labels, but it may be useful to consider the possible consequences of his labelling; in particular, we should attempt to understand the dynamics involved in labelling clients and their families as 'problems', because a social worker's definition of the 'problem' will influence the strategies he employs in his dealings with his clients.

Taber (1970) points out that social workers have traditionally employed three types of 'problem' concepts: the disease concept, the social concept and the behaviourist concept. The disease concept suggests that family problems be seen as manifestations of pathological processes in individuals. The problems which the family may have are merely secondary consequences of the pathology of individual members of the family. If the individual pathology of family members can be treated—perhaps by long-term casework—then family functioning will be restored.

The social concept of problems adopts a sociological approach by seeing them as a product of social structures and social control; the family has a problem because it does not conform to the norms of the wider society, and the social worker's task is to encourage conforming behaviour in the family, such as paying the rent, sending the children to school and expediting the father's return to work.

The behaviourist concept of problems focuses on the overt observable behaviour of some or all family members which is defined as undesirable. If the behaviour of these clients is modified successfully, some of the family's problems are solved. Such an approach is outlined earlier in this book.

All these approaches take the existence of a problem for granted, but differ in their explanation of its aetiology and therefore employ different social work techniques in helping the family. However, the 'problem-definition' itself is a phenomenon that we should also attempt to explain.

Family 'problems' are not 'natural' things which emerge as a product of individual and social processes. Instead, they are categories, names or labels which families, social workers or other people apply to a situation within the family; the labels used will then serve as a guideline as to how social workers and others should define, treat and control the family; they will influence the expectations they will have of each other, thereby structuring their social relationships. For example, if a family situation, such as a child refusing to go to school, is defined as a 'marital problem', this label structures the situation for members of the family and the social workers. The label will influence the kind of social work which the practitioner will do with the family; for example, he will be less likely to be concerned with community action such as forming a tenants' association, or with marshalling resources for the family, than with attempting to increase communication between the husband and wife. It is in this way that the problem-definition is both a cause and a consequence of the type of label applied in a situation.

Taber suggests that one skill which the social worker may have above all others is his capacity to interfere with problem-definitions—in other words, to apply different labels to situations or to enable clients to come to some agreement about the problem-definition. Any action of the social worker which increases the communication between key actors over problem-definitions would be appropriate. The social worker may increase communication by bringing together people with opposing views about the problem forming a committee, advocating on behalf of the client or providing intensive casework. This may mean, respectively: arranging a meeting with the husband and wife so that they can discuss how the family problems are created by their own poor relationships rather than by some pathology within their child; organizing a committee whose members can fight for additional resources for their estate because their difficulties arise more from inadequate housing than from their own individual pathology; advocating for more money for a client from the social security officer through pointing out that a physically ill father is not workshy; or finally, through casework and insight-giving, helping a client to redefine his problem so that he need no longer be paranoid about his wife's feelings towards him once he realizes that her reactions are influenced by the relationship she experienced with her own father.

Problem-definitions in social work must be considered within the structural context of social welfare institutions in complex societies. Social workers may not be as free in the labels they use as the above account may imply. For example, some social workers may too readily choose psychological labels for complex social problems whose roots lie in the institutional arrangements of society. People with housing and income problems may be labelled 'socially inadequate', thereby deflecting attention from society to the under-privileged person. Handler (1968) suggests that caseworkers use psychological labels in a way that covers up their coercive techniques with clients in respect of housing, social security and other official agencies. Labelling in social work is indispensable, but it is important that we are aware of some of the unintended consequences it produces.

However, the problem may sometimes be one of a communication gap, or differences over problem-definition and problem solution, between social worker and client (Mayer and Timms 1969). For example, these authors present evidence that clients expect the social worker to tell them whether they are doing right or wrong and to instruct them how to change their behaviour. Such clients are often surprised and puzzled at the social worker's insight-oriented approach to their problems. Because the social worker and the client provide different explanations of their problems, and thereby apply different labels to their situation, they create different meanings out of the same situation; they name and place the behaviour of the participants in the situation in different ways; because they speak a different language, their explanations of an event are at variance and their solutions follow different courses. Incongruent interpersonal labelling is, therefore, problematic, and increased communication might bring about a change in the labels, a redefinition of the problem, or a fresh strategy for solving the problem. Ultimately, in such a case, a change in the label has brought about changes in the situation and the person's behaviour and this in itself may constitute a solution of the problem.

We are not suggesting that changing the labels will *always* change a person's behaviour. As we have seen, labelling does not go on 'in the air'; it is firmly rooted in individual and social situations. Changing the labels without changing the personal and social supports which buttress them is unlikely to be very effective. The labelling perspective is one means of describing extremely complex phenomena; merely using different labels will not always be sufficient for bringing about change. Increased communication, improved social supports and resources, behaviour modification and insight-giving will also be necessary in many cases.

A labelling approach to social and personal problems may appear to be more amenable than an abstract social structural explanation of such events to social engineering. At one level this may be so because the labelling perspective focuses on the importance of people's reactions towards each other for their future behaviour, personality development and possible deviant careers. The behaviour of people, including their labelling devices, may seem to be easier to modify than, say, complex social institutions. We suggested earlier in the chapter three ways of delabelling deviants. However, four major factors would make us very cautious of advocating the wholesale, uncritical adoption of labelling theory by the social engineer.

Firstly, labelling may generate relatively irreversible processes. Writing about schizophrenia, Bateson (1967) says that, 'Once precipitated into psychosis, the patient has a course to run . . . Once begun, a schizophrenic episode would appear to have as definite a course as an initiation ceremony—a death and rebirth—into which the novice may have been precipitated by his family or by adventitious circumstances, but which in its course is largely steered by endogenous process' (p. xiv). Thus, ignoring, tolerating or normalizing a psychotic episode is unlikely to remove the acute 'symptoms' or to reverse the schizogenic process. Changing the labels may not automatically or directly modify a person's immediate behaviour.

However, this is not to imply that different labels and differential societal reactions to psychotic episodes will have no influence in the long run. As we have seen, patterns of labelling are important determinants of entry into chronic mental illness or 'secondary deviance'. For example, if a psychiatrist informs a patient's relatives that she is 'schizophrenic', the family may adopt the schizophrenic label themselves in their own relations with their daughter, thereby confirming her deviant status. The provision of a label has altered their own behaviour and attitudes towards their daughter, and this in turn has consequences for their daughter's deviant career; their collusion with the label may be the vital factor in her entry into 'secondary deviance'. Withholding the label from the relatives may avert chronic mental illness in such a case. Labelling theory helps the 'social engineer' in this kind of situation.

Secondly, it may be 'cruel' to change the label applied to a person, because the label will confer a status on him and this status carries with it expected patterns of behaviour, rights and obligations. The schizophrenic label may provide a refuge for someone from an intolerable social situation, and the label legitimates his entry into a sick role which carries with it the right to shed some of the responsibilities and anxieties of intolerable social situations. A 'sick' label may provide hospital protection for a socially inadequate person. A 'criminal' label may provide shelter for a few days for the vagrant. Ultimately, we cannot talk about 'labelling' in the abstract; careful analysis of the complex social and personal situation of the people involved will point to the relevance, limits and possibilities of changing labels in society.

Thirdly, human beings are not automata; their reactions to and acceptance or rejection of labels will affect how successful behaviour modification through changing labels will be.

Therefore, fourthly, the complex issue of social engineering and behaviour modification is hedged around with ethical, political and social questions; these must affect the kinds of decisions to be made about changing an individual's behaviour. Some of these issues have been considered elsewhere in this book. Consideration must always be given to such factors as: available resources, society's values, willingness and power of clients and relatives or 'significant others', tolerance levels in the community, and the endemic and ubiquitous nature of labelling in both conforming and deviant situations. Ultimately we must be aware that if we change the labels or refuse to apply them, then some people are going to have to look elsewhere for solutions to their complex personal and social problems.

In conclusion, labelling theory is still insufficiently systematic in its operational definitions and hypotheses (Gibbs 1971). There are still many contradictions and gaps in its empirical findings, especially in respect of the reputed class, racial and sexual biases in labelling (Cohn 1963, Gross 1967, Terry 1967). The perspective must not be applied globally to deviant phenomena. For example, exchange theory may more usefully explain persistent middle class delinquency which often escapes societal reaction (Box and Ford 1971). Several promising studies have linked labelling theory with organizational analysis (Smith 1971, Stoll 1968, DeWolfe 1969) and it is this type of study which might wrest labelling theory from its essentially tautological and ideological foundations (Cohen 1971, Phillipson 1971).

5

Insight

THE CONCEPT OF INSIGHT

Social casework is a wide and complex method ranging from activities directed at changing the client's environment (for example, through re-housing or the provision of financial aid) to the use of psychological methods designed to increase his understanding of how he himself may be contributing to a situation of difficulty. Whether the social worker is to be regarded primarily as friend, administrator, reformer, educator or therapist is a continuing and so far unresolved (perhaps unresolvable) issue, but it is evident that whatever social workers do, in so far as their professional practice is concerned with disturbed interpersonal relationships it must include a considerable counselling or therapeutic component. In the past, social work has owed much to psychodynamic theories of personality, and has derived from these a treatment orientation in which the achievement of insight plays an important part as a way of assisting the client to deal more effectively with problems of social and interpersonal functioning.

Within recent years, however, the effectiveness of insight therapies has been very much questioned, particularly by those engaged in the treatment of neuroses by behavioural methods, and it therefore seems appropriate to re-evaluate the role of insight in social work intervention in the light of the very different approach outlined in the earlier chapters of this book. If social work lays claim to effectiveness, empirical research in the clinical psychological field which has bearing on this obviously has important implications for social work education and practice.

The term 'insight' is itself, however, extremely ambiguous. 'Among the unclarities which are of utmost clinical importance and which cause utmost confusion is the term 'insight,' wrote Zilboord (1952). 'It came from nowhere, so to speak. No one knows who employed it first and in what sense.' We can distinguish at least four different senses. Insight may describe a quality of general perceptiveness or empathic understanding ('he has insight'). It may refer to a client's appreciation that he has a problem ('insight as to illness', in psychiatric terms) or to his understanding of the nature of the problem, and its consequences for himself or others. In Gestalt psychology insight refers specifically to the sudden appreciation of a solution to a previously insoluble problem, through a reorganization of the perceptual field in such a way that familiar elements take on a new pattern. Lastly, it may refer, as in psycho-dynamic psychology, to an understanding of unconscious intra-psychic conflicts and their infantile origins.

This chapter will first attempt some clarification. In it we shall discuss the concept of insight as it is used in a general context; as it appears in Gestalt psychology and psychoanalysis; and finally, as it relates specifically to social work. We shall then go on to consider the role of insight in behaviour change.

Insight as a Special Kind of Human Understanding

The word insight is of course far older than the relatively modern science of psychology and in its most general sense frequently has a religious, scientific or philosophical, rather than a psychological, connotation. The term is used to indicate the perception or understanding of the hidden qualities or meanings underlying observed phenomena. In the Oxford English Dictionary it is defined as penetrating 'with the eye of the understanding into the hidden characteristics or hidden nature of things; a glimpse or view below the surface'. This implies more than observation (even than particularly acute or perceptive observation), and more than the intuitive apprehension of latent phenomena; it requires an intelligence which orders and organizes percepts through some form of explanation. Lonergan (1958) in his comprehensive study of insight likens it to a detective story; in such a story the reader is given all the clues, but reaching the solution involves 'a quite distinct activity of organizing intelligence that places the full set of clues in a unique explanatory perspective.' (p. ix.)

Two stories are often quoted as examples of insight. The first is that of Archimedes, who solved a knotty problem involving the displacement of water while in his bath, and rushed naked through the streets of Syracuse crying 'Eurika!'. The other example is of Newton, said to have been led to an understanding of the laws of gravity through observing an apple fall from a tree. Certain elements are common to these two stories which illustrate further characteristics of insight, the analysis of which is owed to Lonergan (pp. 3-6). Insight here

1. Comes as a solution to a problem with which the mind is already deeply engaged;
2. Comes suddenly and unexpectedly. The experience might be expressed as 'Aha,' or 'I've got it!';
3. Is a function of inner conditions, rather than external circumstances—baths had been taken before and apples had fallen before, without the same insight;
4. Pivots between the concrete and the abstract. The particular concrete instance in both these cases led to the construction of a general scientific law of universal applicability;
5. Passes into the habitual texture of one's mind. Once the insight is acquired,

one's perceptual stance alters, so that it cannot again be lost. Once achieved it appears simple, obvious and beyond dispute.

From this discussion, insight emerges as a special kind of understanding which (a) involves the capacity to see hidden meanings or patterns underlying manifest phenomena, and (b) in the scientific field is characteristically (though not necessarily) related to problem solution.

Lonergan's own analysis pursues the theme through such diverse fields as metaphysics, psychology, physics and theology at increasingly complex conceptual levels ('insight into insight') until it reaches an ultimate religious synthesis, understood in terms of Thomistic theology and based on the conclusion that *omnia Deum appetunt*. This leads far beyond the scope of the present discussion, however, and although the concept of insight might with great profit be carried into the fields of science and literature, for further elucidation in relation to casework we must turn to psychology.

The Gestalt Concept of Insight

The Gestalt concept shows similarities to the sense discussed above in that it is also related to problem-solving, though for Lonergan insight is essentially an achievement of human understanding. Kohler (1925) postulated the occurrence of insight to explain the suddenness with which animals in experimental situations suddenly appeared to find the solution to a difficult problem. In one such experiment a chimpanzee was placed in a cage and chained; within reach was a stick. A banana was then placed outside the chimpanzee's reach, which was limited by the length of the chain. After several unsuccessful attempts to grasp the banana, the chimpanzee used the stick to draw the fruit within his reach. The animal, it is said, was experiencing insight, that is, a re-organization of the perceptual field in such a way that familiar elements take on new meanings and solutions to formerly insoluble problems become possible. The solution is held to be more than the sum of the components, but to depend on a conception of the whole in which sticks and banana are both elements. Thus reaching a solution is more than a simple trial and error process, and involves insight in the sense of establishing previously unrecognized connections which point to a solution. Kohler argues that once insight is achieved, the need for further trial-and-error learning is obviated; that is, the insight is generalized to similar situations in the future. Thomson (1959) has clearly demonstrated the ambiguities inherent in Kohler's concept, pointing out that insight is used in two separate senses, '(a) as a description of a pattern of behaviour observed in some problem solving situations; (b) as a name of a postulated psychological process which controls behaviour.' (p. 38). Among the difficulties (and there are many) are the problem of how to categorize behaviour which displays all the characteristics of insight, yet produces an erroneous solution. Must insight be 'right'? And if we accept Kohler's hypothesis, are we any nearer an explanation of what actually happens, what new factors bring about a changed perceptual organization? Reeves (1969) is similarly critical, since she considers that insight

may constitute a misleading hypothesis and concludes that 'it remains somewhat uncertain precisely what Gestalt psychologists claim in asserting that it
exists, and also whether a case for its existence is established.' (pp. 274-5.)

Despite these difficulties, the concept of insight *is* in practice used to describe
a kind of understanding which involves the appreciation of previously unrecognized patterns and links between events. Thus it is useful, even though its
theoretical basis remains unclear, and it is of great relevance to contemporary
psychotherapy in relation to the problem of therapeutic change. While loosely
used in the sense of self-knowledge or self-awareness, it is evident that insight
does not mean exactly the same thing to all therapists. Those with a background in academic psychology such as Schonbar (1965) are likely to use the
term in a specifically Kohlerian sense. For the behavioural psychologist such as
Bandura (1969) (who prefers to use the term 'awareness' to avoid ambiguity)
insight is primarily a cognitive process which involves the recognition and
labelling of behavioural events or sequences of events. This type of awareness
would seem to have much in common with the kind of process described by
Kohler in that it also involves the recognition of previously hidden patterns and
leads to altered behaviour and the solution of some adaptive problem. The
behavioural view of insight and the criticisms made of it as a therapeutic aim
are discussed in greater detail below.

Psychodynamic therapists, on the other hand (using psychodynamic to refer
to those psychoanalytic and related theories which emphasize the effects of
intra-psychic conflicts and unconscious motivation on behaviour), understand
insight in relation to that new knowledge of himself and of previously unconscious aspects of his personality which the patient gains in the course of
analytic work. For the psychoanalyst in particular insight means something very
different from the cognitive process described by Kohler, and we shall examine
the psychoanalytic concept next. This is of particular relevance for social work,
which has understood insight primarily in psychodynamic terms.

Insight in Psychoanalysis

We might expect to find in the psychoanalytic literature a clearer definition
which would clear away some of the sea-mists surrounding it in social work. It
becomes evident, however, that psychoanalytic writing is no less fraught with
imprecision and difference of interpretation. The main source of this confusion
appears to be that the term is used in the general sense of self-knowledge by some
authors, but with a precise technical meaning by others.

Rycroft (1968) points out that the term was not in fact used by Freud but
was a later import into psychoanalysis (p. 73). In the early years the effective
therapeutic elements in psychoanalytic treatment were seen as the lifting of the
infantile amnesias, the uncovering of repressed instinctual forces (the id) kept in
check by a process of repression, and the re-direction of the released energies
into new and less damaging forms of behaviour. The aim of analysis was seen
as 'making the unconscious conscious,' and was summed up in the often quoted

remark, 'Where id was, there shall ego be'. The later work on the ego and the recognition of other defence mechanisms besides repression (for example, projection, isolation, displacement, introjection and so on) led to a new interest in the integrative function of the ego, particularly by the analysts Hartmann, Kris and Loewenstein. A paper by Loewenstein in 1956 contended that 'Freud's original formulation of the aim of psychoanalytic therapy—to lift amnesias—was sufficient as long as only the undoing of the effects of repression was considered. But since psychoanalysis came to consider the results of other defensive mechanisms as well, the need has also arisen to encompass such processes as the re-establishment of connections, for instance, and the correction of distortions produced by various mechanisms of defence. We refer here to the important role of the synthetic and organizing function in the therapeutic process. Under these circumstances we are justified, I believe, in supplementing the term "bringing to consciousness" by the more comprehensive one of "gaining of insight" when we wish to designate the results of changes in the ego which make warded-off mental functions available to the conflictless sphere of the ego. This term comprises both the bringing to consciousness and the re-establishment of connection.' (pp. 460-1).

The concept of insight is central to psychoanalytic technique as described by Menninger, where a very specific definition occurs. He defines it as 'the recognition by the patient (1) that this or that aspect of his feelings and attitudes, this or that technique of behaviour, this or that role in which he casts other people, is *of a pattern*; (2) that this pattern, like the footprint of a bear which has lost certain toes in a trap, originated long ago and stamps itself on every step of his life journey; it is present in his contemporary reality situation relationships, and it is present in his analytic relationship; (3) that this pattern originated for a reason which was valid at the time, and persisted despite changes in some of the circumstances which originally determined it; (4) that this pattern contains elements which are offensive and injurious to others as well as expensive and troublesome to the patient.' Further, 'Insight is not just seeing that something in the analytic situation is similar to something in childhood, or seeing that something in childhood is reflected in the activities of his contemporary situation, or seeing that something in his contemporary situation is a reflection of something in the analytic situation. In the proper sense of the word and in the useful sense for psychoanalytic techniques, *insight is the simultaneous identification of the characteristic behaviour pattern in all three of these situations together with an understanding of why they were and are used as they were and are.*' (Menninger 1958, p. 147.) Thus insight involves a triple connection—childhood, contemporary extra-analytic relationships, and analytic situation—and the re-establishment of the links between them. In the strict psychoanalytic sense, insight always refers to unconscious conflicts and their origins in early infantile life, particularly (bearing in mind Freud's views on the development of neuroses) before the age of six.

Other analysts broaden the concept of insight to include not only an awareness of how the present is shaped by the past and the repressed but still active infantile conflicts and fantasies, but also the dynamic changes associated with this understanding. Loewenstein wrote: 'We know that such insight is gained only after certain dynamic changes have occurred and that gaining of insight, in its turn, leads to other dynamic changes.' (1956, p. 461). In this sense, insight concerns the total personality and culminates in a reorganization of the ego; it occurs as part of a gradual reconstructive process. The same concern with change in behaviour is also implicit in French's distinction between *introspective* and *problem-solving insight* (French 1958). Introspective insight is 'know why', the awareness of a previously repressed wish or thought influencing current behaviour, but this is only half the story; the other half is 'know how', or problem-solving insight—translating this knowledge into new and more satisfying solutions in the real world. Thus French includes in this concept not only insight in the more common usage (as, for example, that of Menninger) but also the *outcome* of insight and the resumption of the learning process interrupted in infancy, leading to the development of more adult patterns of behaviour. Indeed the distinction between analysis and other forms of therapy has been drawn in terms of this very factor of the therapeutic effects brought about by insight; what is specifically psychoanalytic, it has been claimed, is 'dynamic changes produced by insight gained from interpretation'. (Loewenstein 1951, p. 3).

From the above discussion, it will be evident that insight is not seen merely as a cognitive or intellectual process, but as a dynamic factor leading to profound personality change. Indeed, the kind of insight which brings about no such modification would not be regarded as 'true' insight by analysts, and one of the criteria for deciding whether or not a patient had achieved this insight would be in terms of his subsequent behaviour. A distinction is often made between *intellectual insight*, which is a cognitive type of awareness without therapeutic value (and may even be resistance to genuine insight), and *emotional insight*, which includes a strong affective accompaniment or abreaction. As Richfield (1954) has pointed out, the concept of 'emotional insight' is in itself full of difficulties, and the way in which it is believed to bring about change is by no means clear, but most psychodynamic therapists would accept that it is the *affective* component in insight which matters. Jung likened it to the difference between an illness one reads about and an illness which one has—it is only the experience (not the intellectual appreciation) of insight which in the end brings about some psychological change. 'In psychology,' Jung wrote, 'one possesses nothing unless one has experienced it in reality. Hence a purely intellectual insight is not enough because one knows only the words and not the substance of the thing from the inside.' (1959, p. 33.)

Insight cannot be gained solely by interpretation or by confronting the patient with the meaning of his behaviour in dynamic terms. Resistance has to be overcome and the new understanding translated, little by little, into changed behaviour. The term *working-through* is used to describe the repeated recall and discussion of previously dissociated material until it becomes fully assimilated by the ego and a dynamic factor for change. Fromm-Reichmann, for instance, uses the word 'awareness' for the intellectual grasp of new understanding, but reserves the term 'insight' for the 'integrated curative type of understanding', which, she holds, comes about as a result of the process of working-through and which alone is therapeutically effective. Thus 'insight' cannot properly be applied (in the psychoanalytic sense) to a single flash of understanding, but only to a much more gradual reconstructive process wherein the understanding is worked on and assimilated (Fromm-Reichmann 1953).

The same therapeutic primacy is not given to insight by all analysts, however, and it will be noted that the above paragraphs have drawn particularly on the work of ego-psychologists. In Britain, the work of Fairbairn, Winnicott and others has drawn attention to the importance of other therapeutic factors and, in particular, emphasis has been placed not only on what is re-enacted in the analytic situation—the infantile residues present in the transference—but on what is new—the development of an authentic relationship with the analyst. In a paper given to the 1961 Congress of the International Psycho-analytical Association, Sacha Nacht laid emphasis on the importance of the analyst's personality and his 'deep inner attitude' towards the patient, though this he saw not as a substitute for insight, but as a prerequisite. It is the analyst's capacity to provide the acceptance and kindness which the patient has not had, and his ability to *be* the good object the patient is seeking, which enables the patient to learn new patterns of relationship.

Nonetheless at the same Congress, Hanna Segal took her stand firmly on the conviction that insight is at the root of all lasting therapeutic personality change, and that this is the sine qua non of analytical treatment. She maintained that psychoanalytic insight differs from all other forms of insight (for example, that possessed by the ordinary well-integrated intuitive person, or the perceptive historian or artist). 'It involves a conscious knowledge of archaic processes, normally inaccessible to the most intuitive person, through reliving in the transference the very processes that structured one's internal world and conditioned one's perception.' Insight into the deepest layers of the unconscious and the primitive fantasies with which Kleinian theory is concerned comes primarily through experience of the transference and, says Segal, it is not retained after the termination of the analysis (Segal 1961, p. 217).

Despite the variations of meaning and the confusions surrounding the term, it is evident that for most analysts insight gained through psychoanalytic interpretation is at the heart of the therapeutic process, whatever other curative factors may be also involved. While the above discussion has drawn only on the work of the psychoanalysts (since their influence on casework has been greatest), for all analytic schools the progressive understanding of the unconscious roots of behaviour leading to a greater measure of conscious awareness and control is a central and crucial value. The conceptualization of the *content* of the unconscious mind (and therefore of analytic interpretation) varies of course greatly between the different schools. For Melanie Klein, it is the archaic infantile fantasies which shape the inner world of the adult; for Adler, the struggle for power; and for Jung, not only the personal unconscious, in the Freudian sense, but the archetypal unconscious material which becomes accessible during the individuation process in the later stages of analysis. In analytical psychology, therefore, the ego does not have the primacy it has for the psychoanalysts (particularly the ego-psychologists) but is gradually replaced by a new centre of the personality which is termed the Self. These different theoretical approaches lead to differences in interpretation, and the techniques for exploring the unconscious mind also vary. Nonetheless, the *concept* of the unconscious mind is common to all, and in all the same high value is placed on the gradual penetration into the hidden recesses of the personality and the progressive development of insight.

Summary

In summarizing the discussion thus far, we note that insight may refer to

(a) a *quality* of mind, or psychological attribute of the person ('possessing insight'),

(b) a specific *act* of understanding of a special kind ('the achievement of insight', 'to have gained an insight'),

(c) a particular kind of psychological *process* ('experiencing insight').

Although, as this discussion has shown, the concept is by no means easy to define, this analysis leads us to distinguish three senses in which it is commonly used, all of which we shall find to occur in the social work literature.

1. *Insight* in its most general sense, and as it characterizes the work of scientists, poets, critics, or any other activity of human understanding, involves the capacity to see below the surface, and to apprehend truths which are normally hidden from sight; it requires the ability to 'see into the heart of things'. In relation to scientific work, it is usually connected with problem solution, and thus refers to an essentially intellectual or cognitive activity. Insight is more than observation: it includes an appreciation of the relationships between or underlying observed phenomena (and thus some form of explanatory theory), but seems to depend more on intuition than on reasoning. While the *process* by which insight occurs is psychological in nature (and thus has been a particular area of study for psychologists) the *phenomena* with which it is concerned may be of any kind. For this reason we distinguish a special kind of insight which we term 'psychological insight'.

2. *Psychological insight* is concerned with the understanding of psychological processes. It is related primarily to self-knowledge, but may also be concerned with the understanding of others or inter-personal relationships. It involves the same capacity to perceive or infer patterns of relationship or hidden significance behind manifest phenomena as described above. When used *psychodynamically*, however, it has reference to the appreciation of feelings by experiencing them, and thus is not a predominantly intellectual process. In relation to self-knowledge, therefore, insight includes affect as well as cognition, and it is this affective element ('emotional insight') which is held to distinguish insight from other forms of understanding. In relation to others or to interpersonal dynamics

insight may also have an affective component and is often said to involve the capacity for empathy.* At the same time, the special characteristic of insight is that it links events or feelings in some explanatory way, and thus has an intellectual as well as an emotional component.

Social workers' understanding of the nature of psychological insight has been greatly enriched by a psychodynamic approach to personality and the kinds of insight owed ultimately to psychoanalysis and its derivatives. In our view, however, the term 'psychological insight' should include but should not be restricted to an understanding of the unconscious aspects of behaviour, nor is it most usefully linked to a specific theoretical approach. We shall therefore use the term in a broader and more eclectic sense to indicate a perceptive psychological awareness tied to no particular theoretical orientation. Thus both the emotional insight associated with a psychodynamic approach, and the more cognitive type of insight referred to by behavioural psychologists, would be aspects of psychological insight. It is useful to differentiate this generic use of the term from the more technical meaning it has in psychoanalysis, our third category.

3. *Psychoanalytic insight*, as we define it, has reference primarily to those aspects of behaviour which are unconsciously determined; in particular, intrapsychic conflicts or unconscious fantasies and their infantile roots. In this context 'psycholoanalytic' is to be understood (following Rycroft) as referring not to Freud's theories only, but to those psychodynamic theories and therapies (whether Jungian, Freudian, Kleinian, or other) which in Rycroft's words 'assume the existence of unconscious mental processes, which concern themselves with the elucidation of motives and which make use of transference', and which can be distinguished from the organic school of psychiatry and from behavioural psychology (Rycroft 1966, pp. 9-10). The special characteristic of psychoanalytic insight is its linking of the present with the past, and its appreciation of the contribution of early experiences to contemporary behaviour. While the achievement of this kind of insight is not restricted to the analytic treatment situation, it comes in the main through interpretation, especially of transference phenomena, and through the use of specialized techniques such as free association and the analysis of dreams and fantasies. A good deal of the material with which psychoanalytic insight is concerned therefore is not accessible to consciousness nor to ordinary introspection since it is subject to some form of censorship or is repressed. It is concerned with aspects of mental functioning which are buried and are dynamically unconscious (Freud 1915), rather than merely temporarily out of mind or unrecognized (preconscious).

The difference between psychological and psychoanalytic insight may be clarified by illustration. A social worker involved in family therapy might understand what was going on at different levels. He might become aware of

---

* *Empathy*: rendering of G. *einfuhlung*, in + feeling. 'The power of projecting one's personality into (and so fully comprehending) the object of contemplation.' *Concise Oxford Dictionary*.

the interactions happening here and now between members of the family, or between the members and himself. He might point this out, explaining it in terms of role, communication, or perhaps games theory, thus helping them to a greater awareness of the nature of their current inter-relationships. Much family therapy involves psychological insight of this nature, which is not in any sense 'psychoanalytic'. On the other hand, the social worker might become aware of the impact of unconscious feelings on the current situation. This (if he were psychodynamically-oriented) he might understand in terms of transference of feelings deriving from childhood, though as a social worker he would not attempt to take on the role of analyst by exploring their roots. The second kind of explanation is bound up with psychoanalytic theory in a way that the first is not, and the client's understanding of it would form a very different kind of insight.

To avoid misunderstanding, two points should be borne in mind. The first is that an insight is not, in our sense of the term, necessarily 'psychoanalytic' because it is expressed by a psychoanalyst. In actual practice, the therapist, be he analyst or not, is likely to develop and try to communicate all sorts of insights, and the level at which he does so will be a matter of deliberate choice. In the family therapy situation, for example, the therapist must often decide whether he will interpret what is going on in psychoanalytic terms (i.e. in relation to the past) or in terms of current interactions. Secondly, while many social workers do acquire psychoanalytic insight about themselves (and may use this indirectly in their work) the kind of insight they try to help their clients acquire is rarely of this nature, and is much more likely to be the kind of psychological insight concerned with current interpersonal functioning (see below). Thus in a recent book Wittenberg (1970), discussing the relevance of Kleinian theory to social casework, sees psychoanalytic insight as helpful in understanding the current situation, but does not envisage the caseworker's job as involving exploration of the past; thus it is not, in her view, the caseworker's function to try to help the client acquire psychoanalytic insight. (p. 8.) And while in the view of some authors (Halmos 1958, Winnicott 1959) it is part of the function of social work training to help students develop psychoanalytic insights, this is with a view to increasing their capacity to understand their clients, and does not imply an expectation that the development of insight of this kind will be an aim of their practice.

THE ROLE OF INSIGHT IN CASEWORK

An Historical View

In the early years of casework, emphasis was placed on helping the client through the power of friendship and personal influence, through advice and guidance, or in dealing with pressing economic or environmental needs. This is not to suggest that psychological or personality aspects were totally ignored (though they were deemed to be those of 'character') and one of the avowed aims of the Charity Organization Society in Great Britain was to strengthen character and assist the client to regain the road to independence. Annette Garrett, writing in 1949, pointed out that the attempt to modify personality was 'not a recent and revolutionary undertaking of caseworkers but an evolutionary development of aims present from the beginning'. (Garrett 1949.) The advent of Freudian theory to casework at the end of the first world war did not therefore wholly change the face of social work; what it did was to alter the emphasis and place intra-psychic problems and conflicts, rather than the environment, in central focus. While much of the literature of that time was clearly concerned with assimilating the new psychology, no doubt in practice this was incorporated into the framework of more traditional and practical methods of work. To suggest, as some critics have (Wootton 1959), that caseworkers lost both their hearts and their judgements to the seductive influences of psychoanalysis is probably an overstatement. But that psychoanalysis did indeed make a profound impact, particularly in the United States, is apparent from even a cursory glance at the literature of the time. Not only did psychoanalytic theory offer a framework for understanding human behaviour, especially in its more irrational aspects, but it also offered hope of changing attitudes and behaviour in a systematic and more effective way. Through techniques aimed at increasing his understanding of himself and his unconscious motivations, it was hoped that the client could be assisted to greater self-awareness and thereby enabled to achieve a greater measure of rationality and control over his own behaviour and life situation. The appeal of the new approach has been expressed with great clarity by Charlotte Towle: 'The concept of man as a rational being dominated the caseworker's early thinking on the (casework) relationship; therefore intellect was expected not only to govern thinking and doing, but also to fashion it. The caseworker accordingly relied heavily on imparting information and on appealing to reason in effecting change in behaviour. Psychological insight, however, brought a focus on the irrational self. It gave prominence to the point of view that feelings fashion thinking and prompt action. Therefore rational behaviour was contingent on a change in feeling.' (Towle 1964, p. xi.) From the nineteen thirties on, psychoanalytic theory with later modifications remained a potent influence on professional training and practice in social work.

The development of insight is a corner-stone of analytic therapy, and in view of the extensive influence the psychoanalysts wielded in the casework field, it is not surprising that it came to be seen as an important objective of casework also, though never as its sole or even central objective. American literature on treatment classifications shows unmistakably this debt to psychoanalysis, and particularly to the psychology of the ego developed after the publication of 'The Ego and the Id' in 1923, the 'New Introductory Lectures' in 1933 and Anna Freud's 'The Ego and the Mechanisms of Defence' in 1936. 'The focus on the ego,' Lucille Austin wrote in a well known paper in 1949, 'was more readily useful to casework in its efforts to influence adaptive capacities than was the early emphasis on the "unconscious". This new theory also made for shifts in psychoanalytic technique, placing greater weight on current reality adaptations as well as the analysis of the childhood neuroses. Hence the two professions, casework and psychoanalysis, drew closer together in their common aims. Each profession reached its present formulation of methods of psychotherapy within the disciplines of its own practice but with extensions, by both, in areas of responsibility and treatment skills. The meeting ground, psychotherapy, is a more practical therapy than psychoanalysis and a more comprehensive therapy than our former "intensive" casework.' (Austin 1948, p. 326.)

In keeping with this psychotherapeutic orientation, casework treatment classifications, particularly in the 1940's, emphasized the internal world rather than the external environment of the client. From reading articles such as that of Austin (still widely quoted) it is difficult to avoid the impression that the environmental aspects of casework are passed over rather quickly in order to get to the real heart of the process, the psychological work. Austin does however distinguish two main methods: *social therapy*, which 'consists primarily of the use of techniques designed to influence positively various factors in the environment, and of the effective use of social resources'; and *psychotherapy*, which aims 'to bring about some modification of behaviour and attitudes and rests on a diagnosis of the total personality'. It is the psychotherapeutic aspect of social work which most clearly interests her and it is evident that self-understanding is considered to play a fundamental role in bringing about beneficial changes. Following Alexander and French (1946), psychotherapy is said to rely on two main techniques, supportive therapy and insight therapy, and a third intermediate category, designated experiential therapy, which uses a mixture of the two. While supportive work does not aim at change but rather the maintenance of present strengths, insight therapy aims at considerable reconstruction of the personality or aspects of it. The differences between intermediate and insight therapy are not always clear, since the former also utilizes the transference situation and transference interpretations in developing self-knowledge. The main difference would seem to be that insight is not the main aim in intermediate therapy and that understanding develops not so much through reductive or genetic inter-pretations as through reflections on current experience and interpersonal relationships. It will 'work' through a corrective experience with the case-worker, the roots of which may remain unconscious. Insight or uncovering therapy, on the other hand, is aimed at fundamental personality change through insight and understanding. Part of the interest of Mrs. Austin's paper, historically, is that she sees caseworkers as using *all* these methods, though the last two only with psychiatric consultation and support on the basis of advanced training.

Much the same range of methods, though differently classified, occurs in Florence Hollis' 'Women in Marital Conflict' (1949). This classification, which has since been substantially modified, had the great merit of being derived from a content analysis of actual casework interviews. The classification is four-fold and consists of Environmental Modification, Psychological Support,

Clarification (also called Counselling) and Insight Development. The first two are self-explanatory. Clarification is said to include understanding, with or without strong feeling accompaniment, and it is directed at the client's ability to perceive more clearly and cope more adequately with himself in his environment. It is always combined with support. In insight development, on the other hand, the worker 'is helping the individual to become aware of factors below the level of consciousness, which are adversely affecting his current behaviour, in particular, repressed infantile conflicts'. This sounds like psychoanalysis, but at that period Hollis drew a distinction between casework insight and psychological insight in terms of depth. 'In insight development we deal with transference feelings but not to the depth involved in the transference neurosis. We reach and comment on suppressed material and those unconscious thoughts and feelings that are not deeply repressed. We do not reach the unconscious layer of psychosexual motivation or infantile repression though we may deal with their derivatives. Analysis, on the other hand, involves the use of deeply unconscious material . . .' (Hollis 1949, p. 153.) In her 'Casework' (1964) she discusses the relation between casework and the unconscious more specifically, and revises her earlier views quite sharply. While she holds that a knowledge of unconscious processes is essential to effective casework practice, she considers that generally caseworkers do not deal with unconscious material, in the psychoanalytic sense. 'There was a period in the late forties when many of us believed that casework in "insight development" has as its aim the bringing of true unconscious material to consciousness. I am inclined to think that for the most part we were confusing "unconscious" with "not conscious" and were actually dealing with preconscious suppressed material.' (Hollis, 1964, p. 138.) Her own attempts, and those of the F.S.A.A. Committee on classification, to locate instances of 'insight' development in the strict sense produced very few indeed, even when agencies were asked for examples of their 'deepest' work. Her theoretical explanation links casework procedures with the work of Kris and others on the preconscious (Kris 1950); thus she does not see caseworkers as concerned with psychoanalytic insight in the sense defined above. In the same book and in a series of articles, a revised classification of casework procedures has been published, with a six-fold division. This avoids the crudity of the support versus insight-giving approach, and does justice to her conception of social work treatment procedures as being ranged along a continuum in which a number of different techniques are blended together. These can be distinguished for the purpose of conceptual analysis, though the distinctions may not be apparent to the practitioner engaged in the casework interview. The categories are:

A. Sustaining procedures—communications of a supportive, encouraging or sustaining type, verbal or non-verbal; e.g. the sympathetic comment.

B. Direct influence—advice or encouragement directed to promoting some form of behaviour; e.g. 'It might be wise to consult a solicitor.'

C. Exploration–ventilation–description—exploration concerning the client or his situation (often factual) or encouraging the expression of feeling in relation to it.

D. Person–situation reflections—promoting thought about and understanding of the client's person–situation gestalt in the present or adult past. This would include discussion of strengths or difficulties in current inter-personal functioning but *not* the possible childhood origins of these.

E. Reflection on personality dynamics—helping the client to understand his own personality patterns, characteristics and dynamics in a more generalized way than in D above; for example, his use of defensive manoeuvres.

F. Reflection upon developmental factors, or on early life events which may be connected with his present behaviour. (Hollis 1967a, b).

Of these the last three are concerned with the development of insight or self-understanding though research evidence suggests that very little casework intervention is in fact carried on at the level of the last two categories and that discussion of current patterns of interpersonal functioning is likely to be more central (see p. 141). Hollis' book is widely used on social work training courses, and indicates the role which insight may be considered to play in current social work practice, though the above categories are only concerned with the content of casework *interviews*, and other important aspects of intervention concerned, for example, with altering the client's environment, are not included in it.

The assimilation of psychoanalytic theory into the social work field came more slowly in Britain. Even so, Elizabeth Irvine, writing in 1956, described it as leading to a period of renaissance, and maintained that psychoanalysis had a major contribution to make to the solution of the problems encountered by the social worker (Irvine 1956a). The inculcation of psychoanalytic theory has come about in various ways, through the teaching of psychodynamic psychology on training courses, particularly of a generic type, and through courses of advanced casework training such as that provided at the Tavistock Clinic since 1951. Textbooks in current use often use either an explicitly psychoanalytic framework or draw upon analytic theories and concepts (Ferard and Hunnybun 1962, Hollis 1964.) Two important papers which refer to insight-oriented techniques derived from psychoanalysis are 'Transference and Reality in Casework Relationship' (Irvine 1956b) and 'The Function and Use of Relationship in Psychiatric Social Work' (Goldberg 1953).

Because of the past concentration on the therapeutic aspects of casework (and in particular on insight as the primary means of modification and change) interpretation has, particularly among analytically oriented caseworkers, enjoyed a special prestige. In the last ten years this imbalance has been subjected to a good deal of critical scrutiny and a more balanced view of the place of insight is beginning to emerge. Margaret Brown pointed out (1964) that the essence of casework skill lay in appropriately meeting a wide range of needs through a wide range of activities rather than in depth of interpretive skill. 'Skill in casework,' she wrote, 'does not lie in the use of a small range of techniques directed towards the development of insight in the client, though this does demand skill of a kind, but in the careful assessment of the social situation, personality structure, stage of development and sources of anxiety of each individual and then in the sensitive, discriminating application of appropriate methods of help. Depending on the needs of the client we may at various times be warm or detached, active or passive, directive or permissive, verbal or silent, moralistic or non-judgmental in our approach.' (p. 34.)

Her view was generally (though not wholly) supported by Elizabeth Irvine, who in an important paper in 1964 finally laid this particular ghost. There she recognised that interpretation, because of its intensive study by analysts, had tended to emerge as the figure against a ground of 'simple supportive and directive work'. She conceptualized casework at that time as a continuum of responses ranging from interpretation to largely non-verbal interaction in terms of practical help, gifts, loans and so on. 'If we look at it this way, we by-pass all those meaningless discussions about whether casework can be combined with the exercise of authority or the giving of practical and material aid. Casework becomes a total interaction within which action is seen to have an aspect of non-verbal communication, and words to be one of the many forms of helpful activity.' (p. 40.)

The present emphasis is therefore very much on the differential application of a broad range of helping procedures, and Elizabeth Irvine, while particularly interested in the appropriate use of interpretation, which she sees as well adapted to the needs of neurotic clients, has also been concerned to develop an account of casework which is sufficiently broad to be appropriate to very different types of clients and need.

The current direction is towards a broadly based professional social work role which includes the use of group, community and even political methods. This kind of conceptualization has rendered obsolete the earlier narrow identification of social work with a clinically-oriented treatment role and has resulted, in some quarters at least, in a more sociological orientation, in which therapeutic concepts such as insight are no longer central.

The Extent of Insight-oriented Procedures in Casework

This discussion has drawn mainly on theory, and there is not a great deal of evidence as to what actually happens in social work interviews in Britain, nor the role which insight in fact plays as a treatment goal. A recent study by Mayer and Timms (1969) noted that there is 'a pervasive, although possibly decreasing, tendency in the field of social work to rely on psychodynamic concepts in explaining behaviour. As a consequence, cognitive elements (beliefs, thoughts, opinions) receive little attention and are apt to be viewed as epiphenomena, as derivatives of something deeper, and therefore unlikely to produce any decisive effects of their own on behaviour.' (p. 38.) This tendency was evident in the workers' predilection for methods involving the development of insight in their clients, regardless of whether or not this fitted the client's own definition of his problem and expectation of help, or of its appropriateness to working-class as opposed to middle-class clients. These workers were very much concerned, in fact, with psychological insight as a primary treatment aim. This study was concerned with an agency generally regarded as psychodynamic in orientation, and this may to some extent explain the discrepancy between Mayer and Timms' findings and those of recent work in the United States, which suggests that casework is *not* generally concerned with promoting insight, at least in the sense that the psychoanalyst understands it.

In Hollis' analysis of fifteen marital cases two significant tendencies emerged:

1. The psychotherapeutic role envisaged for caseworkers in papers such as that of Austin in the 1940's was not characteristic of this small group of cases. A very small part was played in the interviews by either reflection on personality patterns or early life experience. The communications of worker and client for those two categories E and F) did not exceed an average of 2.6% per interview. There was very little F material, and in seven of the fifteen cases, none at all.

2. By far the greatest proportion of client communications fell in category C (description–ventilation) and of worker communications in either C or D (reflective consideration of the client–situation configuration). In all a third of the verbal content was directed to the development of understanding of the client's current person–situation gestalt.

Hollis concluded that her study 'clearly shows that in so far as the third to fifth interviews can be inferred to be typical of the total casework treatment process, emphasis is, as predicted, on description–ventilation and on reflection concerning the here and now rather than on the study of general personality dynamics and causation in terms of early development. It also supports the hypothesis that a small amount of the latter two is undertaken in a wide range of cases and suggests that this type of treatment very infrequently reaches major proportions. It also suggests that those who criticize caseworkers for preoccupation with the internal dynamics of the personality may be unfamiliar with the true nature of casework treatment.' (Hollis 1968a p. 43).

Although these findings related to a small and unrepresentative sample, they are supported by three other studies (Mullen 1968, Pinkus 1968, Reid 1968), using the Hollis or a similar classification. Again the proportion of E and F communications was small. Table 3 summarizes their findings.

In Reid's research carried out at the Centre for Social Casework Research, the tendency noted by all these investigators emerges very clearly; there was very little emphasis in casework interviews on helping the client to gain awareness of his patterns of behaviour beyond the limits of specific roles. Most of the communications were directed at helping the client understand the roles of family members, and the interaction between them (Reid 1968). The similarity between these findings is very striking and throws new light on the objectives and techniques of casework intervention. In general it appears that caseworkers deal with conscious or relatively easily recalled material, and

Table 3—*Distribution of Social Worker Communications in Interviews (Mullen 1968)*

Treatment Procedure	Proportion of Worker Communication			
	Mullen	Hollis	Reid-CSS	Pinkus
Sustainment: A	·027	·081	·043	·050
Direct Influence: B	·052	·036	·040	·015
Exploration–Description– Ventilation: C	·368	·398	·463	·508
Person–Situation Configuration: D	·459	·457	·354	·313
Personality Reflection: E	·005	·013	·014	·050
Early Life Reflection: F	·014	·015	·020	·016
Other	·073	—	·066	·048
TOTAL	·998	1·000	1·000	1·000

discussion in the casework interview tends to be of a kind which explores, describes or reflects upon the client's current situation and relationships, without attempting to illuminate his present behaviour in terms of infantile and unconscious determinants.

The particular purpose of social casework is to 'help people who are suffering from some impairment or breakdown in their adequate social functioning and to restore, reinforce or enhance the performance of their daily life tasks'. (Perlman 1960.) To do this the caseworker operates predominantly on a reality level and concerns himself with current life situations and interpersonal relationships, and not primarily (as a psychotherapist would) with unconscious conflicts or the sources of psychopathology. In general then, the social worker, in so far as he is trying to promote insight, is likely to be concerned with it in a general psychological, rather than a specifically psychoanalytic, sense, though there are, of course, social workers operating in psychiatric or psychoanalytically-oriented settings (for instance, the Institute of Marital Studies at the Tavistock Centre) to whose work analytic theories and concepts are directly applicable. This work, however, demands training and skills far beyond those normally acquired in a first professional course.

THE ROLE OF INSIGHT IN BEHAVIOUR CHANGE

The importance attached to the development of insight in casework appears to have two quite distinct foundations. The first is an ethical and ideological one, the second pragmatic. Insight, for social workers, was an ethically welcome alternative to the paternalistic and authoritarian methods used in the early days of casework. Whereas the giving of advice or direction implies a belief on the part of the worker that he knows better than his client what is good for him, and thus a certain arrogance, insight oriented casework is based on the assumption that the client can work out his own solutions, given a greater measure of understanding. It thus appears less derogatory to the dignity of the person seeking help, since it seeks to emphasize rather than diminish his independence and responsibility as a human being. This belief in individual worth and dignity is a crucial value in social work, and part of the appeal of insight and evocative approaches it is ineffective in achieving change, at least in relation to About the moral values underlying this approach to treatment, psychotherapeutic research has, of course, nothing to say.

The second reason for the emphasis on insight is that it is believed to be more effective than, for example, behavioural or directive methods. This is a question which can be subjected to empirical investigation. Unfortunately, there is little evidence from the social work research field which has bearing on this point, though such studies as have been made of the effectiveness of casework and counselling have not given grounds for great optimism (Meyer 1965). Work from the psychotherapeutic field is, however, much more extensive and has a direct bearing on the casework process in so far as this also depends for its efficacy on the use of psychological methods.

The concept of insight has been fundamental to most traditional psychotherapeutic approaches, which, whether Freudian, analytically-oriented, Sullivanian, or simply eclectic, have all stressed the development of consciousness or awareness by the patient into aspects of his motives or behaviour which were previously hidden from him. Underlying this is the assumption that behaviour, and especially neurotic behaviour, is significantly motivated, but in ways not apparent to the patient himself. The development of insight is regarded as a necessary condition of therapeutic change, and many of the techniques of the therapeutic interview are designed to facilitate the acquisition of insight, through interpretation, or exposure to the patient of what he is doing, albeit unconsciously, in the therapeutic situation. Insight has thus been considered an essential goal, and thought to result in greater understanding and control of previously 'blind', irrational or compulsive behaviour.

Here, however, comes the crunch. Not only, as we have demonstrated, is the *concept* of insight extremely ill-defined, but the *process* by which it is thought to mediate change is equally inexplicit. Indeed, a forthright critic of insight therapies such as Bandura would claim that not only has the assumption that insight leads to change never been validated, but that the evidence increasingly suggests that by comparison with other therapeutic approaches it is ineffective in achieving change, at least in relation to specific and comparatively isolated conditions such as phobias.

The attacks on psychodynamic or insight therapies have come in the main from those concerned with the application of strategies of behavioural change based on theories of learning. Although a full account of these strategies is given in earlier chapters, it will be useful here to contrast briefly the approaches of what London (1964) has designated 'Action' and 'Insight' therapists.

Behavioural and Psychodynamic Approaches: 'Action' and 'Insight'

Although the term 'behavioural' refers simply to the systematic application of knowledge drawn from any field of experimental psychology, much of this work derives from learning theory and is based on the premise that a neurotic 'symptom' is learned behaviour which can be eradicated by extinguishing or re-educative procedures. Exponents of this approach do not exclude the possible infantile origins of, for example, phobias, but would hold that what is important is the extent to which the original trauma has been reinforced or modified by subsequent learning. The psychodynamic view is that the symptom points to an underlying unconscious conflict and can only be adequately treated through the resolution of this conflict; if the symptom is treated directly, the conflict will simply manifest itself in some other way, through a process of symptom-substitution.

For the behaviourist as well as for the dynamic therapist, a crucial concept is that of anxiety. Much behaviour therapy is designed to eliminate anxiety and its accompanying maladaptive responses, but the *origin* of the anxiety is relatively unimportant. The psychodynamic approach differs in that the origin is *all*-important and is seen to lie predominantly in early relationships or childhood events, of which the anxiety condition is a symptom or (as in Freud's case of little Hans' phobia of horses) a symbolic representation. Thus cure can come only through the genetic reconstruction of the unconscious conflict causing anxiety. In practice these different theoretical accounts of the nature of the anxiety lead to different therapeutic strategies. The behaviourist is likely to attempt directly to reduce the patient's fear; the insight therapist will attempt to understand, and to help the patient understand, the underlying reasons for his fear, in order to eliminate it in this indirect way. The insight therapist would in general consider that, while some forms of neurotic behaviour *are* simply learned responses which can be extinguished through behavioural methods, this is much too simple a view of most neuroses which he would regard as reflections of far more fundamental and pervasive emotional difficulties. His interest is therefore less in the symptom than the person with the symptom. For such a therapist, the presenting symptom may quickly lead on to an exploration of the total personality of the patient. Storr discusses the problem of agoraphobia, which he sees as linked with a persistent childhood dependence characteristic of the patient's whole adaptation to life, rather than as merely a difficulty in being alone in an open space. From his discussion it must be obvious, he writes, 'that the study of a phobia may, and often should, lead to a consideration of the patient's whole personality and relations with other people; and that abolition of the single symptom of agoraphobia, even if this were possible, would not relieve the patient of the bulk of her emotional problems' (Storr 1966, p. 57). The majority of phobias, he maintains, 'do not spring from isolated traumatic incidents, but are intimately connected with the patient's style of life and his whole development from childhood onwards' (p. 56).

While much of the work referred to here relates to clinical practice, caseworkers also encounter severe anxiety and its manifestations, for instance school or situational phobias, and they may use different conceptual models and, therefore, different strategies in attempting to treat them. An interesting example of a social worker helping an agoraphobic client through reducing her anxiety and helping her to acquire new skills in social situations is described by Heimler (1962, pp. 171-8, 'Joan'). Though not explicitly analysed as a learning process, his way of helping his client seems to be more readily explicable in behavioural than in psychodynamic terms.

The behaviourist makes two main criticisms of insight therapies. The first has to do with the validity of psychodynamic hypotheses, and is based on a scepticism about the therapeutic value of insight into determinants of behaviour which lie in the past and which are inferred and not directly observable. The second questions the traditional belief in the necessity of insight as a condition of therapeutic change and the neglect of strategies based on other theoretical accounts of the origin of neurotic symptoms. These will be dealt with in turn.

On the first point Bandura (1969) conceives the psychotherapeutic process as one of social persuasion rather than genuine self-discovery, and contends that psychotherapeutic patients are highly amenable to influence of this kind. In his view, the psychotherapeutic process is to be seen as one in which the patient progressively accepts the therapist's opinions in place of his own ideas about himself, and the higher the prestige of the therapist, the more likely is the patient to change his self-attitudes to accord with the therapist's interpretations, even where these are erroneous. There is ample evidence, he maintains, 'that psychotherapists selectively reinforce conformity to their own opinion about the causes of behaviour, and that clients can readily secure their therapists' appreciation and approval by reiterating the appropriate insights.' (p. 98.) In Bandura's view, therefore, 'Insight into the presumed psychic determinants of interpersonal responses is of questionable validity and has little effect on behaviour', and what effect it has is to be attributed to a conversion process, in which the client adopts the therapist's point of view. 'Reports that clients have achieved self-awareness generally mean, in behavioural terms, that clients have learned to label social stimulus events, past and present causal sequences, and their own response in terms of the predilections and language of their therapists.' (p. 94.) It should be noted that 'labelling' does not necessarily have a negative connotation, and can have a positive function in that language allows for foresight and symbolic rehearsal of future behaviour, and plays an important role in cognitive learning. There is evidence that changes in verbal behaviour (verbal conditioning) do occur in psychotherapy, but the evidence for generalization to non-verbal behaviour in the natural environment is slender (Bandura 1969, pp. 258–9). This is closely related to the problem of insight, since an insight expressed verbally within the therapeutic situation is only of therapeutic value if it is translated into altered behaviour outside it—a problem of which most psychotherapists are only too well aware.

On the second point the evidence for the effectiveness of a behavioural approach in relation to specific clinically definable conditions is certainly impressive, and good summaries of the current position can be found in Bandura (1969) and Meyer and Chesser (1970). This research undoubtedly presents a formidable challenge to insight therapies, which so far have been unable to claim anything like comparable results. There are also other difficulties in examining the role of insight; in particular, how far is it a sole or necessary precondition of change? Further, how is 'true' and effective insight to be distinguished from that which is 'false', or merely intellectual understanding? Hobbs (1962) points out that insight is often defined in psychotherapy ex post facto, in that if change occurs, the insight was genuine and if not, it was false. But there are many instances where insight of itself, however complete, seems to have little effect on behaviour. In Hobbs' view, insight is to be seen as the result rather than as a condition of change, and as relief of difficulties and problems occurs, insight as to their causation may develop. Therapeutic change may therefore occur quite independently of insight. A similar view is put forward by Alexander and French (1946), namely, that insight is to be regarded as a consequence rather than a cause of change. A case in which insight developed after considerable improvement had already occurred is described by Melitta Schmideberg (1965, 1967), that of a school teacher whom she treated for exhibitionism. 'In this case,' she writes, 'insight into the past came several years after treatment stopped. Whether a cured patient develops insight spontaneously, or prefers to forget, depends largely on the type of personality and cultural background. In treating this patient, I have tried, in the main, to reorientate his values, develop his self-control, teach him how to handle himself and those around him and to show confidence in his ability to do so as well as some personal concern.' Storr (1966) acknowledges also that while psychoanalysis does bring insight it is uncertain how far insight either relieves distress or modifies behaviour. Insight of itself, Storr believes, is insufficient; he no doubt has in mind here the educative role of the analyst implicit in Jung's well known view that every neurosis involves, at root, fundamental ethical problems, and unless these are faced openly and decisively with a sense of responsibility, no cure can come about. (Jung 1933, p. 223; Jung 1949.)

So far we have been considering the criticisms made of insight therapies. But there is also systematic evidence that awareness can be a potent factor in facilitating learning and change, though not necessarily a sole or sufficient one; its role however appears to be complex and not yet fully understood. The comparative neglect of insight and of cognitive and symbolic processes in the literature of behaviour therapy has been pointed out by several authors (London 1964, Meyer and Chesser 1970, Peterson and London 1965) as a significant omission. In the main, behaviour therapists 'condition, extinguish, sensitize, desensitize, train and retrain their subjects in exclusive reference to behavioural functions. There is little or no emphasis on comprehension, understanding, hindsight, foresight, or insight in any of their work.' (Peterson and London 1965, p. 289.) Insight as there used has not of course the technical meaning assigned to it by the psychoanalyst, who relates it particularly to unconscious processes, but refers rather to 'reasonably accurate knowledge of the origins and consequences of one's own behaviour'. Bandura prefers to use the term 'awareness', defined as correct verbalization of response-reinforcement contingencies, but it is clear that despite linguistic differences this is not something wholly other than the insight of dynamic psychotherapy. Such awareness may operate in a number of ways. The sheer provision of accurate information may correct a false and erroneous belief and bring about considerable change in behaviour; prejudice, for instance, may be diminished by new information which challenges the prejudiced belief. And in human beings (pre-eminently capable of rational and purposive action) comprehension of a situation, knowledge of cause and effect sequences, and of one's own behaviour and its consequences, may have a dramatic effect on manifest behaviour. Thus to ignore the role of insight is just as mistaken as to restrict attention wholly to it. It would seem that the relative neglect of insight by behaviour therapists until recently has occurred partly in reaction to the over-emphasis on it in traditional psychotherapy, and partly because of their pre-occupation with directly observable behaviour, particularly in laboratory studies of animals.

As Bandura notes, the potential of symbolic factors for therapeutic change has not been fully exploited, although classical behaviour therapy procedures rely heavily on cognitively-produced effects; for example, symbolic rehearsal of behaviour in imagination forms part of systematic desensitization and of some aversive techniques. Such imaginative rehearsal or fantasy is surely evidence of the powerful effects of symbolic arousal on manifest behaviour. Even so it would appear that the use made of higher-order processes in behaviour therapy is relatively unsophisticated by contrast with the wealth and richness of the human symbolic processes and inner mental experience portrayed in language and art.

Common Ground between Action and Insight Therapies

A few years ago the controversy between the two appeared to have led to a situation of irreconcilable conflict between mutually exclusive approaches (Mowrer 1969). But three areas are now emerging as of common importance. These are the increasing interest by behaviour therapists in the role of insight; the growing appreciation by psychodynamic therapists of the role of learning in therapy; and the concern of both with current adaptational problems. A fourth area of common importance, the therapeutic relationship, is considered in the next chapter.

As we have noted, behaviour therapists are now paying considerable attention to the role of psychological insight in the control of behaviour. The place for insight has been cogently argued by several authors not particularly sympathetic to psychodynamic theories of therapeutic change and it would appear that in behaviour therapy, increasing attention is currently being paid to cognitive factors in the therapeutic process and also to those aspects of behaviour which are unconscious. Insight is of particular importance where a distressing symptom is maintained because of the secondary and often unconscious benefits the patient derives from it, for example, in gaining the sympathy and attention of others. In such a case, a direct attack on a specific maladaptive response is likely to be ineffective unless the associated conditions are dealt with also. Partly for this reason, very careful diagnostic assessment is stressed by behaviour therapists and although psychodynamic language is not used, it is evident that the clinical phenomenon is no different from that described by analysts as 'secondary gain'. Similarly, both behaviour and insight therapists consider that anxiety plays a crucial role in the development of neurotic disorders, and that many neurotic conditions operate as defences against an underlying anxiety (Freud 1940, Meyer and Chesser 1970). Here the overt condition can be viewed as secondary.

Secondly, psychodynamic therapists are increasingly interested in learning factors in therapy, and in trying to distinguish differences which are primarily semantic from those which are fundamental and inescapable differences in orientation and technique. Wolf (1966) and Marks and Gelder (1966) have both attempted to find common ground between psychodynamic and behaviour theory, and in 1963 Alexander made an explicit re-interpretation of analytic theory in learning terms. The two approaches are not in fact as inconsistent as might at first appear. Reference has already been made to the emphasis in psychoanalysis on 'working-through' as an essential component in change, and this can be viewed as part of an educative process in which different adaptations are tried out in the therapeutic situation, with the acceptance and encouragement of the therapist. For example, the abnormally shy or diffident person is not only helped to understand *why* he is shy, but to try himself out in more assertive roles within and outside the therapeutic situation. When this occurs, direct influence is being brought to bear to achieve what to both therapist and patient is a mutually desirable end. Indeed Freud himself viewed analysis as, in part, 'after education'—interrupting and correcting the pattern of disturbed relationships begun in childhood. Thus he recognized the influence inherent in the transference situation, and acknowledged that the analyst serves as an authority and parental substitute, as well as teacher and educator, though he warned also against the analyst's misuse of this influence to try to create men in his own image (Freud 1940).

A third common factor is the concern of therapists with the present reality-situation of the patient. The aim of any therapy is to fit the patient for life, not to pursue insight for its own sake. This is particularly stressed by Alexander (1963). 'The understanding of the past should always be subordinated to the problems of the present. Therapy is not the same as genetic research. Freud's early emphasis upon the reconstruction of past history was the result of his primary interest in research. The interest in past history at the expense of the present is the residue of the historical period when research in personality dynamics of necessity was a prerequisite to developing a rational treatment method.' (p. 443.) Alexander in fact sees one of the great dangers of analytic treatment as a tendency to get stuck in the past while evading the adaptive issues of the present. A somewhat similar view was expressed by Melitta Schmideberg in the letter already quoted on 'The Relevance of Insight'. Formerly a noted psychoanalyst, she states: 'Modern psychotherapy is dominated by the belief that "insight", and in particular remembering the past, is the most important curative factor ... Slowly over the years I have come to the conclusion that neither "insight" nor "working-through" the past or unconscious phantasies are the most relevant therapeutic agents and that dwelling too exclusively on pathology and evoking unhappy memories does more harm than good. It seems more likely that the attachment to the therapist, utilized for clinical-socializing aims, is what matters. Occasionally, such discussions of the past may help to gain this attachment, but are effective only if used for this purpose. Often, however, such attachment may be gained more effectively by helping the patient with his immediate problems.' (1967). While this may be an expression of an extreme view (of which the statement by Hanna Segal above represents the opposite extreme) it is consonant with current research findings, particularly those of the Rogerian school, which will be further discussed below. The concern with current adaptational problems is particularly characteristic of psychoanalytic ego-psychology, which is now the dominant analytic orientation in American social work training. As Boehm has pointed out, the psychology of the ego, concerned as it is with reality perception and with the relation of the individual to his environment, as well as to his own instinctual make-up, is particularly apposite for a social work which is concerned with social functioning and the restoration of impaired capacity for role performance (Boehm 1958).

To conclude, although social work has leaned heavily on psychodynamic theory and on the strategy of change (i.e. insight) for which this provides the rationale, factors associated with a learning approach are being taken into account in recent social work writing (Jehu 1967, Jehu and Sluckin 1970, Thomas 1967) which offer new possibilities for effective helping. This provides a useful addition to social work method, though psychological insight will undoubtedly continue to play an important part in strategies of casework intervention and should not be undervalued. The type of insight which is directly related to bringing about some change in behaviour may be understood either in terms of cognitive psychology, or in terms of psychodynamic theories. While the second has been particularly influential in social work, the kind of cognitive insight which is related to problem-solving in the here-and-now appears to play an important role in actual casework practice, though it has been sadly neglected in theoretical accounts. Since the knowledge base of social work must relate to professional practice, it is important that the concept of psychological insight should not be understood in an exclusively psychodynamic sense but should be expanded to include those more cognitive aspects discussed above.

6

The Helping Relationship

Perhaps no other concept has received such attention in the social work literature or appeared with such frequency as that of 'the relationship'. Perlman (1960) defines this as 'a condition in which two persons with some common interest between them, long-term or temporary, interact with feeling' (p. 65) whether this feeling be of warmth and attraction or of antagonism. Not only is the help the social worker has to offer mediated through a personal relationship, so that this can facilitate or hinder the problem-solving process, but relationship and interaction with others is in itself essential to psychological growth. Relationship has therefore an intrinsic as well as an instrumental significance. 'That is why,' writes Perlman (1960), 'the casework process, like every other process intended to promote growth, must use relationship as it basic means. The labours of mind and body involved in problem-solving may feel less arduous when they take place within the warmth and security of a strong relationship; the will to try may be spurred and sustained by th helpfulness and hopefulness it conveys; and far below the surface of con sciousness the person may absorb from him to whom he feels related that sens of oneness and yet of separate worth which is the foundation of inner security and self-esteem.' (p. 65). Thus a good deal of stress has been placed on th expressive aspects of the social work relationship and its sustaining or suppor tive function, and indeed, a great deal of the interaction which takes plac between client and worker appears to be of this supportive kind (Hollis 1968).

The concept of the professional relationship is not of course of exclusive concern to social work, but is one which it shares with many other helping professions, notably teaching, psychotherapy and the ministry. None the less, a remarkable amount of social work writing has been devoted to a consideration of this concept (Ferard and Hunnybun 1962, Perlman 1957). In training it is a central concern, and on many British training courses at the present time the neophyte social worker will cut his teeth on 'The Casework Relationship (Biestek 1957). In the foreword to that work, Biestek claims that 'the unique importance of the professional interpersonal relationship between the person seeking help from a social agency and the caseworker is universally recognized in contemporary practice. The relationship is the soul of social casework. It i the principle of life which vivifies the processes of study, diagnosis and treatment and makes casework a living, warmly human experience. It would b hard to exaggerate the importance of the relationship in casework, not only because it is essential to effective casework, but also because it is the practical living out of our basic convictions about the value and dignity of the human person. It is based upon a philosophy of life which is both realistic and idealistic, which encompasses matter and spirit, reason and faith, time and eternity.' Foremost among the many skills the student will be expected to acquire during training is the ability to establish and use constructive working relationships, even in adverse situations or with reluctant or antagonistic clients. Much of his fieldwork teaching will be concerned with this, and should he fail in this essential skill, no amount of knowledge, intelligence or practical ability will compensate. Practical experience in social work education indicates the preoccupation of students with the professional relationship—the extent to which it is to be distinguished from friendship, how far it is compatible with the exercise of authority, and in what ways it implies detachment or emotional distance, all issues which have been examined in recent publications (Foren and Bailey 1968, Timms 1968).

It is the purpose of this introduction simply to indicate the crucial importance which some foremost exponents of social work (more especially casework) practice have assigned to the concept of relationship rather than to examine what they say about it. But although its importance has been acknowledged since the days of Octavia Hill, it is difficult to discuss without imprecision, sententiousness or a kind of quasi-mysticism (from which the above quotations are not exempt). As Eileen Younghusband has succinctly expressed it in her introduction to the British edition of Biestek (1961), 'Attempts to describe or analyse the nature of the relationship between persons and the use of this relationship by the social worker to help the client are beset with pitfalls. On the one hand they may sound like sentimental waffle or wishful thinking, or attempts to give high-sounding titles to simple processes; while on the other hand those who struggle with this task are sometimes accused of cold dissection or an indifferent detachment from the urgent sorrows of men.' Given this, one might expect to find at the very least a certain confusion in social work writing on relationship, a confusion which critics have not been slow to expose (Wootton 1959).

The major criticism which has been levelled at social workers, however, is not their confusion about what a helping relationship is, nor their imprecision in its conceptual analysis, but that they are preoccupied with it at all. In the view of Sinfield (1969) the concern with the expressive component in social work has led to a devitalizing of the action-oriented instrumental role which he conceives as proper for the social worker of today, and like Wootton (1959) he would prefer social workers to be a little less high-minded and rather more effective. These general criticisms cannot receive detailed discussion here, and we must confine ourselves to noting that they have undoubted validity. In selection for training it seems likely that the personality attributes of intuition, responsiveness and understanding have in the past been over-emphasized to the detriment of the more assertive and active qualities necessary to the exercise of

—BM • •

authority, problem-solution, and effective social action. The concern with this last aspect in the current literature, however, suggests that this balance is at least being corrected, if not swung the other way. For this reason, it is important to recognize that research in psychotherapy has become increasingly concerned with relationship factors and the results suggest that the traditional concern with this in the helping professions has been well-founded. If we neglect this aspect in favour of an exclusively action-oriented role, we are in danger of demolishing the scientific foundations on which social work practice can be solidly grounded. The remainder of this chapter will be concerned with the consideration of some of this research and what it can contribute in a scientific way to the understanding and analysis of relationship. Inevitably this discussion will smack of 'cold dissection', but its implications for social work education and practice are of profound importance.

The Psychotherapeutic Relationship

Different psychotherapeutic schools lay emphasis on different therapeutic factors—conditioning, insight, self-actualization—but a new convergence of therapeutic interest emerges very clearly from recent research. This focuses on the centrality of the relationship as a crucial factor in the therapeutic process, no matter what the theoretical orientation of the therapist, and the importance, for good or ill, of the therapist's own attitudes and personality. At the centre of therapy is a continuing interpersonal interaction which profoundly affects the outcome of the whole process. After reviewing the evidence, Goldstein et al. (1966) conclude that there is wide agreement on the centrality which must be accorded the therapeutic relationship in the overall therapeutic transaction, though there is disagreement as to the specific nature and implications of this relationship (p. 75).

Psychoanalytic therapy has long been concerned with *transference*, those distortions of the patient's perception of his analyst which the patient brings to therapy, and which give rise to powerful and irrational emotional responses. The exposing of these distortions and tracing them back to their roots in the past (notably to the patient's relationship with his parents) is a basic component of all analytic treatment. The essential features of transference reactions are that they are repetitions of the past and that they are inappropriate to the present (Greenson 1965). Increasingly, however, the analytic relationship has been recognized as a highly complex interactional process between two people in which the therapist's own emotional reactions and personality may be as significant as those of the patient. Thus in psychoanalysis there has been a renewed interest in the therapeutic significance of the *counter-transference*, first discussed by Freud in 1895 (see Sandler 1970b, Szasz 1963, Zetzel 1956).

Attention has also been directed to the *non-transference* or reality elements in the therapeutic relationship (Greenson and Wexler 1969, Irvine 1956b, Szasz 1963). Alexander (1963) stresses the significance of the difference between the old family conflicts and the actual doctor–patient relationship, which allows a 'corrective emotional experience' to take place, and regards this as the cardinal therapeutic factor. The therapist's present response to the patient's emotional problems (which is different from the response of the patient's parents in the past) allows the maladaptive emotional patterns to be altered and brought under the control of the ego. Similarly, in a paper given to the International Congress of Psychotherapy in 1964, Ronald Laing (who has been influential in social work in this country) pointed out that while the distinctive contribution of psychoanalysis has been its illumination of the carry-overs from the past distorting current relationships, and the insight into this which the patient can gain through analysis of the transference, none the less, the tendency is increasingly 'to focus not only on transference, not only on what has happened before, but on what has never happened before, on what is new. Thus, in practice, the use of interpretations to reveal the past, or even to reveal the past-in-the-present, may be used as only one tactic and, in theory, there are efforts to understand better and to find words for the *non*-transference elements in psychotherapy.' (Laing 1964, pp. 39-40.) The psychotherapist is primarily a human being, and only secondarily a psychological expert. 'Psychotherapy,' Laing writes, 'must remain *an obstinate attempt of two people to recover the wholeness of being human through the relationship between them.*' (p. 45). Thus Laing shares with existential writers such as Rollo May a belief in an authentic encounter between patient and therapist as an inescapable feature of any constructive psychotherapeutic relationship.

Relationship has also received attention in psychotherapy research (notably by Goldstein 1962, Goldstein and Dean 1966, Goldstein et al. 1966 and by Strupp and others in a series of papers). It has long been recognized that the patient's expectations of his therapist can in themselves have a powerful effect on outcome. So also can the therapist's own expectations of the degree of improvement to be anticipated. 'The therapist, as a function of his life experiences, approaches each initial interview with needs, expectations, and wishes of his own . . . if his expectations are sufficiently realized, he will consider the situation as "rewarding", and a "warm" attitude towards the patient is likely to develop. More specifically, if in an initial interview the prospective patient approximates the therapist's conception of an "ideal patient", he may develop a warm attitude towards the patient.' (Wallach and Strupp 1960). Thus therapist and patient can both elicit positive or negative responses from each other, and the relationship can be seen as reciprocally contingent in nature. Goldstein et al. (1966) maintain that the therapist's attractiveness to the patient increases his influence over the patient and that this interpersonal attractiveness can be deliberately increased with consequent therapeutic gain (p. 73 ff.).

Relationship factors may also have been of significance in early outcome studies, such as those referred to by Eysenck (1960) in which treated (experimental) groups were compared with untreated (control) groups. Goldstein (1962) questions the whole concept of 'spontaneous remission' and argues that, even where no formal treatment is instituted, the attention the patient receives from psychiatrist, psychologist or social worker during the diagnostic phase may in itself have beneficial effects. The comparison, he suggests, is not therefore strictly between treated and untreated groups, but between those treated in formal psychotherapy, and those treated by a kind of informal non-specific therapy operating in the history-taking stages. This is somewhat similar to the classic 'Hawthorne effect' of social psychology; in the Hawthorne experiments, concerned with the effects of changes in illumination level on work output, the investigators found that output rose and was maintained at a high level, even when light conditions were reduced to approximately moonlight level. This somewhat startling finding was afterwards explained in terms of uncontrolled human relations factors which were operating unknown to and unrecognized by the researchers, and which countered the effect of the deliberately induced experimental variables. These human relations factors were the interest and friendly attention of the researchers, which contributed to an increased sense of morale and cohesion in the experimental workgroup. (Mayo 1933, Roethlisberger and Dickson 1939.)

Paul's (1966) study of the effects of three different procedures (desensitization, insight therapy and attention-placebo therapy) in the treatment of college students for performance anxiety produced some surprising findings which also point towards the importance of non-specific factors and give support to Goldstein's thesis. In his study the percentage of 'successful' cases ran at approximately 50% for both the insight and the attention-placebo groups. Relating these findings to the outcome studies discussed by Eysenck, Paul comments: 'Despite the acknowledged incomparability of all these studies, the relative consistency of results seems to be greater than chance; the gaining of insight from traditional eclectic or analytic psychotherapy does not appear to have been any more beneficial for neurotic individuals than the effects gained from the reassurance, suggestion, and support given by non-professional psychotherapists. In agreement with these findings, the present study, making use of the same criteria with the same amount of contact, and the same therapists, finds the same perecentage of "successful" cases for both insight and attention-placebo groups.' (pp. 73-4). The conclusion to be drawn, he suggests, is *not* that the comparison between the treated and untreated groups has little to do with the effectiveness of therapy, *nor* that psychotherapy is ineffective, but rather that traditional insight-oriented psychotherapy is no more efficient in bringing about change than the non-specific factors of attention, interest, etc. Paul's 'insight-therapy' consisted of only five sessions—hardly considerable enough to satisfy many practising therapists—but the study was well controlled. These findings give strong support to the importance of the therapist's sheer concern and attention, no matter what treatment is offered.

A study of treatment of habitual smokers by Koenig and Masters (1965), while it also found patients' rating of the personal characteristics of the therapist to be significant, provides a cautionary tale. Here the therapists were rated on intelligence, warmth, tolerance, liking of subject, attractiveness, helpfulness, skill and consideration of others. These factors were indeed significantly correlated with outcome at the conclusion of treatment, but in an *inverse* direction to that predicted. The more positively the therapist was seen, the less did the subject succeed in changing his smoking behaviour in the desired direction. In other words, the therapist who is attractive, warm, intelligent is not necessarily more effective as a therapist, and may even be less so.

In general, the behaviour therapy literature shows little interest in relationship factors, though the therapist is seen by Bandura (1969) as a powerful source of reinforcement in conditioning procedures and may also provide a model. Wolpe (1958), however, recognizes it as a common element in therapy and devotes considerable attention to 'interview-induced emotional responses'. He notes a 'strong clinical impression that patients who display strong positive emotions towards me are particularly likely to show improvement *before* special methods for obtaining reciprocal inhibition of anxiety are applied'. (p. 194). He quotes the case of Mr U, a thirty-year-old machinist who was very nervous about looking people, and particularly his boss, in the face. In this case, considerable improvement occurred during the history-taking interviews and before the therapist had undertaken any active specific therapy; in particular, he reported improvement in interpersonal situations and his fear of his boss had diminished. Wolpe comments that it is obvious 'that certain anxieties of great importance in his life had been overcome, apparently merely as a result of the patient having subjected himself to psychotherapeutic interview, without deliberate measures on the part of the therapist contributing in any way to the improvement.' (p. 195).

Meyer and Chesser (1970) include a discussion of current research bearing on this topic and acknowledge that relationship variables may affect the outcome of behaviour therapy, though their work is concerned primarily with the discussion of specific behavioural techniques. The therapeutic relationship is, by contrast with behavioural procedures, difficult to control for, and no doubt partly for this reason has not received very much attention in the behavioural literature, though Wilson et al. discuss in their 1968 paper the necessity for conceptual analysis of the factors involved in the therapeutic relationship in learning terms: for example, the control of behaviour through influence, placebo effect and other aspects touched on above. It has, however, in the past been one of the major criticisms of behaviour therapy that therapeutic gain is accounted for in terms of procedures which can be relatively easily measured, while the part played by factors which are less specific and difficult to control remains unclear. Meyer and Chesser suggest that such factors play a greater role in some types of treatment and with some types of patient than in others; for example, in patients with interpersonal anxiety, and in treatments using operant conditioning or modelling, the therapeutic relationship may play a larger role than it does in the desensitization of a patient with a monosymptomatic phobia. In their view, as systematic knowledge of the way in which relationship variables operate becomes available, this should be incorporated within the theoretical framework of behaviour therapy.

For some of the most illuminating discussion of the therapeutic relationship, however, we must look to the work of Carl Rogers and, more recently, Truax,

Carkhuff, Berenson and others. This work, which is of fundamental importance for social work education and practice, seems to have received scarcely a passing glance in British social work literature, although it has made considerable impact on the school counselling training programmes at Reading and Keele Universities.

Rogers considers far more important than technique or interpretation the interpersonal relationship between therapist and patient as the crucial therapeutic experience. It is the quality of this relationship, he holds, which is the significant factor in determining effectiveness and fostering growth and actualization. He had come to believe, he wrote in 1962, that 'the quality of my encounter is more important in the long run than is my scholarly knowledge, my professional training, my counselling orientation, the techniques I use in the interview'. (p. 154). It is the experiential nature of the relationship, facilitated (or obstructed) by the attitude of the therapist, which determines its value to the client. At that time, Rogers attempted to analyse those therapist/counsellor attitudes which facilitated growth and actualization in the client, and distinguished three. In the first place, the counsellor must be *congruent,* that is, he must be open and genuine, not hiding himself behind his professional role, but responding in a genuine human way. Essentially congruence involves being real, but it also implies the counsellor's ability to listen to, understand and accept his own feeling reactions in the interpersonal situation. The second condition is that of *empathy,* that the counsellor is sensitively and accurately tuning in to the client's private world, without an overlay of his own feelings of anxiety, hostility or fear getting in the way, so that he can communicate his understanding of what to the client may be only imprecisely recognized or understood. The third condition is *positive regard*, by which he means a 'warm, positive and accepting attitude towards what *is* in the client'. This is an essentially mature attitude which involves a genuine but non-possessive warmth, and the establishment of a relationship in which the client is significant simply as himself. Furthermore, this regard should be unconditional, in that it is non-evaluative, and is not withheld should the client express feelings of which the counsellor may himself disapprove.

To Rogers it is not the counsellor's skill in interpretation leading to insight which is the primary change factor but the creation of a *psychological climate conducive to growth.* Similarly, *failure* to provide these conditions may prove actually harmful. Rogers holds that 'A relationship characterized by a high degree of congruence or genuineness in the counsellor, by sensitive and accurate empathy on the part of the counsellor, by a high degree of regard, respect and liking for the client by the counsellor, and an absence of conditionality in this regard, will have a high probability of being an effective, growth-promoting relationship'. (Rogers 1962, p. 162). This has implications for social work training, since it emphasizes different factors from those generally stressed in psychoanalytically oriented therapy, namely, interpretation leading to insight. More especially, it highlights the fundamental importance of the counsellor's own personality and attitudes.

A considerable body of research has now been undertaken (Carkhuff 1967, Carkhuff and Berenson 1967, Truax and Carkhuff 1966) which supports the conclusion that these three core dimensions, together with a fourth, *concreteness* or specificity of expression or problem-solving, can be related to constructive change in all psychotherapeutic systems.

None of these dimensions is without difficulty and ambiguity, though they receive a somewhat more precise definition in Truax and Carkhuff's 1967 investigation. *Accurate empathy* 'involves more than just the ability of the therapist to sense the client or patient's "private world" as if it were his own. It also involves more than just his ability to know what the patient means. Accurate empathy involves both the therapist's sensitivity to current feelings and his verbal facility to communicate this understanding in a language attuned to the client's current feelings.

'It is not necessary—indeed it would seem undesirable—for the therapist to *share* the client's feelings in any sense that would require him to feel the same emotions. It is instead an appreciation and a sensitive awareness of those feelings. At deeper levels of empathy, it also involves enough understanding of patterns of human feelings and experience to sense feelings that the client only partially reveals.' (1967, p. 46). As Carkhuff has expressed it elsewhere (1969a, p. 36) an empathic response is one which adds significantly to the expressions of another person in such a way as to express accurately feelings several levels below what the other was aware of or able to communicate.

As regards the second condition, of *non-possessive warmth* or *unconditional positive regard*, Truax's (1966) study of Rogerian interviews shows that even Rogers was not as 'unconditional' as his writing suggests and that, in fact, the therapist's warmth was given selectively and therefore conditionally on the therapist's approval; for instance, patient responses indicating self-exploration, a problem-orientation, or discrimination about himself and his feelings (what Shapiro (1969) has called 'good' patient behaviour) tended to elicit such approval. Similarly, when the patient expressed himself in a style similar to that of the therapist, the therapist was more empathic, more warm and accepting, and less directing than if he expressed himself in a style different from that of the therapist. The selective use of empathy and warmth is therefore consistent with a behavioural view of psychotherapy as involving differential reinforcement. In a later work, Carkhuff appears to have modified considerably Rogers' original concept of 'warmth', and emphasizes that in using such terms as warmth and respect he is not indicating a passively receptive quality, nor is he equating it with 'unconditional positive regard' or 'non-retaliatory permissiveness' (1969a, p. 36). He is attempting to delineate rather an attitude of respect for the person as having significance, value and potential in himself, which is consistent with encouraging or disapproving of certain of his actions.

The concept of *genuineness,* or self-congruence, is again difficult to define accurately. It does not indicate that the therapist is acting non-professionally, but that his responses are sincere and without professional 'phoniness'; it does not mean overtly and freely expressing all he feels but avoiding the inauthenticity of denying his feelings or responding defensively. ' "Being himself" simply means that at the moment the therapist is really what his response denotes. It does not mean that the therapist must disclose his total self, but only that whatever he does show is a real aspect of himself, not a response growing out of defensiveness or a merely "professional" response that has been learned and repeated.' (Truax and Carkhuff 1967, p. 68 ff.).

Shapiro (1969) has reviewed the evidence and concludes that these three conditions are associated with good therapeutic results. Furthermore, experiments with training non-professionals as counsellors have shown that it is possible in comparatively short periods of time to train lay persons to demonstrate high levels of these conditions and provide constructive growth experiences for their clients (Truax and Carkhuff 1967). The approach therefore has promising practical implications.

Action-oriented Dimensions

The work described above is still developing. As already indicated, to the three Rogerian conditions a fourth has been added—specificity or concreteness in problem-solving. In a recent work (Carkhuff 1969b) a revised model of helping processes has been presented. To the facilitative dimensions of warmth and responsiveness are added dimensions which are more evidently action-oriented; these refer to the more active and assertive contributions in which counsellor rather than client takes the initiative, and which may involve specific suggestion, confrontation or direction. Both the facilitative components of sensitivity and responsiveness and the action-oriented, assertive components must be present in any effective helping relationship.

The helping process may be conceptualized as having two phases. First, a downward or inward phase, and second an upward or outward phase (Carkhuff 1969b, pp. 28 ff.). In the first phase, emphasis is on the client's self-exploration and experiencing; at this time the counsellor will concentrate more on the facilitative dimensions (empathic understanding, warmth, respect, concreteness). As the relationship becomes established and deepens, the way is open for the therapist to take more initiative, particularly in confronting the client with discrepancies in his behaviour. In the second phase, the action-oriented dimensions take on more significance, and the problems which brought the client are more directly addressed. 'Now we understand. What are we going to do about it?' This has been termed the phase of *emergent directionality*, in which there is concern with solutions to real life problems. In this phase, several possible modes of helping are open to the therapist, for example, the systematic use of behavioural techniques such as counter-conditioning, or modification of the environment to facilitate the client's actualization of his growth potential. This requires both good assessment ability and flexibility in the use of a wide range of treatment procedures on the part of the helper.

Some support for the validity of this model comes from Bierman (1968), who studied process movement along the two dimensions of active–passive and affectional–rejecting. Most therapists initially attempted to function in a passive-affectional manner, but those who moved from passive-affectional to an active-affectional mode of functioning had the most constructive effects. In addition, those who functioned initially most effectively in a passive-affectional manner moved in the direction of greater activity, whereas those who were least effective initially moved towards rejection, either active or passive. Only a few of the many possible dimensions have been examined in this way, but the work of Truax, Carkhuff et al. is providing solidly based foundations for a more scientific approach to helping troubled people. No doubt, further progress will be made along these lines.

This approach is eclectic and wedded to no particular theoretical account of the psychotherapeutic process, though the influence of Rogers is clearly strong. It is built upon a central core of conditions shared by all interview therapies, and on systematic research; but it is intended as a basis for therapy, not the last word in therapy, and acknowledges the distinctive contributions made by other systems and the significance of other additional dimensions. Lest it sound simple, it must be added that the role of the therapist emerges as a demanding one; not only must he be conversant with theory and research and himself skilled in interpersonal relations, but he must also be 'a fully functioning whole person'; unless he is this, he has no right to offer himself as a therapist, nor will he be effective.

The two-phase model is applicable to any form of interpersonal helping. But in social work the concern with insight and self-understanding has perhaps led to a preoccupation with the first, more passive of these phases. The Carkhuff model draws attention not only to the 'insight' but the 'action' component in any helping process, and reminds us that whatever our concern with a supportive relationship, this is only a means to an end, that is, the client's enhanced ability to function effectively in his environment and to cope with the reality problems which confront him.

Conclusion

As noted earlier in this book, social work has to a considerable extent drawn for its theoretical base on psychoanalytic theories and concepts. To this, the casework relationship is no exception, and attention has already been drawn to the discussions in Ferard and Hunnybun (1962), Hollis (1964 and Perlman (1957) which are psychoanalytically based. While we know of no author who has seen the casework relationship in purely analytic terms, or who has not been aware of the essential differences in function between therapist and social worker, it remains true that a great deal of the analysis of the caseworker–client relationship has been in terms of the analytic concepts of transference and counter-transference. In other words, this analysis has tended to be in terms of those distortions of perception or inappropriate reactions which derive from the past and are present to some degree in every object relationship. This has been the primary focus of analytic interest and interpretation ever since Freud's analysis of the Dora case (Greenson and Wexler 1969). Despite the more recent interest in the real or non-transference elements in the therapeutic relationship referred to above, the analysis of the transference remains crucial in the analytic situation; and indeed, for the Kleinian analyst, *every* interaction between patient and analyst is seen as transference or counter-transference (Greenson and Wexler 1969). The analytic model therefore focuses primarily on the infantile or neurotic elements in this interaction, and those authors who have given most attention to the nature of the more real personal encounter between analyst and patient (Fairbairn 1958, Laing 1964) may be regarded as somewhat outside the mainstream of analytic orthodoxy.

Further, Sandler (1970a) has demonstrated the dilutions and distortions which may occur when technical words developed within and specific to a particular clinical situation are transposed to other non-clinical contexts. For these and other reasons, we must be wary of adapting for social work use concepts appropriate to a very different situation and often precisely defined for use within it. Other concepts which have been transposed in this way, with unfortunate results, are those of *resistance* and *acting out*, both of which tend to be used very loosely in the social work literature; the first is often used to refer to any kind of opposition or reluctance on the part of the client, and the second to explain, usually inaccurately, any kind of aggressive behaviour.

In relation to casework–client interactions, therefore, the psychoanalytic model has severe limitations. The work of Carl Rogers and the client-centred school offers a different model stressing other dimensions, namely, therapist qualities such as warmth, acceptance, genuineness and empathy. In so far as the casework relationship includes a therapeutic element, it must take account of work such as this which has a solid research base.

Even so, however, analysis of any relationship in scientific terms alone must remain unsatisfactory and partial as a guide to action. Our conception of what is desirable in relationships between persons cannot depend solely on answers to such questions as, What is effective? or What is therapeutic? but on the value that is placed on human personality, and on our conception of the nature of man and of interpersonal encounters. This has to do with values and the ethical bases of action and goes far beyond the scope of scientific analysis. For a deeper understanding of relationship, therefore, social work needs to draw not only on the behavioural sciences, but on the more comprehensive view of man contained in the work of such writers as Buber and Tillich, whose concern is not with the client, the patient, the 'problem' or the deviant, but with man in his wholeness. This dimension, important as it is, must however lie outside the scope of our present concern with therapeutic change.

7

Ethical Implications of a Behavioural Approach

In this chapter some ethical issues arising from a behavioural approach in social work practice are considered. Discussion of the implications of a scientific, determinist view of human behaviour is followed by consideration of two major issues in the treatment situation—the choice of methods, particularly the exercise of influence and control by the worker, and the choice of goals to be achieved. Finally, some wider social implications are examined.

Freedom and Determinism in Human Behaviour

Much of the argument concerning the ethics of a behavioural approach revolves around the worker's attempt to be scientific. In addition to factual questions (which are outside the scope of this chapter) regarding the susceptibility of human behaviour to scientific study, it is frequently asserted that a scientific approach in this sphere is degrading and de-humanizing, and that strict cause–effect interpretations of behaviour leave no scope for questions of value, moral choice or moral judgment in human affairs. Whether the scientific study of anything can be regarded as by definition degrading is a matter of personal morality about which there can be little discussion. Anatomy and physiology were subject to similar criticism in their formative years and there are no doubt those who regard psychologists as the 'grave-robbers' of the twentieth century. Underlying the criticism of cause–effect theories of behaviour is the age-old controversy concerning determinism and freewill in human activity. The social worker adopting a behavioural approach, wedded inevitably to a determinist view, is criticized above all for apparently regarding people as machines to be programmed, manipulated and controlled at the will of the controller.

It is tempting in this context, though perhaps insufficient, to defend the determinist view by pointing out that traditional casework theory and practice is equally determinist, to the extent that it is founded on psychoanalytic theory. Freud would certainly have been sympathetic to the comment made by Skinner (1956), a leading exponent of behaviour control, that caprice is only another name for behaviour for which we have not yet found a cause.

This is not the place for a full discussion on the philosophy of determinism, but for our purpose two points might usefully be borne in mind. Firstly, determinism in this context should not be equated with fatalism, namely, the belief that whatever one does, Y consequences will follow. The determinist view is that *if* one does X *then* Y will follow—the individual is an integral part of the causal chain, not a helpless piece of driftwood in the tide of Fate. Secondly, physical laws do not *force* objects to behave in certain ways but merely *describe* how in fact they do behave under certain conditions. There is no need to postulate that psychological 'laws' compel us to act against our will.

The determinist view, briefly stated, is that behaviour, like all other events in nature, is lawfully related to antecedent and attendant events and that such relationships may be quantitatively described. Immergluck (1964) points out that this belief has been indispensable in liberating psychology from its metaphysical ancestry and in bringing it into the fold of natural science. Within this framework, there is no room for a concept of freewill, in the sense of an ability on the part of an individual to choose to act independently of his past and present conditions. It is, however, meaningful to talk of Brown having more freedom of action than Jones in a given situation, in the sense that Brown, by virtue of a more fortunate heredity and life history, has a wider range of alternative courses of action potentially available. Goldiamond (1963) argues that increasing an individual's freedom means, in behavioural terms, setting up conditions in which a wider range of response alternatives is available. Another aspect of 'freedom' within a determinist view is the recognition that a person's behaviour is a contributing factor to subsequent causal events—again, it is important to remember that not all the determinants of behaviour are external, in so far as there are internal processes within the individual, acting on and reacting to the environment.

There can of course be no final proof of either the freewill or the determinist viewpoints and philosophers have long since agreed that it makes sense to argue on questions of ethics and morals whichever view is adopted. In practice, social workers and others concerned with human welfare act as if their clients' behaviour were determined, and will find themselves increasingly compelled to do so as we move beyond the stage where the findings and methods of science are applied to human affairs only in a sort of remedial patchwork (Skinner 1956). Immergluck (1964) makes the point that our confusion arises only when we are unwilling to accept the logic of this approach and concede, rather grudgingly, the validity of a determinist view 'only up to a point'. Given that the individual's conception and birth at least are determined for him, at what point does 'freewill' emerge? We believe that schizophrenia is caused, and its causes are energetically sought; but, if schizophrenia is caused, why should healthy behaviour or creativity not be? The sense of professional inadequacy felt by social workers when unable to 'explain' or 'understand' their clients' behaviour implies a belief that all would be revealed to us if only we had more knowledge or skill.

Whichever viewpoint we adopt, we are faced with a paradox, well expressed by Carl Rogers (1961)—'In our pursuit of science we are fools if we do not assume everything that occurs is a portion of a cause-and-effect sequence, and that nothing occurs outside of that ... but ... if we adopt that point of view in our living as human beings, in our confrontation with life, then that is death.' (p. 575). In his discussion of this paradox, Immergluck distinguishes two levels of perception, the experiential and the experimental, which allow us simultaneously to feel free personally but to regard the behaviour of others as determined and explicable. He suggests that the feeling of freedom which we have in relation to our own behaviour is probably an illusion, but one which is necessary to our self-image, which appears to demand some feeling of inner spontaneity, a psychological conviction that one is not helplessly trapped by past and present circumstances, and that one can, after all is said and done, transcend one's own determining confines.

Control in the Treatment Situation

The preceding discussion on freewill and determinism, though superficial from a philosophical point of view, may be thought more prolonged than is necessary for the present purpose, but it is intended to prepare the ground for consideration of an aspect of the behavioural approach which perhaps more than any other comes under critical attack, namely, the degree of active control exercised in the treatment situation. As a preliminary, it may be as well to mention the more lurid arguments raised by some critics—that behaviour therapists are cold, unfeeling creatures, technicians rather than helping persons (why not both?), unconcerned for their patients as sentient, 'whole persons', and motivated consciously or unconsciously by a lust for power. Behaviour therapists are doubtless as fallible, personally and professionally, as other mortals but generalized fantasies of this kind, which perhaps say more about the critic himself than about the subject under discussion, contribute nothing to the debate. Clearly, the principles and procedures used in a behavioural approach can be employed to threaten human freedom and dignity or to enhance it therapeutically.

Within the treatment situation, two elements may usefully be distinguished—the choice of goals and the selection and application of procedures to achieve these goals. To take the latter topic first, the behaviourally-oriented worker attempting to bring about behaviour change appears to occupy a different world from the psychoanalyst, whose aim is to help release the patient's unconscious material into the realm of consciousness and to allow him to work out his own salvation. Equally remote, apparently, is the non-directive counsellor of the Carl Rogers school, who sees himself as providing a protected, accepting relationship within which the client may engage in self-exploration and self-actualization. Presented in these terms, it is not difficult to see why a behavioural approach is commonly regarded as coercive, manipulative and totalitarian; and why the more traditional approaches are thought to uphold the individual's right to self-determination, and the principles of Western democracy in general. There appears to be a clear choice between behaviour therapy as a means of control and psychoanalytic therapy as a means to freedom.

It follows from the discussion on determinism, however, that human behaviour is already under the control of a multiplicity of external and internal forces—it is not a question of the therapist imposing controls where none existed before. As Bandura (1969) puts it, 'All behaviour is inevitably controlled, and the operation of psychological laws cannot be suspended by romantic conceptions of human behaviour, any more than indignant rejection of the law of gravity can stop people from falling' (p. 85). The matter to be decided in the treatment situation is not *whether* behaviour is to be controlled but where the controlling forces lie and to what extent it is appropriate for the worker to assume some part in these forces.

The inevitability of influence in a therapeutic setting is well documented (Frank 1961). Kanfer (1965) identifies two features of psychotherapeutic interaction which make the patient especially vulnerable to manipulation or control; the patient's discomfort or distress, which create dependency in relation to the therapist, and the content of the therapist–patient interaction. A common element in all therapeutic interactions is the therapist's insistence that the patient should talk about private experiences, fears, attitudes and beliefs that are not normally shared with other people. As a consequence of such 'confession', the patient becomes increasingly vulnerable to control by the therapist. Privacy, which represents the bulwark of democracy in that it allows for variability and divergences in attitude and belief, is surrendered in the psychotherapeutic hour. An additional factor often overlooked in discussions of the ethical implications of behaviour control is that most people enter treatment only as a last resort, hoping to modify patterns of behaviour that are distressing to themselves and to others. Bandura (1969) suggests that therapists might often be better employed fretting over their own limited effectiveness in helping people than in agonizing and fantasizing about their potential powers.

Various writers have drawn attention to the fact that, although attempts by one individual to control the behaviour of another date back to the Garden of Eden, the last few years have seen a sudden increase in public concern over this issue, in such fields as advertising and propaganda. Two main reasons are suggested for this development: the greater effectiveness of present-day methods, and the trend away from negative and towards positive techniques of control. Skinner (1956) examines our failure to recognize the elements of control in such time-honoured social measures as education, moral discourse and persuasion. Such measures are felt to be acceptable in that they make only partial contributions to the control of behaviour and, to the extent that they are frequently ineffective, we may be able to convince ourselves that they do not represent control at all. Control measures which run the risk of being effective arouse our strong disapproval and are labelled 'propaganda', 'brainwashing' and so on.

On the second source of concern, the use of positive reinforcement, Kanfer

(1965) suggests that, if anything, there is more anxiety about positive controls than about our traditional, aversive controls such as threats, coercion and punishment. Aversive control may be less worrying because the person on the receiving end is aware of what is happening and may be able to adopt counter-measures; because aversive control is less easily imposed or maintained by a small group—the controllers have to be bigger, stronger or more numerous than the controlled; and because such measures affect only public behaviour and are of limited value in 'thought control'. Positive control does not have these limitations—people respond fairly easily to promises, rewards and reassurance, and may be expected to do so even more readily as techniques of control become more sophisticated and lose some of their amateurish, transparent quality. The experimental evidence is inconclusive at present but it seems possible for a person's behaviour to be modified without full awareness on his part of what is happening to him.

Those who oppose the use of reinforcement techniques on ethical grounds, even in situations where the patient knows and agrees to the procedure, argue that desirable behaviour should be intrinsically satisfying and that the deliber-ate use of reinforcement is an insult to the personal integrity of human beings, degrading them to the level of laboratory rats pressing levers for pellets of food. As Bandura (1969) points out, the fact that behaviour is strongly influenced by its consequences is not a phenomenon created by behavioural scientists, any more than physicists are responsible for the laws of gravity. (In passing, we might wonder whether it is similarly degrading to human dignity that people should be subject to the laws of gravity, just like rats.) For those who need it, there is comfort to be gained from the knowledge that where operant tech-niques are crudely applied, and the incentives are inappropriate to the indi-vidual's developmental level (for example, attempting to reinforce adult behaviour with pellets of food), the treatment is not just insulting but ineffective.

Confronted with recent research findings on interpersonal behaviour, it is hardly possible for psychiatrists and social workers of whatever school to continue to deny the high degree of influence and control which they exert, deliberately or otherwise, over their patients and clients. Carl Rogers, the apostle of the non-directive approach, has conceded that 'In client-centred therapy, we are deeply engaged in the prediction and influencing of behaviour, or even the control of behaviour. As therapists, we institute certain attitudinal conditions and the client has relatively little voice in the establishment of these conditions' (Rogers and Skinner 1956, p. 1063). However, one writer has attacked the behavioural approach for ignoring the potentially damaging effects of manipulation, not just on the patient but on the would-be manipulator too. 'The essential factor in the psychotherapeutic situation', he writes, 'is a loving, honest and spontaneous relationship between the therapist and the patient.' (Jourard 1959, p. 174). Faced with such a heart-warming picture, it was perhaps unkind of Krasner (1962) to remark that apparent spontaneity on the therapist's part may very well be the most effective means of manipulating behaviour. The therapist is an individual programmed by training into a fairly effective behaviour control machine—a machine which is most likely to be effective when it least appears to be one.

Rogers contends that non-directive therapy, of the kind he advocates, exercises a benevolent control which eventually leaves the patient under his own internal, 'self-actualized' control and no longer subject to the psychotherapist's influence. However, the proof of the therapy is in the outcome. Studies of people treated by Rogerian therapists have revealed that, far from being 'individuated' and 'self-actualized', these clients have been as thoroughly conditioned and converted to the belief system, jargon and interpretations of reality favoured by their therapists as are the products of Freudian or Jungian analysis to the orientation of their respective therapists (Truax 1966). It is known that the patients of Freudian or Jungian analysts have Freudian or Jungian dreams, as appropriate. One is reminded of those subjects of laboratory experiments who, while apparently engaging in 'free association', are prevailed upon quite unwittingly to specialize in uttering plural nouns in response to almost inaudible, but strategically-placed, grunts from the experimenter. 'Selective reinforcement' is not the exclusive preserve of those who talk about it.

The influence of the therapist does not stop short at the client's symptoms or overt behaviour but extends deep into the realm of values and beliefs. Most social workers would doubtless agree with Watson (1958) that to speak of a value-free or amoral therapy is a contradiction in terms. Psychotherapy, in its endeavour, in Watson's words, 'to make lost, unhappy and unproductive people able to lead more meaningful, more useful and more satisfying lives' (p. 574), is in itself a highly ethical undertaking. Even the most non-directive therapist would hardly allow his client to jump out of a skyscraper window in pursuit of self-realization if it were in the therapist's power to prevent this. What is less easily grasped by social workers, in so far as the idea clashes with accepted casework principles, is the extent to which the worker's own values may be communicated to and absorbed by the client. The study of Rogerian patients already mentioned is one example. Another, possibly more disturbing, is that by Rosenthal (1955) which showed that patients who were rated by their therapists as 'improved' moved significantly in the direction of the values held by their therapist; while patients rated as 'unimproved' moved equally significantly in the opposite direction. Clearly there is much food for thought in the apparently cynical definition of insight quoted by Carstairs in a recent symposium—'When psychiatrists describe a patient as having achieved insight, this simply means that the patient now agrees with the therapist' (Porter 1968, p. 133).

Uncomfortable though the idea may be for social workers, they are in a position of control over their clients, however partial and incomplete such control may be, and the first essential is to recognize the power and responsibility of that position. Recognition of the responsibility and of its serious implications for social work theory and practice is a difficult step to take, and it is hardly surprising that some workers, particularly those reared in the ideology of 'non-directiveness', seem tempted to solve the problem by denying its existence. It is hardly more satisfactory to recognize the fact of control but to renounce it in a therapeutic situation (an approach adopted by Rogers in theory though not, as we have seen, put into practice) in the hope that the client will himself take control. As Skinner commented in his famous debate with Rogers, 'Control passes not to a "self" but to forces in other parts of the client's world' (Rogers and Skinner 1956, p. 1065). This sentiment is echoed by Homme and Tosti (1965) in rather more technical language—'Either one manages the contingencies or they get managed by accident. Either way there will be contingencies, and they will have their effect.' (p. 16). The basic moral question for social workers, to quote Bandura (1969) again, 'is not whether man's behaviour will be controlled, but rather by whom, by what means, and for what ends' (p. 85).

Before turning to the question of ends or goals, it is perhaps appropriate at this point to mention two methods of treatment which are particularly singled out for attack because they represent the extremes of positive and negative control, the token economy regime and aversion therapy. Each method illustrates the commonplace observation that the consideration of means cannot be entirely separated from consideration of ends, insofar as the choice of means will determine to a greater or lesser extent the nature of the goals achieved.

The token economy method involves defining certain forms of inmate behaviour as desirable and rewarding these, as described in Chapter 2. Obviously this is open to the kinds of criticism on ethical grounds which have already been discussed in relation to positive reinforcement procedures in general. Here again, we are not faced with a straight choice between patients being controlled in a token economy ward or being left uncontrolled in an ordinary ward. Patients in psychiatric wards are already subject to control by means of a frequently unspecified (and unofficial) system of rewards and punishments from the ward staff. A common criticism of mental hospitals is that the kinds of behaviour rewarded tend to be those which are conducive, not to the patient's rehabilitation in the outside world but to 'good order' in the ward, and to passive, apathetic obedience on the part of the patient. Undoubtedly there is a risk of token economy measures being similarly distorted, though the fact that so much attention is paid to specifying explicit procedures and goals should provide some safeguard against such distortion. As a method of treatment, the token economy regime is in its infancy, with many technical problems to be solved. However, from an ethical point of view, provided that the regime is geared to preparing the patient for life outside, or at least to improving the quality of his life within the institution, it is difficult to see any convincing objection to its use.

Aversion therapy, in which the pain and discomfort of electric shock or induced nausea are applied in order to bring about behaviour change, is for many people a major stumbling-block to their acceptance of a behavioural approach. Indeed, some critics, whose superficial acquaintance with the subject has led them to regard behaviour therapy as nothing but aversion therapy, have felt compelled to dismiss behaviour therapy 'en bloc' as beyond the pale of permissible treatment methods in a civilized society. An ethical problem peculiar to aversion therapy is that the infliction of pain and suffering is deliberate and central to the treatment, not just an unfortunate side-effect as in the case of many medical and surgical measures. Many behaviour therapists will readily admit that aversive techniques are in some cases applied in an ethically objectionable manner that justifies the severest censure. Occasionally, exceedingly noxious procedures are employed which are out of all proportion to the demands of the situation and when a much lower intensity of suffering would achieve the desired results. Crude measures of this kind, Bandura comments, are inclined to instil in the patient an understandable aversion to therapy and therapists rather than to the condition which prompted the treatment. Rachman and Teasdale (1969), conscious of the very real dangers of aversion therapy, maintain that such methods should be used only with the full knowledge and consent of the patient and only if no alternative measures are available. Adoption workers, faced with the problem of assessing the degree of freedom available to a mother in consenting to her child's adoption, will echo the authors' anxiety over the validity of the patient's 'consent' in some situations. Rachman and Teasdale resist the notion of treatment under coercion—for example, in making parole dependent on the offender's willingness to undergo aversion therapy—and draw attention to the now well-established finding that people coerced into accepting treatment rarely respond well in any case. For many patients, of course, the brief discomfort occasioned by a programme of aversion therapy is minor compared to the repeated imprisonment, social disgrace, disruption of family life or indeed the self-condemnation which generally result from uncontrollable and injurious behaviour. In these circumstances, patients should at least be given the opportunity to choose.

The fact that at the particular moment in time there may be no alternative treatment in existence raises an ethical problem for wholesale opponents of aversion therapy—is it right to withhold the only available, effective treatment because it happens to be ethically uncongenial to the therapist? (Social workers are familiar with the parallel situation where a doctor refuses to recommend abortion or even to provide contraceptive help for a sick or over-burdened mother.) A case reported by Risley (1968) illustrates the ethical dilemma in a particularly dramatic form as the patient was a six-year-old psychotic girl who suffered many serious injuries from dangerous climbing activities which she engaged in continuously. In this case, where ironically the pain of therapy was considerably less than that of the self-inflicted injuries, aversion therapy was employed as a last resort when other measures had failed, literally to save the child's life. In another life-saving exercise (Lang and Melamed 1969) the patient was a nine-month-old boy weighing 12 lb., the result of chronic ruminative vomiting. Several treatment measures had been employed without success and conditioning procedures were used as a final attempt (in the words of the physician's clinical notes) 'in view of the fact that therapy until now has been unsuccessful and the life of the child is threatened by continuation of this behaviour'. The success of aversion therapy in these and similar cases must be set against the consequences of the other available methods—close physical restraint during childhood, self-mutilation, or even death.

A distinction is drawn by Rachman and Teasdale between punishment (in the technical sense relating to the treatment administered) and a punitive attitude, which need not and indeed should not accompany treatment. The distinction, a perilous one (and doubtless damned in the eyes of experts on other people's unconscious motivation), will make sense to any social worker who, for example, has had to decide to bring a client to court as part of a treatment plan. The behaviour therapist, unlike the social worker, has at least the consolation of being reasonably sure that the punishment-treatment prescribed will be appropriate and perhaps effective.

A number of writers, including Rachman and Teasdale, express the view that aversive techniques will in time be supplanted by methods of a more positive kind which are ethically less suspect. In the meantime, this is clearly an area of behaviour therapy which needs continual scrutiny if abuses are to be avoided, though our thinking, and any social policy flowing from it, is not helped by the kind of blanket condemnation of aversion therapy which brands its practitioners automatically as no better than licensed torturers.

Selection and Definition of Goals

Turning to the question of the choice of goals, it is evident that the behaviourally-oriented worker shares with workers who adhere to other theoretical orientations two major problems—the varying abilities of clients to determine for themselves the goals of treatment, and the need somehow to balance the possibly conflicting needs and desires of the client and of the wider society. In conditions where behaviour therapy has so far been most commonly used—the treatment of phobias by systematic desensitization—both therapist and client are clear on what needs to be done and a conflict of values is unlikely to arise. Treatment takes the form of a joint exploration by therapist and client of the nature of the problem and the agreed application of the requisite procedures.

In situations of this kind, the worker employing a behavioural approach is spared an important but rarely-discussed ethical problem which permeates the work of his psychodynamic colleague, and which is related to the latter's criticism of behavioural treatment for merely removing 'symptoms' and ignoring 'underlying causes'. Consideration of the relative merits of symptomatic treatment and insight-therapy in terms of outcome is outside the scope of this book but it is appropriate to compare the ethical implications of the two approaches. The insight therapist, 'endowed with a tradition of depth-probing' (Kanfer 1965, p. 193) and focusing not on the behaviour of the client but on inferred inner (and largely unconscious) states, frequently takes the position that the client does not know what his real problems are and that these can be revealed only by a lengthy series of interpretive interviews. Having re-defined the client's problem and the goal to be achieved (not always with the client's knowledge or consent, at least in the early stages), the therapist becomes engaged, not in rendering assistance in a circumscribed area, but in attempting to change the patient's total pattern of living.

There would be nothing ethically objectionable, as Bandura (1969) points out, in a therapist offering a particular brand of insight to interested clients, provided two qualifications were made clear: first, that the insights they are likely to attain reflect the therapist's own belief system; and, secondly, that the attainment of such insight is unlikely to lead to much improvement in the 'symptoms' which originally led the client to seek treatment. It is only fair to point out in this connection that many present-day insight therapists are curtailing their aims in the field of symptom relief and turning their attention more to clients whose problems are existential rather than behavioural.

For the behaviourally-oriented worker, more ethical problems arise from situations where the client's difficulties, often of an interpersonal nature, are such that the client himself can either see no solution or is less readily aware of ways in which his behaviour might be modified as a means of reaching a solution. The 'difficult', 'immature', problem family father, unable to control his temper when confronted with authority figures, might be shaped into automatic obedience to authority, however unreasonable its demands might be—a course of treatment in keeping with the popular image of the behaviour therapist. Alternatively, the therapist might see his function as being to help the client explore, develop and experiment with a wider range of behavioural responses to such difficult situations, thus enabling the client to express himself in a more coherent, positive and more effective manner. The worker in the role of advocate for his client—a role which is exercising social workers greatly at the present time—might, by exploiting learning techniques, bring his client to a point where the major responsibility for advocacy passes from worker to client, to the obvious benefit of all concerned. A similar use of such techniques to strengthen and enhance client self-control in the field of marital counselling is discussed in the paper by Goldiamond (1963) mentioned earlier. Here again, as in the treatment of simple phobias, although the technical problems for the worker are probably greater, the emphasis on specific behaviour, rather than on underlying causes, allows the client more scope for autonomy and initiative in treatment, and a more ethically satisfying degree of freedom and dignity as a person.

Much more difficult to resolve at the ethical level are situations where the client sees no need for treatment (for himself, at least) or where he defines the treatment goals in a way which is unacceptable, on professional or wider social grounds, to the worker. In some cases, such as the prevention of suicide or acts of cruelty towards children, the worker's intervention, though involving ethical judgment, is unlikely to be subjected to serious disagreement. The consensus of ethical opinion is here sufficiently strong to allow the worker to act almost without hesitation—conversely, failure to act would incur serious criticism. In other situations, particularly in relation to deviant but non-criminal behaviour or in matters affecting the life-style of the client (choice of marriage partner occupation and so on), society's attitudes are ambiguous and the worker is likely to fall back on his own personal experience and values for guidance.

We have already seen that the beliefs and values of the worker are inevitably transmitted to the client in the course of treatment and it is clear that the worker's values similarly play a part in determining the choice of goals. What is important here is that personal and professional bias and agency policy should be made explicit and not represented to the client as fragments of scientific or divine revelation.

Some Wider Issues

It is evident that the behaviourally-oriented and the analytically-oriented worker share similar and important ethical problems—by what right, and according to what standards, may we intervene in people's lives, with or without their consent, and to what purpose? These dilemmas are not to be resolved simply by adopting one or other of the available treatment models, despite anxious and persistent claims from the analytically-inclined that their's is the straight way to democracy while the behavioural approach is a broad highway to Hell. The truly alarming feature of such glib pronouncements is that they betray, not just lack of understanding of the behavioural approach (which is no sin, to be sure), but a surprising lack of insight on the part of the analytically-oriented worker into the nature of his own work, particularly the degree of control which he exercises in the treatment situation.

The danger that the worker's power may be misused is perhaps more noticeable in a behavioural approach, where ends and means are more carefully defined and where control by the worker is exercised explicitly and perhaps more effectively. The totalitarian possibilities of behavioural methods are undeniably frightening in comparison with the more familiar world of psychoanalysis, which, as Goldiamond (1963, p. 234) argues, may be regarded like Dolfuss's Austria as 'dictatorship mitigated by sloppiness'. To equate freedom with sloppiness of control is no longer appropriate as we move into a world where the possibilities of efficient behaviour control, at individual and social levels, are developing rapidly.

The issue for social workers is not the use or non-use of control but where the control lies in any given situation and to what end it should be used. The notion of social workers as agents of social control, much discussed at the moment, cuts both ways, and, in their role as mediators between client and community, social workers may seek to adapt their behaviour-modification techniques so that they may be directed not only at clients but at councillors and committees too. Mention has already been made of the use of learning techniques to enhance self-assertion in clients, which could add greatly to the impact of programmes of client participation and community action.

Social workers as citizens must also face the age-old question, *quis custodies custodiet?*—in this context, who will control the controllers? Skinner argues in a number of published papers that a necessary defence against tyranny is the fullest possible exposure of the control techniques which are in operation. Ironically, in playing his part in publicising these techniques, he has come under fire for allegedly advocating the tyranny he fears. The argument of Skinner and others is that once control procedures are identified it becomes possible to set up counter-controls to keep the former in check. Control in interviews, for example, is by no means all one way and research has established what interviewers have often suspected, that the interviewee plays a part in shaping the interviewer's behaviour. The situation is perhaps best illustrated in the famous cartoon which has achieved the distinction of being included in a number of psychology textbooks—the cartoon shows one laboratory rat saying to another, 'Boy, do we have this guy conditioned—every time I press the bar down, he drops a pellet in!'.

Behaviour therapists themselves are actively engaged in bringing to public notice the ethical problems of the human welfare business which affect workers of all theoretical persuasions. The behaviourally-oriented worker and the non-directive therapist share ultimately the same problem: behaviour modification—to what end? client self-actualization—to what end? Watson (1958) argues that the first moral obligation of the helping professions is to be competent, an obligation which involves keeping up with research findings and new developments in their field. He argues strongly for their education in philosophy as an antidote to the inevitable limitations of any one theoretical framework. Now that the development of behavioural and other techniques is perhaps enabling social workers to be, not just well-meaning, but effective as well, the need for continuing appraisal and re-appraisal of means and ends becomes increasingly urgent.

Summary

This chapter discusses some of the ethical problems of behaviourally-oriented social work practice. Consideration of the implications of a scientific and determinist view of human behaviour, and of some relevant research in counselling and psychotherapy, leads to the suggestion that social workers need to become aware of the degree of control which they exercise over clients, in both the methods and goals of treatment. The ethical problems of social work intervention are largely similar for all social workers of whatever theoretical persuasion. Finally, some wider issues are discussed, stressing the need to understand the philosophical and political implications of social work.

References

Ackerman, N. W., Beatman, F. L., and Sherman, S. N. (1961). *Exploring the Base for Family Therapy*. Family Service Association of America, New York.

Alexander, F. (1963). 'The dynamics of psychiatry in the light of learning theory', *American Journal of Psychiatry*, **120**, 440–8.

Alexander, F., and French, T. M. (1946). *Psychoanalytic Therapy*. Ronald Press, New York.

Allen, K. E., Hart, B. M., Buell, J. S., Harris, F. R., and Wolf, M. M. (1964). 'Effects of social reinforcement on isolate behaviour of a nursery school child', *Child Development*, **35**, 511–18.

Allen, S. (1968). 'Some theoretical problems in the study of youth', *Sociological Review*, **16**, 319–31.

Anant, S. S. (1967). 'A note on the treatment of alcoholics by a verbal aversion technique', *Canadian Psychologist*, **8**, 19–22.

Anant, S. S. (1968). 'Verbal aversion therapy with a promiscuous girl: Case report', *Psychological Reports*, **22**, 795–6.

Ashem, B., and Donner, L. (1968). 'Covert sensitization with alcoholics: A controlled replication', *Behaviour Research and Therapy*, **6**, 7–12.

Atthowe, J. M. Jr., and Krasner, L. (1968). 'Preliminary report on the application of contingent reinforcement procedures (token economy) on a "chronic" psychiatric ward', *Journal of Abnormal Psychology*, **73**, 37–43.

Austin, L. (1948). 'Trends in differential treatment in social casework', *Journal of Social Casework*. Reprinted in Kasius, C. (Ed), *Principles and Techniques in Social Casework*. Family Service Association of America, New York: 1950, 324–38.

Ausubel, D. P. (1963). *The Psychology of Meaningful Verbal Learning*. Grune and Stratton, New York.

Ayllon, T., and Azrin, N. H. (1964). 'Reinforcement and instructions with mental patients', *Journal of the Experimental Analysis of Behaviour*, **7**, 327–31.

Ayllon, T., and Azrin, N. H. (1968). *The Token Economy: A Motivational System for Therapy and Rehabilitation*. Appleton-Century-Crofts, New York.

Ayllon, T., and Haughton, E. (1962). 'Control of the behaviour of schizophrenics by foods', *Journal of the Experimental Analysis of Behaviour*, **5**, 343–52.

Ayllon, T., and Haughton, E. (1964). 'Modification of symptomatic verbal behaviour of mental patients', *Behaviour Research and Therapy*, **2**, 87–9.

Ayllon, T., and Michael, J. (1959). 'The psychiatric nurse as a behavioural engineer', *Journal of the Experimental Analysis of Behaviour*, **2**, 323–4.

Ayllon, T., Smith, D., and Rogers, M. (1970). 'Behavioural management of school phobia', *Journal of Behaviour Therapy and Experimental Psychiatry*, **1**, 125–38.

Bailey, K. G., and Sowder, W. T. (1970). 'Audiotape and videotape self-confrontation in psychotherapy', *Psychological Bulletin*, **74**, 127–37.

Bandura, A. (1969). *Principles of Behaviour Modification*. Holt, Rinehart and Winston, New York.

Bandura, A., Blanchard, E. B., and Ritter, B. (1968). *The Relative Efficacy of Desensitization and Modeling Approaches for Inducing Behavioural, Affective and Attitudinal Changes*. Unpublished manuscript, Stanford University.

Bandura, A., Grusec, J. E., and Menlove, F. L. (1967). 'Vicarious extinction of avoidance behaviour', *Journal of Personality and Social Psychology*, **6**, 16–23.

Bandura, A., and Menlove, F. L. (1968). 'Factors determining vicarious extinction of avoidance behaviour through symbolic modeling', *Journal of Personality and Social Psychology*, **8**, 99–108.

Barlow, D. H., Leitenberg, H., and Agras, W. S. (1969). 'The experimental control of sexual deviation through manipulation of the noxious scene in covert sensitization', *Journal of Abnormal Psychology*, **74**, 596–601.

Bateson, G. (1963) *The Naven*. Stanford University, Stanford.

Bateson, G. (1961). 'Perceval's narrative', in Ackerman, N. W., Beatman, F. L., and Sherman, S. N., (Eds.), *Exploring the Base for Family Therapy*. Family Service Association of America, New York, 116–22.

Becker, H. S. (1970). 'Notes on the concept of commitment', *American Journal of Sociology*, **66**, 32–40.

Becker, H. S. (1963). *Outsiders: Studies in the Sociology of Deviance*. The Free Press, New York.

Becker, H. S. (1964). *The Other Side: Perspectives on Deviance*. Collier-Macmillan, London (a).

Becker, H. S. (1964). 'Personal Change in Adult Life'. *Sociometry*, **27**, 40-53 (b).

Becker, H. S., and Strauss, A. L. (1956). 'Careers: Personality and adult socialization', *American Journal of Sociology*, **LXII**, 253–6.

Beech, H. R. (1969). *Changing Man's Behaviour*. Penguin, Harmondsworth.

Beecher, H. K. (1955). 'The powerful-placebo', *Journal of the American Medical Association*, **159**, 1602–5.

Benedict, R. (1934). *Patterns of Culture*. Houghton Mifflin, New York.

Bentler, P. M. (1962). 'An infant's-phobia treated with reciprocal inhibition therapy', *Journal of Child Psychology and Psychiatry*, **3**, 185–9.

Bentler, P. M. (1968). 'Heterosexual behaviour assessment: 1. Males', *Behaviour Research and Therapy*, **6**, 21–5 (a).

Bentler, P. M. (1968). 'Heterosexual behaviour assessment: 11. Females', *Behaviour Research and Therapy*, **6**, 27–30 (b).

Berger, S. M. (1968). 'Conditioning through vicarious instigation', *Psychological Review*, **69**, 450–66.

Bergin, A. E. (1969). 'A self-regulation technique for impulse control disorders', *Psychotherapy: Theory, Research and Practice*, **6**, 113–18.

Bierman, R. (1967). *Therapist Activity–Passivity and Affection–Rejection in Therapeutic Psychotherapy*. Holt, Rinehart and Winston, New York.

Biestek, F. P. (1961). *The Casework Relationship*. Allen and Unwin, London.

Boehm, W. (1968). 'The construction of psychoanalysis and social work education', in Younghusband, E. (Ed.), *Education for Social Work*. Allen and Unwin, London. 86–97.

Bott, E. (1957). *Family and Social Network*. Tavistock Publications, London.

Boyd, H. S., and Sisney, V. V. (1967). 'Immediate self-image confrontation and changes in self-concept', *Journal of Consulting Psychology*, **31**, 291–4.

Brim, O. G. Jr. (1960). 'Personality as role learning', in Iscoe, I., and Stevenson, H. (Eds.), *Personality Development in Children*. University of Texas Press, Austin, 127–59.

Brim, O. G., and Wheeler, S. (1966). *Socialization after Childhood*.Wiley, New York.

Brehm, J. W., and Cohen, A. R. (1962). *Explorations in Cognitive Dissonance.* Wiley, New York.

Brown, G. D., and Tyler, V. O. (1968). 'Time out from reinforcement: A technique for dethroning the "Duke" of an institutionalised delinquent group', *Journal of Child Psychology and Psychiatry*, **9**, 203–11.

Brown, M. A. G. (1966). 'A review of casework methods' in Younghusband, E. (Ed)., *New developments in Casework.* Allen and Unwin, London, 11–46.

Buber, M. (1947). *Between Man and Man.* Routledge and Kegan Paul, London.

Buber, M. (1965). *The Knowledge of Man.* Allen and Unwin, London.

Buehler, R. E., Patterson, G. R., and Furniss, J. M. (1966). 'The reinforcement of behaviour in institutional settings'. *Behaviour Research and Therapy*, **4**, 153–62.

Buckley, W. (1967). *Sociology and Modern Systems Theory.* Prentice Hall, Englewood Cliffs, N.J.

Burgess, J. D. (1967). 'Systematic socialization: A programmed environment for the habilitation of antisocial retardates'. *Psychological Record*, **1**, 461–76.

Burchard, J. D. (1969). 'Residential behaviour modification programs and the problem of uncontrolled contingencies: A reply to Lachenmeyer'. *Psychological Record*, **19**, 259–61.

Burchard, J., and Tyler, V. (1965). 'The modification of delinquent behaviour through operant conditioning'. *Behaviour Research and Therapy*, **2**, 245–50.

Bykov, K. M. (1957). *The Cerebral Cortex and the Internal Organs.* Translated and edited by W. H. Gantt. Chemical Publishing Co, New York.

Cahoon, D. D. (1968). 'Symptom substitution and the behaviour therapies: A reappraisal'. *Psychological Bulletin*, **69**, 149–56.

Campbell, D. T., and Stanley, J. C. (1966). *Experimental and Quasi-experimental Designs for Research.* Rand McNally, Chicago.

Campbell, D., Sanderson, R. E., and Laverty, S. G. (1964). 'Characteristics of a conditioned response in human subjects during extinction trials following a single traumatic conditioning trial'. *Journal of Abnormal and Social Psychology*, **68**, 627–39.

Caprio, F. S. (1954). *Female Homosexuality.* Citadel Press, New York.

Carkhuff, R. R. (1957). *The Counselor's Contribution to Facilitative Processes.* Parkinson, Urbana, Ill.

Carkhuff, R. R. (1969a). *Helping and Human Relations. Vol. I.* Holt, Rinehart and Winston, New York.

Carkhuff, R. R. (1969b). *Helping and Human Relations. Vol II.* Holt, Rinehart and Winston, New York.

Carkhuff, R. R., and Berenson, B. G. (1967). *Beyond Counseling and Therapy.* Holt, Rinehart and Winston, New York.

Cautela, J. R. (1965). 'Desensitization and insight'. *Behaviour Research and Therapy*, **3**, 59–64.

Cautela, J. R. (1967). 'Covert sensitization'. *Psychological Reports*, **20**, 459–68.

Cautela, J. R. (1970). 'Covert reinforcement'. *Behaviour Therapy*, **1**, 33–50.

Cautela, J. R., and Kastenbaum, R. (1967). 'A reinforcement survey schedule for use in therapy, training and research'. *Psychological Reports*, **20**, 1115–30.

Chittenden, G. E. (1942). 'An experimental study in measuring and modifying assertive behaviour in young children'. *Monographs of the Society for Research in Child Development*, **7**, No 1 Serial No 31.

Cicourel, A. C. (1968). *The Social Organisation of Juvenile Justice.* Wiley, New York.

Clark, D. F. (1963). 'Treatment of a monosymptomatic-phobia by systematic desensitization'. *Behaviour Research and Therapy*, **1**, 89–104 (a).

Clark, D. F. (1963). 'Fetishism treated by negative conditioning'. *British Journal of Psychiatry*, **109**, 404–7 (b).

Cloward, R. W., and Ohlin, L. E. (1960). *Delinquency and Opportunity*. The Free Press, New York.

Cohen, A. K. (1955). *Delinquent Boys: The Culture of the Gang*. The Free Press, New York.

Cohen, H. L. (1968). 'Educational therapy: The design of living environments', in Shlien, J. M. (Ed). *Research in psychotherapy*. Vol III. American Psychological Association, Washington, D.C. 21–53.

Cohen, H., Filipiczak, J. A., and Bis, J. S. (1966). *Contingencies Applicable to Special Education of Delinquents: Establishing 24-hour Control in an Experimental Cottage*. Institute for Behavioural Research Inc., Silver Spring, Maryland, mimeographed.

Cohen, H. L., Goldiamond, I., Filipczak, J., and Pooley, R. (1968). *Training Professionals in Procedures for the Establishment of Educational Environments*. Educational Facility Press for Institute for Behavioural Research, Silver Spring, Maryland.

Cooper, A. J. (1963). 'A case of fetishism and impotence treated by behaviour therapy'. *British Journal of Psychiatry*, **109**, 649–52.

Davison, G. C. (1968a). 'Elimination of a sadistic fantasy by a client-controlled counter-conditioning technique'. *Journal of Abnormal Psychology*, **73**, 84–90.

Davison, G. C. (1968b). 'Systematic desensitization as a counter-conditioning process'. *Journal of Abnormal Psychology*, **73**, 91–9.

Davison, G. C. (1969). 'Appraisal of behaviour modification techniques with adults in institutional settings', in Franks, C. M. (Ed). *Behaviour Therapy*. McGraw-Hill, New York. 220–78 (a).

Davison, G. C. (1969). 'Self-control through "imaginal aversive contingency" and "one-downmanship" ' in Krumboltz, J. D., and Thoresen, C. E. (Eds). *Behavioural Counseling: Cases and Techniques*. Holt, Rinehart and Winston, New York (b).

Davison, G. C., and Valins, S. (1969). 'Maintenance of self-attributed and drug-attributed behavior change'. *Journal of Personality and Social Psychology*, **11**, 25–33.

Diehl, H. S., Baker, A. B., and Cowan, D. W. (1940). 'Cold vaccines, further evaluation'. *Journal of the American Medical Association*, **115**, 593–4.

Dittes, J. E. (1957). 'Extinction during psychotherapy of G. S. R. accompanying "embarrassing" statements'. *Journal of Abnormal and Social Psychology*, **54**, 187–91 (a).

Dittes, J. E. (1957). 'Galvanic skin responses as a measure of patients' reaction to therapist's permissiveness'. *Journal of Abnormal and Social Psychology*, **55**, 295–303 (b).

Downes, D. M. (1966). *The Delinquent Solution*. Routledge and Kegan Paul, London.

Duncan, C. P. (1959). 'Recent research on human problem-solving'. *Psychological Bulletin*, **56**, 397–429.

Durkheim, E. (1938). *The Rules of Sociological Method*. Collier Macmillan, London.

Eaton, J. W., and Weil, R. J. (1955). *Culture and Mental Disorders*. The Free Press, New York.

Epstein, R. (1966). 'Aggression toward outgroups as a function of authoritarianism and imitation of aggressive models'. *Journal of Personality and Social Psychology*, **3**, 574–9.

Erikson, K. T. (1957). 'Patient role and social uncertainty: A dilemma of the mentally ill'. *Psychiatry*, **20**, 263–75.

Erikson, K. T. (1964). 'Notes on the sociology of deviance' in Becker, H. S. (Ed). *The Other Side*. Collier Macmillan, London, 9–23.

Eysenck, H. J., and Rachman, S. (1965). *The Causes and Cures of Neurosis*. Routledge and Kegan Paul, London.

Fairbairn, W. R. (1958). 'On the nature and aims of psychoanalytical treatment'. *International Journal of Psychoanalysis*, **39**, 374–85.

Fairweather, G. W. (1964). *Social Psychology in Treating Mental Illness: An Experimental Approach*. Wiley, New York.

Fairweather, G. W., Sanders, D. W., Maynard, H., and Cressler, D. L. (1969). *Community Life for the Mentally Ill: An Alternative to Institutional Care*. Aldine, Chicago.

Fenichel, O. (1945). *The Psychoanalytic Theory of Neurosis*. Norton, New York.

Ferard, M. L., and Hunnybun, N. K. (1962). *The Caseworkers Use of Relationships*. Tavistock Publications, London.

Field, M. G., and Aronson, J. (1968). 'The institutional framework of soviet psychiatry', in Weinberg, S. K. (Ed). *The Sociology of Mental Disorders*, Staples, London. 351–6.

Foote, N. (1951). 'Identity as a basis for a theory of motivation'. *American Sociological Review*, **16**, 14–21.

Foren, R., and Bailey, R. (1968). *Authority in Social Casework*. Pergamon, Oxford.

Frank, J. D. (1961). *Persuasion and Healing*. John Hopkins Press, Baltimore.

Frank, J. D. (1968). 'The influence of patients' and therapists' expectations on the outcome of psychotherapy'. *British Journal of Medical Psychology*, **41**, 349–56.

Frank, J. D., Gliedman, L. W., Imber, S. D., Stone, A. R., and Nash, E. W. Jr. (1959). 'Patients' expectancies and relearning as factors determining improvement in psychotherapy.' *American Journal of Psychiatry*, **115**, 961–8.

Freeman, H. (1969). 'Community care'. *New Society*, April, 560–1.

Freeman, H. L., and Kendrick, D. C. (1964). 'A case of cat phobia: Treatment by a method derived from experimental psychology', in Eysenck, H. J. (Ed). *Experiments in Behaviour Therapy*. Macmillan, New York, 51–61.

French, T. M. (1958). *The Reintegrative Process in a Psychoanalytic Treatment. The Integration of Behaviour. Vol III*. University of Chicago Press, Chicago.

Freud, A. (1936). *The Ego and the Mechanisms of Defence*. Hogarth Press, London.

Freud, S. (1915). *The Unconscious. The Standard Edition of the Complete Psychological Works of Sigmund Freud. Vol 14*, The Hogarth Press and the Institute of Psychoanalysis, London, 161.

Freud, S. (1940). *An Outline of Psychoanalysis*. Hogarth Press, London.

Freund, K. (1963). 'A laboratory method for diagnosing predominance of homo- or heteroerotic interest in the male'. *Behaviour Research and Therapy*, **1**, 85–93.

Freund, K. (1965). 'Diagnosing heterosexual pedophilia by means of a test for sexual interest'. *Behaviour Research and Therapy*, **3**, 229–34.

Friedlander, K. (1947). *The Psychoanalytical Approach to Juvenile Delinquency*. Routledge and Kegan Paul, London.

Friedman, D. (1966). 'Treatment of a case of dog phobia in a deaf mute by behaviour therapy'. *Behaviour Research and Therapy*, **4**, 141–2.

Friedman, H. J. (1963). 'Patient-expectancy and symptom reduction'. *Archives of General Psychiatry*, **8**, 61–7.

Fromm-Reichmann, F. (1953). *Principles of Intensive Psychotherapy*. Allen and Unwin, London.

Gallup, G. G. Jr. (1968). 'Mirror-image stimulation'. *Psychological Bulletin*, **70**, 782–93.

Garrett, A. (1950). 'Historical survey of the evolution of casework'. Journal of Social Casework, 1949, June. Reprinted in Kasius, C. (Ed). *Principles and Techniques in Social Casework*. Family Service Association of America, New York, 393–411.

Garvey, W. P., and Hegrenes, J. R. (1966). 'Desensitization techniques in the treatment of school phobia'. *American Journal of Orthopsychiatry*, **36**, 147–52.

Geer, J. (1965). 'The development of a scale to measure fear'. *Behaviour Research and Therapy*, **3**, 45–54.

Gelder, M. G., and Marks, I. M. (1968). 'Desensitization and phobias: A cross-over study'. *British Journal of Psychiatry*, **114**, 323–8.

Gelder, M. G., Marks, I. M., and Wolff, H. H. (1967). 'Desensitization and psychotherapy in the treatment of phobic states: A controlled enquiry'. *British Journal of Psychiatry*, **113**, 53–73.

Gewirtz, J. L. (1961). 'A learning analysis of the effects of normal stimulation, privation and deprivation on the acquisition of social motivation and attachment', in Foss, B. M. (Ed). *Determinants of Infant Behaviour. Volume I.* Methuen, London, 213–90.

Goffman, E. (1961). *Asylums.* Doubleday, New York.

Goldberg, E. M. (1966). 'The function and use of relationship in psychiatric social work', in Younghusband, E. (Ed). *New Developments in Casework.* Allen and Unwin, London, 95–107.

Goldiamond, I. (1965). 'Justified and unjustified alarm over behavioural control'. 1963, in Milton, O. (Ed). *Behavior Disorders: Perspective and Trends.* J. B. Lippincott Co., Philadelphia.

Goldiamond, I. (1965). 'Self control procedures in personal behaviour problems'. *Psychological Reports*, **17**, 851–68.

Goldstein, A. P. (1962). *Therapist-patient expectancies in Psychotherapy.* Pergamon, Oxford.

Goldstein, A. P., and Dean, S. J. (1966). *The Investigation of Psychotherapy: Commentaries and Readings.* Wiley, New York.

Goldstein, A. P., Heller, K., and Sechrest, L. B. (1966). *Psychotherapy and the Psychology of Behaviour Change.* Wiley, New York.

Gove, W. R. (1970). 'Societal reaction as an explanation of mental illness: An Evaluation'. *American Sociological Review*, **35**, 873–84.

Greenson, R. R. (1965). 'The working alliance and the transference neurosis'. *Psychoanalytic Quarterly*, **34**, 155–81.

Greenson, R. R., and Wexler, M. (1969). 'The non-transference relationship in the analytic situation'. *International Journal of Psychoanalysis*, **50**, 27–39.

Greenwald, H. (1958). *The Call Girl.* Ballantine, New York.

Grinker, R. R., and Spiegel, J. P. (1945). *Men under Stress.* McGraw-Hill, New York.

Halmos, P. (1958). *Personal Involvement in Learning about Personality.* Sociological Review Monograph, No. 1.

Hagman, C. (1932). 'A study of fears of children in the pre-school age'. *Journal of Experimental Psychology*, **39**, 260–9.

Handel, G. (1968). *The Psychosocial Interior of the Family.* Allen and Unwin, London.

Handler, F. (1968). 'The Coercive Children's Officer'. *New Society*, October, 485–7.

Hargreaves, D. H. (1967). *Social Relations in a Secondary School.* Routledge and Kegan Paul, London.

Hart, J. D. (1966). *Fear Reduction as a Function of the Assumption and Success of a Therapeutic Role. Unpublished Master's Thesis.* University of Wisconsin.

Hartmann, D. (1969). 'Influence of symbolically modeled instrumental aggression and pain cues on aggressive behaviour'. *Journal of Personality and Social Psychology*, **11**, 280–8.

Hawkins, R. P., Peterson, R. F., Schweid, E., and Bijou, S. W. (1966). 'Behaviour therapy in the home: Amelioration of problem parent-child relations with the parent in a therapeutic role'. *Journal of Experimental Child Psychology*, **4**, 99–107.

Heimler, E. (1962). *A Link in the Chain.* Bodley Head, London.

Henry, F. W. (1941). *Sex Variants.* Hoeber, New York.

Hobbs, N. (1962). 'Sources of gain in psychotherapy'. *American Psychologist*, **17**, 741–7.

Holder, C. E. (1969). 'Temper tantrum extinction: A limited attempt at behaviour modification'. *Social Work (U.K.)* **26**, 8–11.

Holland, C. J. (1970). 'An interview guide for behavioural counseling with parents'. *Behaviour Therapy*, **1**, 70–9.

Hollis, F. (1949). *Women in Marital Conflict*. Family Service Association of America, New York.

Hollis, F. (1964). *Casework: A Psychosocial Therapy*. Random House, New York.

Hollis, F. (1967). 'Explanations in the development of a typology of casework treatment'. *Social Casework*, **XLVIII**, 335–41 (a).

Hollis, F. (1967). 'The coding and application of a typology of casework treatment'. *Social Casework*, **XLVIII**, 489–97 (b).

Hollis, F. (1968). 'A profile of early interviews in marital counseling'. *Social Casework*, **XLIX**, 35–43 (a).

Hollis, F. (1968). 'Continuance and discontinuance in marital counseling and some observations on joint interviews'. *Social Casework*, **XLIX**, 167–74 (b).

Homme, L. E. (1965). 'Perspectives in psychology: XXIV Control of coverants, the operants of the mind'. *Psychological Record*, **15**, 501–11.

Homme, L. E., and Tosti, D. T. (1965). 'Contingency management and motivation'. *Journal of the National Society for Programmed Instruction*, **4**, 14–16.

Hooker, E. (1961). 'The homosexual community'. *Proceedings of the XIV International Congress of Applied Psychology*. Munksgoord, Copenhagen.

Immergluck, L. (1964). 'Determinism-freedom in contemporary psychology—an ancient problem re-visited'. *American Journal of Psychology*, **19**, 270–81.

Irvine, E. E. (1956). 'Renaissance in British casework'. *Social Work, (U.K.)* **13**, 187–94 (a).

Irvine, E. E. (1956). 'Transference and reality in the casework relationship'. *British Journal of Psychiatric Social Work*, **3**, 15–24 (b).

Irvine, E. E. (1966). 'A new look at casework', in Younghusband, E. (Ed). *New Developments in Casework*. Allen and Unwin, London, 38–46.

Jehu, D. (1967). *Learning Theory and Social Work*. Routledge and Kegan Paul, London.

Jellinck, E. M. (1946). 'Clinical tests on comparative effectiveness of analgesic drugs'. *Biometrics*, **2**, 87–91.

Johnson, S. M., and Brown, R. A. (1969). 'Producing behaviour change in parents of disturbed children'. *Journal of Child Psychology and Psychiatry and Allied Disciplines*, **10**, 107–21.

Jones, H. (1965). *Crime and the Penal System*. University Tutorial Press, London.

Jones, H. E. (1931). 'The conditioning of overt emotional responses'. *Journal of Educational Psychology*, **22**, 127–30.

Jones, M. C. (1924). 'A laboratory study of fear: The case of Peter'. *Pedagogical Seminar*, **31**, 308–15 (a).

Jones, M. C. (1924). 'The elimination of children's fears'. *Journal of Experimental Psychology*, **7**, 383–90 (b).

Jourard, S. (1959). 'I-thou relationship versus manipulation in counseling and psychotherapy'. *Journal of Individual Psychology*, **15**, 174–9.

Jung, C. G. (1959). *Aion*. Routledge and Kegan Paul, London.

Jung, C. G. (1961). *Modern Man in Search of a Soul*. Routledge and Kegan Paul, London.

Jung, C. G. (1969). Foreword to: Neumann, Erich. *Psychology and a New Ethic*. Hodder and Stoughton, London.

180

Kanfer, F. H. (1965). 'Issues and Ethics in Behavior Manipulation'. *Psychological Reports*, 185–96.

Kanfer, F. H., and Phillips, J. S. (1970). *Learning Foundations of Behaviour Therapy*. Wiley, New York.

Kanfer, F. H., and Saslow, G. (1969). 'Behavioral diagnosis'. In Franks, C. M. (Ed). *Behavior Therapy*. McGraw-Hill, New York, 417–44.

Katkin, E. S., and Murray, E. N. (1968). 'Instrumental conditioning of autonomically mediated behaviour: Theoretical and methodological issues'. *Psychological Bulletin*, **70**, 52–68.

Kimble, G. A. (1961). *Hilgard and Marquis' Conditioning and Learning*. Appleton-Century-Crofts, New York.

Kinsey, A. C., Pomeroy, W. B., and Martin, C. E. (1948). *Sexual Behaviour in the Human Male*. Saunders, Philadelphia.

Kitsuse, J. I., and Cicourel, A. V. (1963). 'A note on the use of official statistics'. *Social Problems*, **11**, 131–9.

Klein, J. (1965). *Samples from English Culture*. Routledge and Kegan Paul, London.

Koenig, M. P., and Masters, J. (1965). 'Experimental treatment of habitual smoking'. *Behaviour Research and Therapy*, **3**, 235–43.

Kohler, W. (1925). *The Mentality of Apes*. Routledge and Kegan Paul, London.

Kraft, T., and Al-Issa, I. (1965). 'The application of learning theory to the treatment of traffic phobia'. *British Journal of Psychiatry*, **111**, 277–9.

Kraft, T., and Burnfield, A. (1967). 'Treatment of neurosis by behaviour therapy'. *London Hospital Gazette*, **70**, xxi–xvi.

Krasner, L. (1962). 'Behaviour control and social responsibility'. *American Psychologist*, **17**, 199–204.

Krasner, L. (1968). 'Assessment of token economy programmes in psychiatric hospitals', in Porter, R. (Ed). *The Role of Learning in Psychotherapy*. J. and A. Churchill Ltd., London, 155–74.

Krasner, L. 'Token economy as an illustration of operant conditioning procedures with the aged, with youth, and with society', in Levis, D. J. (Ed). *Learning Approaches to Therapeutic Behaviour Change*. Aldine, Chicago, 74–101.

Krasnogorski, N. I. (1925). 'The conditioned reflexes and the children's neuroses'. *American Journal of Diseases of Children*, **30**, 753–68.

Krasnogorski, N. I. (1933). 'Physiology of cerebral activity in children as a new subject of pediatric investigation'. *American Journal of Diseases of Children*, **46**, 473–94.

Kris, E. (1950). 'On preconscious mental processes'. *Psychoanalytic Quarterly*, **19**, 540–60.

Kris, E. (1956). 'On some vicissitudes of insight in psychoanalysis'. *International Journal of Psychoanalysis*, **37**, 445–55.

Krumboltz, J. D., and Schroeder, W. W. (1965). 'Promoting career exploration through reinforcement'. *Personnel Guidance Journal*, **44**, 19–26.

Krumboltz, J. D., and Thoresen, C. E. (1964). 'The effects of behavioural counseling in group and individual settings on information-seeking behaviour'. *Journal of Counseling Psychology*, **11**, 324–33.

Krumboltz, J. D., Varenhorst, B. B., and Thoresen, C. E. (1967). 'Nonverbal factors in the effectiveness of models in counseling'. *Journal of Counseling Psychology*, **14**, 412–18.

Kushner, M. (1965). 'Desensitization of a post-traumatic phobia', in Ullman, L. P., and Krasner, L. (Eds). *Case Studies in Behaviour Modification*. Holt, Rinehart and Winston, New York, 193–5.

Lachenmeyer, C. W. (1969). 'Systematic socialization: Observations on a programmed environment for the habilitation of antisocial retardates'. *Psychological Record*, **19**, 247–57.

Laing, R. D. (1967). 'The Psychotherapeutic Experience' in the *Politics of Experience*. Penguin, Harmondsworth, 39–48.

Lang, P. J., and Lazovik, A. D. (1963). 'The experimental desensitization of a phobia'. *Journal of Abnormal and Social Psychology*, **66**, 519–25.

Lang, P. J., Lazowick, D. J., and Reynolds, D. J. (1965). 'Desensitization, suggestibility and pseudo-therapy'. *Journal of Abnormal Psychology*, **6**, 395–402.

Lang, P. J., and Melamed, B. G. (1969). 'Avoidance conditioning therapy of an infant with chronic ruminative vomiting'. *Journal of Abnormal Psychology*, **74**, 1–8.

Lasagna, L., Mosteller, F., von Felsinger, J. M., and Beecher, H. K. (1954). 'A study of the placebo response'. *American Journal of Medicine*, **16**, 770–9.

Lawson, A. R. L. (1966). *The Recognition of Mental Illness in London*. Oxford University Press, London.

Lazarus, A. A. (1959). 'The elimination of children's phobias by deconditioning'. *Medical Proceedings (South Africa)*, **5**, 261–5.

Lazarus, A. A. (1961). 'Group therapy of phobic disorders'. *Journal of Abnormal and Social Psychology*, **63**, 504–12.

Lazarus, A. A., and Abramovitz, A. (1962). 'The use of "emotive imagery" in the treatment of children's phobias'. *Journal of Mental Science*, **108**, 191–5.

Lazarus, A. A., and Rachman, S. (1960). 'The use of systematic desensitization in psychotherapy', in Eysenck, H. J. (Ed). *Behaviour Therapy and the Neuroses*. Macmillan, New York, 181–7.

Lazarus, R. S., Speisman, J. C., Mordkoff, A. M., and Davison, L. (1962). 'A laboratory study of stress produced by a motion picture film'. *Psychological Monographs*, **76**, (Whole No. 553).

Lemert, E. M. (1951). *Social Pathology*. McGraw-Hill, New York.

Lemert, E. M. (1967). *Human Deviance, Social Problems and Social Control*. Prentice Hall, Englewood Cliffs, New Jersey.

Lewinsohn, P. M. (1968). *Manual of Instructions for the Behavior Ratings used for the Observation of Interpersonal Behaviour*. Unpublished manuscript. University of Oregon.

Liberman, R. (1970). 'Behavioural approaches to family and couple therapy'. *American Journal of Orthopsychiatry*, **40**, 106–18.

Lindsley, O. R. (1966). 'An experiment with parents handling behaviour at home'. *New Jersey, Johnstone Training Center. Johnstone Bulletin*, **9**, 27–36.

Locke, E. A., Cartledge, N., and Koeppel, J. (1968). 'Motivational effects of knowledge of results: A goal-setting phenomenon?'. *Psychological Bulletin*. **70**, 474–85.

Lovaas, O. I. (1961). 'Interaction between verbal and non-verbal behaviour'. *Child Development*, **32**, 37–44.

Lovaas, O. I. (1964). 'Control of food intake in children by reinforcement of relevant verbal behaviour'. *Journal of Abnormal and Social Psychology*, **68**, 672–8.

Lovaas, O. I., Freitag, G., Gold, V. J., and Kassorla, I. C. (1965). 'Experimental studies in childhood schizophrenia: Analysis of self-destructive behaviour'. *Journal of Experimental Child Psychology*, **2**, 67–84.

Loewenstein, R. M. (1951). 'The problem of interpretation'. *Psychoanalytic Quarterly*, **20**, 1–14.

Loewenstein, R. M. (1956). 'Some remarks on the role of speech in psychoanalytic technique'. *International Journal of Psychoanalysis*, **37**, 460–7.

London, P. (1964). *The Modes and Morals of Psychotherapy*. Holt, Rinehart and Winston, New York.

Lonergan, B. J. F. (1957). *Insight: A Study of Human Understanding*. Longmans, Green and Co., London.

Madsen, C. H., Becker, W. C., and Thomas, D. R. (1968). 'Rules, praise, and ignoring. Elements of elementary classroom control'. *Journal of Applied Behaviour Analysis*, **1**, 139–50.

Mahoney, M. J. (1970). 'Toward an experimental analysis of coverant control'. *Behaviour Therapy*, **1**, 510–21.

Marks, I. M. (1969). *Fears and Phobias*. Heinemann, London.

Marks, I. M., and Gelder, M. G. (1965). 'A controlled retrospective study of behaviour therapy in phobic patients'. *British Journal of Psychiatry*, **111**, 561–73.

Marks, I. M., and Gelder, M. G. (1966). 'Common ground between behaviour therapy and psychodynamic methods'. *British Journal of Medical Psychology*, **39**, 11–23.

Marlatt, G. A. (1968). *Vicarious and Direct Reinforcement Control of Verbal Behaviour in an Interview Setting*. Unpublished Ph. D. thesis. Indiana University.

Marlatt, G. A., Jacobson, E. A., Johnson, D. L., and Morrice, D. J. (1966). *Effects of Exposure to a Model Receiving Varied Informational Feedback upon Consequent Behaviour in an Interview*. Paper presented at a meeting of the Midwestern Psychological Association, Chicago.

Matza, D. (1969). *Becoming Deviant*. Prentice Hall, New Jersey.

May, R. (1950). *The Meaning of Anxiety*. Ronald Press, New York.

Mayer, J. E., and Timms, N. (1969). 'Clash in perspective between worker and client'. *Social Casework*, **50**, 32–9.

Mayer, J. E., and Timms, N. (1970). *The Client Speaks: Working Class Impressions of Casework*. Routledge and Kegan Paul, London.

Mayo, E. (1933). *The Human Problems of an Industrial Civilization*. Macmillan, New York.

McCall, G. J., and Simmons, J. L. (1966). *Identities and Interactions*. The Free Press, New York.

McCord, J., and McCord, W. (1958). 'The effects of parental role model on criminality'. *Journal of Social Issues*, **14**, 66–75.

McGlynn, F. D., Mealiea, W. L., and Nawas, M. M. (1969). 'Systematic desensitization of snake-avoidance under two conditions of suggestion'. *Psychological Reports*, **25**, 220–2.

McGuire, R. J., Carlisle, J. M., and Young, B. G. (1965). 'Sexual deviations as conditioned behaviour: A hypothesis'. *Behaviour Research and Therapy*, **2**, 185–90.

McIntosh, M. (1968). 'The homosexual role'. *Social Problems*, **16**, 182–92.

Mead, M. (1935). *Sex and Temperament in Three Primitive Societies*. Morrow, New York.

Menninger, K. (1958). *Theory of Psychoanalytic Technique*. Imago, London.

Merton, R. K. (1957). *Social Theory and Social Structure*. The Free Press, New York.

Metcalfe, M. (1956). 'Demonstration of a psychosomatic relationship'. *British Journal of Medical Psychology*, **29**, 63–6.

Meyer, H. J., Borgatta, E. F., and Jones, W. C. (1965). *Girls at Vocational High: An Experiment in Social Work Intervention*. Russell Sage Foundation, New York.

Meyer, V., and Chesser, E. S. (1970). *Behaviour Therapy in Clinical Psychiatry*. Penguin, Harmondsworth.

Mills, C. W. (1942). 'The professional ideology of social pathologists'. *American Journal of Sociology*, **XLIX**, 165–80.

Mishel, W. (1968). *Personality and Assessment*. Wiley, New York.

Mishler, E. G., and Scotch, N. A. (1963). 'Sociocultural factors in the epidemiology of schizophrenia: A review'. *Psychiatry*, **26**, 315–51.

Moss, F. A. (1924). 'Note on building likes and dislikes in children'. *Journal of Experimental Psychology*, **7**, 475–8.

Mountney, G. H., Fryers, T., and Freeman, H. L. (1969). 'Psychiatric emergencies in an urban borough'. *British Medical Journal*, **1**, 498–500.

Mowrer, O. H. (1948). 'Learning theory and the neurotic paradox'. *American Journal of Orthopsychiatry*, **18**, 571–610.

Mowrer, O. H. (1960). *Learning Theory and Behaviour*. Wiley, New York.

Mowrer, O. H. (1969). 'Too little and too late'. *International Journal of Psychiatry*, **7**, 536–56.

Mullen, E. J. (1968). 'Casework communication'. *Social Casework*, **49**, 546–51.

Murray, E. J. (1956). 'A content-analysis method for studying psychotherapy'. *Psychological Monographs*, 70 (Whole No. 420).

Nacht, S. (1962). 'The curative factors in psychoanalysis'. *International Journal of Psychoanalysis*, **43**, 206–11.

Nolan, J. D. (1968). 'Self-control procedures in the modification of smoking behavior'. *Journal of Consulting and Clinical Psychology*, **32**, 92–3.

O'Connor, R. D. (1969). 'Modification of social withdrawal through symbolic modelling'. *Journal of Applied Behaviour Analysis*, **2**, 15–22.

O'Leary, K. D., Becker, W. C., Evans, M. B., and Saudargas, R A. (1969). 'A token reinforcement program in a public school. A replication and systematic analysis'. *Journal of Applied Behaviour Analysis*, **2**, 3–13.

Oliveau, D. C., Agras, W. S., Leitenberg, H., Moore, R. C., and Wright, D. E. (1969). 'Systematic desensitization, therapeutically oriented instructions and selective positive reinforcement'. *Behaviour Research and Therapy*, **7**, 27–33.

Orne, M. T. (1962). 'On the social psychology of the psychological experiment: With particular reference to demand characteristics and their implications'. *American Psychologist*, **17**, 776–83.

Park, L. C., and Covi, L. (1965).' Nonblind-placebo trial'. *Archives of General Psychiatry*, **12**, 336–45.

Parsons, T. (1951). *The Social System*. Routledge and Kegan Paul, London.

Patterson, G. R. (1969). 'Behavioral techniques based upon social learning: An additional base for developing behavior modification technologies', in Franks, C. M. (Ed). *Behavior Therapy*, McGraw-Hill, New York, 341–74.

Patterson, G. R., McNeal, S., Hawkins, N., and Phelps, R. (1967). 'Reprogramming the social environment'. *Journal of Child Psychology and Psychiatry*, **8**, 3–4, 181–95.

Patterson, G. R., Ray, R. S., and Shaw, D. A. (1968). 'Direct intervention in families of deviant children'. *Oregon Research Institute Bulletin*, **8**, 9.

Patterson, G. R., Ray, R. S., Shaw, D. A., and Cobb, J. A. (1969). 'Manual for coding of family interactions'. 6th revision. *Oregon Research Institute*, June.

Paul, G. L. (1966). *Insight Versus Desensitization in Psychotherapy*. Stanford University Press, Stanford.

Paul, G. L. (1967). 'Insight versus desensitization in psychotherapy two years after termination'. *Journal of Consulting Psychology*, **31**, 333–48.

Paul, G. L. (1969). 'Outcome of systematic desensitization. I. Background procedures and uncontrolled reports of individual treatment', in Franks, C. M. (Ed). *Behavior Therapy*. McGraw-Hill, New York, 63–104 (a).

Paul, G. L. (1969). 'Outcome of systematic desensitization. II. Controlled investigations of individual treatment, technique variations, and current status', in Franks, C. M. (Ed). *Behaviour Therapy*. McGraw-Hill, New York, 105–59 (b).

Pavlov, I. P. (1927). *Conditioned Reflexes* (Translation by Annep, G. V.) Oxford University Press, London.

Perlman, H. (1951). *Casework, a Problem Solving Process*. University of Chicago Press, Chicago.

Peterson, D. R., and London, P. (1965). 'A role for cognition in the behavioural treatment of a child's eliminative disturbance', in Ullmann, L. P. and Krasner, L. (Eds). *Case Studies in Behaviour Modification*. Holt, Rinehart and Winston, New York, 289–95.

Phillips, E. L. (1968). 'Achievement place: Token reinforcement procedures in a home-style rehabilitation setting for "pre-delinquent" boys'. *Journal of Applied Behavior Analysis*, **1**, 213–23.

Phillipson, C. M. (1971). 'Juvenile delinquency and the school', in Carson, W. G., and Wiles, P. (Eds). 'Crime and Delinquency in Britain—Sociological Readings'. Martin Robertson, London, 236–58.

Pinkus, H. (1968). *Casework Techniques Related to Selected Characteristics of Client and Worker*. Doctoral dissertation. Columbia University.

Porter, R. (Ed). (1968). *The Role of Learning in Psychotherapy*. Churchill, London.

Poser, E. G. (1970). 'Toward a theory of "behavioral prophylaxis"'. *Journal of Behaviour Therapy and Experimental Psychiatry*, **1**, 39–43.

Power, M. J., Alderson, M. R., Phillipson, C. M., Shoenberg, E., and Morris, J. N. (1967). 'Delinquent Schools'. *New Society*, 542–3.

Price, W. H. (1969). 'Sex determination, mental subnormality, crime and delinquency, in males'. *Journal of Mental Subnormality*, **15**, 37–44.

Rachman, S. (1966). 'Sexual fetishism: An experimental analogue'. *Psychological Records*, **16**, 293–6.

Rachman, S., and Hodgson, R. J. (1968). 'Experimentally-induced "Sexual fetishism": Replication and development'. *Psychological Record*, **18**, 25–7.

Rachman, S., and Teasdale, J. (1969). *Aversion Therapy and Behaviour Disorders*. Routledge and Kegan Paul, London.

Rausch, H. L. (1965). 'Interaction sequences'. *Journal of Personality and Social Psychology*, **2**, 487–99.

Ray, R. S., Shaw, D. A., and Patterson, G. R. (1968). *Observation in the School: Description of a Coding Form*. Re-programming Project, Oregon Research Institute.

Razran, G. (1961). 'The observable unconscious and the inferable conscious in current soviet psychophysiology'. *Psychological Review*, **68**, 81–147.

Rehm, L. P., and Marston, A. R. (1968). 'Reduction in social anxiety through modification of self-reinforcement: An instigation therapy technique'. *Journal of Consulting and Clinical Psychology*, **32**, 5, 565–74.

Reid, W. J. (1961). 'A study of caseworkers' use of insight-oriented techniques'. *Social Casework*, **48**, 3–9.

Reiss, A. J. (1961). 'The social integration of queers and peers'. *Social Problems*, **9**, 102–20.

Richfield, J. (1954). 'An analysis of the concept of insight'. *Psychoanalytic Quarterly*, **23**, 390–408.

Rimland, B. (1964). *Infantile Autism*. Appleton-Century-Crofts, New York.

Risley, T. R. (1968). 'The effects and side-effects of punishing the autistic behaviors of a deviant child'. *Journal of Applied Behavior Analysis*, **1**, 21–34.

Roethlisberger, F. J., and Dickson, W. J. (1939). *Management and the Worker*. Harvard University Press, Cambridge, Mass.

Rogers, C. R. (1961). 'Cultural evolution as seen by psychologists'. *Daedalus*, **90**, 570–86.

Rogers, C. R. (1962). 'The interpersonal relationship: The core of guidance'. *Harvard Educational Review*, **32**, 416–29.

Rogers, C. R., and Skinner, B. F. (1966). 'Some issues concerning the control of human behaviour'. Science, 1956, **124**, 1057–66. Reprinted in Ulrich, R., Stachnik, T., and Mabry, J. (Eds). *Control of Human Behavior.* Scott, Foresman and Co., Glenview, Illinois, 301–16.

Rogers, J. M. (1960). 'Operant conditioning in a quasi-therapy setting'. *Journal of Abnormal Social Psychology*, **60**, 247–52.

Rose, A. M. (1962). *Human Behaviour and Social Processes.* Routledge and Kegan Paul, London.

Rosenthal, D. (1955). 'Changes in some moral values following psychotherapy'. *Journal of Consulting Psychology*, **19**, 431–6.

Rosenthal, R. (1966). *Experimenter Effects in Behavioural Research.* Appleton-Century-Crofts, New York.

Rubington, E., and Weinberg, M. S. (1968). *Deviance: The Interactionist Perspective.* Collier Macmillan, London.

Rycroft, C. (1966). *Psychoanalysis Observed.* Constable, London.

Rycroft, C. (1968). *A Critical Dictionary of Psychoanalysis.* Nelson, London.

Salzinger, K. (1969). 'The operant conditioning of verbal behavior in psychotherapy', in Franks, C. M. (Ed). *Behavior Therapy.* McGraw-Hill, New York, 375–95.

Sandler, J., Dare, C., and Holder, A. (1970). 'Basic psychoanalytic concepts: I The extension of clinical concepts outside the psychoanalytic situation'. *British Journal of Psychiatry*, **116**, 551–4 (a).

Sandler, J., Dare, C., and Holder, A. (1970). 'Basic psychoanalytic concepts: III Transference'. *British Journal of Psychiatry*, 116, 667–72 (b).

Schacter, S., and Singer, J. E. (1962). 'Cognitive, social and physiological determinants of emotional state'. *Psychological Review*, **69**, 379–99.

Sheff, T. J. (1966). *Being Mentally Ill.* Weidenfeld and Nicolson, London.

Scheff, T. J. (1967). *Mental Illness and Social Processes.* Harper and Row, New York.

Schmideberg, M. (1965). 'Reality therapy with offenders'. *British Journal of Criminology*, **5**, 168–82.

Schmideberg, M. (1967). 'Conundrum: How relative is "insight?" '. *British Journal of Criminology*, **7**, 243–4.

Schofield, M. (1965). *The Sexual Behaviour of Young People.* Longmans, London.

Schonbar, R. A. (1965). 'Interpretation and insight in psychotherapy'. *Psychotherapy – Theory, Research and Practice*, **2**, 78–83.

Schur, E. M. (1965). *Crimes Without Victims: Deviant Behaviour and Public Policy.* Prentice Hall, New Jersey.

Schwitzgebel, R. L. (1968). 'Survey of electromechanical devices for behaviour modification'. *Psychological Bulletin*, **70**, 444–59.

Schwitzgebel, R., and Kolb, D. A. (1964). 'Inducing behaviour change in adolescent delinquents'. *Behaviour Research and Therapy*, **1**, 297–304.

Segal, H. (1962). 'The curative factors in psychoanalysis'. *International Journal of Psychoanalysis*, **43**, 212–17.

Shapiro, A. K. (1960). 'A contribution to a history of the placebo effect'. *Behavioural Science*, **5**, 109–35.

Shapiro, D. A. (1969). 'Empathy, warmth and genuineness in psychotherapy'. *British Journal of Social and Clinical Psychology*, **8**, 350–61.

Shaw, C. R., and McKay, H. D. (1942). *Juvenile Delinquency and Urban Areas.* Chicago University Press, Chicago.

Shoben, E. J. (1953). 'Some observations on psychotherapy and the learning process', in Mowrer, O. H. (Ed). *Psychotherapy, Theory and Research.* Ronald Press, New York, 120–39.

Sinfield, A. (1969). *Which Way for Social Work?* Fabian Society, London, Fabian Tract No. 393.

Skinner, B. F. (1953). *Science and Human Behaviour.* Macmillan, New York.

Skinner, B. F. (1966). 'Freedom and the control of man'. American Scholar, Winter 1955-6, 25, 47-65. Reprinted in Ulrich, R., Stachnik, T., and Mabry, J. (Eds). *Control of Human Behavior.* Scott, Foresman and Co., Glenview, Illinois, 11-20.

Slucki, H., Adam, G., and Porter, R. W. (1965). 'The operant discrimination of an interoceptive stimulus in rhesus monkeys'. *Journal of the Experimental Analysis of Behaviour,* **8,** 405-14.

Sluckin, A., and Jehu, D. (1969). 'A behavioural approach in the treatment of elective mutism'. *British Journal of Psychiatric Social Work,* **10,** 70-3.

Smith, J. E. (1965). *Encouraging Students to Utilise Their Unscheduled Time More Effectively Through Reinforcement and Model Counseling.* Unpublished Ph.D. thesis. Stanford University.

Solomon, R. L., and Wynne, L. C. (1953). 'Traumatic avoidance learning: Acquisition in normal dogs'. *Psychological Monographs,* **67,** 54.

Solomon, R. L., and Wynne, L. C. (1954). 'Traumatic avoidance learning: The principles of anxiety conservation and partial irreversibility'. *Psychological Review,* **61,** 353-85.

Solyom, L., and Miller, S. (1965). 'A differential conditioning procedure as the initial phase of the behaviour therapy of homosexuality'. *Behaviour Research and Therapy,* **3,** 147-60.

Speisman, J. C., Lazarus, R. S., Mordkoff, A., and Davison, L. (1964). 'Experimental reduction of stress based on ego-defense theory'. *Journal of Abnormal and Social Psychology,* **68,** 367-80.

Spohn, H. E. (1960). 'The influence of social values upon the clinical judgements of psychotherapists', in Peatman, J. G., and Hartley, E. L. (Eds). *Festschrift for Gardner Murphy.* Harper, New York, 274-90.

Stoller, F. H. (1968). 'Focused feedback with video tape: Extending the groups function', in Gazda, G. M. (Ed). *Basic Innovations to Group Psychotherapy and Counseling.* Charles Thomas, Springfield, Illinois.

Storr, A. (1966). 'The concept of cure', in Rycroft, C. (Ed). *Psychoanalysis Observed.* Constable, London.

Strauss, A. (1965). *George Herbert Mead: On Social Psychology.* University of Chicago Press, Chicago.

Strupp, H. H. (1955), 'An objective comparison of Rogerian and Psychoanalytic techniques'. *Journal of Consulting Psychology,* **19,** 1-8.

Strupp, H. H. (1957). 'A multidimensional comparison of therapist activity in analytic and client-centered therapy'. *Journal of Consulting Psychology,* **21,** 301-8.

Stuart, R. B. (1967). *Analysis and Illustrations of the Process of Assertive Conditioning.* Paper presented at 94th Annual Forum of National Conference on Social Welfare.

Stuart, R. B. (1969). 'Token reinforcement in marital treatment', in Rubin, R. D., and Franks, C. M. (Eds). *Advances in Behaviour Therapy, 1968.* Academic Press, New York, 221-30 (a).

Stuart, R. B. (1969). 'Operant-interpersonal treatment for marital discord'. *Journal of Consulting Psychology,* **33,** 675-82 (b).

Stuart, R. B. (1971). 'Behavioural contracting within the families of delinquents'. *Journal of Behaviour Therapy and Experimental Psychiatry,* **2,** 1-11.

Sudnow, D. (1965). 'Normal crimes: Sociological features of the penal code'. *Social Problems,* **12,** 255-70.

Susser, M. (1968). *Community Psychiatry: Epidemiologic and Social Themes.* Random House, New York.

Sutherland, E. H. (1937). *The Professional Thief, by a Professional Thief.* University of Chicago, Chicago.

Sutherland, E. H., and Cressey, D. R. (1960). *Principles of Criminology.* Lippincott, New York.

Szasz, T. S. (1962). *The Myth of Mental Illness.* Secker and Warburg, London.

Szasz, T. S. (1963). 'The concept of transference'. *International Journal of Psychoanalysis,* **44,** 432–43.

Taber, M. (1970). 'Social work as interference in problem definitions'. *Applied Social Studies,* **2,** 59–68.

Tharp, R. G., and Wetzel, R. J. (1969). *Behavior Modification in the Natural Environment.* Academic Press, New York.

Thomas, E. J. (1967). *The Socio-behavioural approach and Applications to Social Work.* Council on Social Work Education, New York.

Thomas, E. J. (1968). 'Selected socio-behavioural techniques and principles: An approach to interpersonal helping'. *Social Work (U.S.A.).,* **13,** 12–26.

Thomas, E. J. (1964). *Selecting Knowledge from Behavioural Science,* in *Building Social Work Knowledge.* National Association of Social Workers, New York, 38–48.

Thomson, R. (1959). *The psychology of thinking.* Penguin, Harmondsworth.

Thoresen, C. E., and Krumboltz, J. D. (1967). 'Relationship of counselor reinforcement of selected responses to external behaviour'. *Journal of Counseling Psychology,* **14** 140–44.

Thorne, G. L., Tharp, R. G., and Wetzel, R. J. (1967). 'Behavior modification techniques: New tools for probation officers'. *Federal Probation,* **31,** 21–7.

Tillich, P. (1952). *The Courage to Be.* James Nisbet, London.

Timms, N. (1968). *The Language of Social Casework.* Routledge and Kegan Paul, London.

Tizard, J., and Grad, J. C. (1967). *The Mentally Handicapped and Their Families.* Oxford University Press, London.

Towle, C. (1964). 'Preface to Hollis, F.' *Casework: A Psychosocial Therapy.* Random House, New York.

Trasler, G. (1962). *The Explanation of Criminality.* Routledge and Kegan Paul, London.

Trice, H. M. and Romar, P. M. (1970). 'Delabeling, relabeling and alcoholics anonymous'. *Social Problems,* **17,** 538–44.

Truax, C. B. (1966). 'Reinforcement and non-reinforcement in Rogerian psychotherapy'. *Journal of Abnormal Psychology,* **71,** 1–9.

Truax, C. B., and Carkhuff, R. R. (1965). 'Personality change in hospitalised mental patients during group psychotherapy as a function of alternate sessions and vicarious therapy pretraining'. *Journal of Clinical Psychology,* **21,** 225–8.

Truax, C. B., and Carkhuff, R. R. (1967. *Toward effective counseling and psychotherapy.* Aldine, Chicago.

Tyler, V. O., and Brown, G. D. (1967). 'The use of swift, brief isolation as a group control device for institutionalised delinquents'. *Behaviour Research and Therapy,* **5,** 1–9.

Uhlenhuth, E. H., Canter, A., Neustadt, J. O., and Payson, H. E. (1959). 'The symptomatic relief of anxiety with meprobamate, phenobarbital and placebo'. *American Journal of Psychiatry,* **115,** 905–10.

Ullman, L., and Krasner, L. (1969). *A Psychological Approach to Abnormal Behaviour.* Prentice Hall, New Jersey.

Ullmann, L. P., Krasner, L., and Collins, B. (1961). 'Modification of behavior through verbal conditioning effect in group therapy'. *Journal of Abnormal and Social Psychology,* **62,** 128–32.

Ullman, L. P., Krasner, L., and Edinger, R. L. (1964). 'Verbal conditioning of common associations in long-term schizophrenic patients'. *Behavior Research and Therapy*, **2**, 15–18.

Valins, S., and Ray, A. A. (1967). 'Effects of cognitive desensitization on avoidance behaviour'. *Journal of Personality and Social Psychology*, **7**, 345–50.

Vernon, M. D. (1962). *The Psychology of Perception*. Pelican, London.

Volgyesi, F. A. (1954). 'School for patients: Hypnosis, therapy and psychoprophylaxis'. *British Journal of Medical Hypnosis*, **5**, 10–17.

Wahler, R. G., and Cormier, W. H. (1970). 'The ecological interview: A first step in out-patient child behavior therapy'. *Journal of Behavior Therapy and Experimental Psychiatry*, **1**, 279–89.

Wallach, M. S., and Strupp, H. H. (1960). 'Psychotherapists' clinical judgement and attitudes toward patients'. *Journal of Consulting Psychology*, **24**, 315–23.

Walton, D. (1960). 'The application of learning theory to the treatment of a case of neurodermatitis'. In Eysenck, H. J. (Ed). *Behaviour Therapy and the Neuroses*. Macmillan, New York, 272–4.

Watson, G. (1958). 'Moral issues in psychotherapy'. *American Psychologist*, **13**, 574–6.

Watson, J. B., and Rayner, R. (1920). 'Conditioned emotional reactions'. *Journal of Experimental Psychology*, **3**, 1–14.

Weinberg, S. K. (1967). *The Sociology of Mental Disorders*. Staples Press, London.

Weiner, H. (1962). 'Some effects of response cost upon human operant behaviour'. *Journal of the Experimental Analysis of Behaviour*, **5**, 201–8.

West, D. J. (1967). *The Young Offender*. Penguin, London.

Wetzel, R. (1966). 'Use of behavioral techniques in a case of compulsive stealing'. *Journal of Consulting Psychology*, **30**, 367–74.

Wheeler, L. (1966). 'Toward a theory of behavioural contagion'. *Psychological Review*, **73**, 179–92.

Whitener, R. W., and Nikelly, A. G. (1964). 'Sexual deviation in college students'. *American Journal of Orthopsychiatry*, **34**, 486–92.

Whiting, J. W. M. (1941). *Becoming a Kwoma*. Yale University, New Haven.

Whiting, J. W. M., and Child, I. L. (1953). *Child Training and Personality*. Yale University, New Haven.

Whyte, W. F. (1937). *Street-corner Society*. University of Chicago, Chicago.

Wilkins, L. T. (1964). *Social Deviance*. Tavistock, London.

Williams, C. D. (1959). 'The elimination of tantrum behaviour by extinction procedures: Case report'. *Journal of Abnormal and Social Psychology*, **59**, 269 (a).

Williams, C. D. (1962). *Extinction and Other Principles of Learning in the Treatment and Prevention of Children's Disorders*. Paper presented at the meeting of the American Psychological Association, St. Louis.

Williams, R. I. (1959). 'Verbal conditioning in psychotherapy.' *American Psychologist*, **14**, 388 (b).

Wilson, G. T., Hannon, A. E., and Evans, W. I. M. (1968). 'Behaviour therapy and the therapist – patient relationship'. *Journal of Consulting and Clinical Psychology*, **32** 103–9.

Winnicott, C. (1959). *The Development of Insight*. Sociological Review Monograph, 2.

Wittenberg, I. S. (1970). *Psychoanalytic Insight and Relationships*. Routledge and Kegan Paul, London.

Wolberg, L. R. (1967). *The Technique in Psychotherapy*. Heinemann, London.

Wolf, E. (1966). 'Learning theory and psychoanalysis'. *British Journal of Medical Psychology*, **39**, 1–10.

Wolf, M. M., Risley, T., and Mees, H. (1965). 'Application of operant conditioning procedures to the behaviour problems of an autistic child', in Ullman, L. P., and Krasner, L. (Eds). *Case Studies in Behaviour Modification*. Holt, Rinehart and Winston, New York, 138–45.

Wolfgang, M. E., and Ferracuti, F. (1967). *The Subculture of Violence*. Tavistock, London.

Wolpe, J. (1954). 'Reciprocal inhibition as the main basis of psychotherapeutic effects'. *Archives of Neurology and Psychiatry*, **72**, 205–26.

Wolpe, J. (1958). *Psychotherapy by Reciprocal Inhibition*. Stanford University, Stanford.

Wolpe, J. (1969). *The Practice of Behaviour Therapy*. Pergamon, Oxford.

Wolpe, J. (1970). 'Transcript of initial interview in a case of depression'. *Journal of Behaviour Therapy and Experimental Psychiatry*, **1**, 71–8 (a).

Wolpe, J. (1970). 'Behaviour analysis of a case of hypochondriacal anxiety: Transcript'. *Journal of Behaviour Therapy and Experimental Psychiatry*, **1**, 217–24 (b).

Wolpe, J. (1970). 'Identifying the antecedents of an agoraphobic reaction: A transcript'. *Journal of Behaviour Therapy and Experimental Psychiatry*. **1**, 299–304 (c).

Wolpe, J., and Lang, P. J. (1964). 'A fear survey schedule for use in behavior therapy'. *Behaviour Research and Therapy*, **2**, 27–30.

Wolpe, J., and Lazarus, A. (1966). *Behaviour Therapy Techniques*. Pergamon, Oxford.

Wootton, B. (1959). *Social Science and Social Pathology*. Allen and Unwin, London.

Worsley, P., Fitzhenry, R., Mitchell, J. C., Morgan, D. H. J., Pons, V., Roberts, B., Sharrock, W. W., and Ward, R. (1970). *Introducing Sociology*. Penguin, Harmondsworth.

Wynne, L. C., and Solomon, R. L. (1955). 'Traumatic avoidance learning: Acquisition and extinction in dogs deprived of normal peripheral autonomic function'. *Genetic Psychology Monographs*, **52**, 241–82.

Yablonsky, L. (1962). *The Violent Gang*. Macmillan, New York.

Younghusband, E. (1961). 'Introduction to Biestick, F. The casework relationship'. Allen and Unwin, London.

Zigler, E., and Child, I. L. (1969). 'Socialization', in Lindsey, G. L., and Aronson, E. *The Handbook of Social Psychology*. 2nd Ed. Addison-Wesley, London, **Vol III**, 450–589.

Zilboorg, G. (1952). 'The emotional problem and the therapeutic role of insight'. *Psychoanalytic Quarterly*, **21**, 1–24.

Zetzel, E. R. (1956). 'Current concepts of transference'. *International Journal of Psychoanalysis*, **37**, 369–76.

Further References

Listed below are further references received at press stage.

Box, S., and Ford, J. (1971). 'The facts don't fit: on the relationship between social class and criminal Behaviour'. *The Sociological Review*, **19**, 31-52.

Cohen, S. (1971). *Images of Deviance*. Penguin, Harmondsworth.

Cohn, Y. (1963). 'Criteria for the probation officer's recommendations to the juvenile court judge'. *Crime and Deliquency*, 262–275, in Garabedian, P. G., and Gibbons, D. C. (1970), *Becoming Delinquent*. Aldine, Chicago.

DeWolfe, T. E. (1969). *Criminal or Mentally Ill: Some Correlates of Labelling Lawbreaking Deviants*. Unpublished. Ph. D. Thesis. University of Houston.

Eysenck. H. J. (1960). 'The effects of psychotherapy', in Eysenck, H. J. (Ed). *Handbook of Abnormal Psychology*. Pitman, London.

Gibbs, J. (1971). 'A critique of the labelling perspective', in Rubington, E., and Weinberg, M. S. (Eds). *The Study of Social Problems*. Oxford University Press, London, 193–204.

190

Gross, S. Z. (1967). 'The prehearing juvenile report: probation officers' Conceptions'. *Journal of Research in Crime and Delinquency*, **IV**, 212–217.

Kanfer, F. H. (1970). 'Self-monitoring: methodological considerations and clinical applications'. *Journal of Consulting and Clinical Psychology*, **35**, 148–152.

Patterson, G. R. (1971). 'Behavioural intervention in the classroom and in the home', in Bergin, A. E. and Garfield, S. L. (Eds). *Handbook of Psychotherapy and Behaviour Change*. Wiley, New York.

Phillipson, M. (1971). *Sociological Aspects of Crime and Delinquency*. Routledge and Kegan Paul, London.

Reeves, J. W. (1969). *Thinking about Thinking*. Martin, Secker and Warburg, London.

Smith, G., and Harris, R. (1971). 'Ideologies of need and the organization of social work departments'. *British Journal of Social Work* (In press).

Stoll, C. S. (1969). 'Images of man and social control'. *Social Forces*, **47**, 119–127.

Terry, R. M. (1967). 'Discrimination in the handling of juvenile offenders by social control agencies'. *Journal of Research in Crime and Delinquency*, **IV**, 218–230.

Winett, R. A. (1970). 'Attribution of attitude and behaviour change and its relevance to behaviour therapy'. *Psychological Record*, **20**, 17–32.

Subject Index

1547